DON'T GIVE YOUR HEART TO A RAMBLER

MUSIC IN AMERICAN LIFE

*A list of books in the series appears
at the end of this book.*

DON'T GIVE YOUR HEART TO A RAMBLER

MY LIFE WITH JIMMY MARTIN, THE KING OF BLUEGRASS

BARBARA MARTIN STEPHENS

FOREWORD BY MURPHY HICKS HENRY

UNIVERSITY OF ILLINOIS PRESS
Urbana, Chicago, and Springfield

Library of Congress Cataloging-in-Publication Data
Names: Stephens, Barbara Martin.
Title: Don't give your heart to a rambler : my life with
    Jimmy Martin, the king of bluegrass / Barbara
    Martin Stephens ; foreword by Murphy Hicks
    Henry.
Description: Urbana : University of Illinois Press,
    [2017] | Series: Music in American life | Includes
    index.
Identifiers: LCCN 2017002331 (print) | LCCN
    2017006574 (ebook) | ISBN 9780252082764 (pbk. :
    alk. paper) | ISBN 9780252099793 (e-book)
Subjects: LCSH: Stephens, Barbara Martin. | Concert
    agents—United States—Biography. | Martin,
    Jimmy. | Bluegrass musicians—United States—
    Biography.
Classification: LCC ML429.S84 A3 2017 (print) | LCC
    ML429.S84 (ebook) | DDC 782.421642092 [B]—dc23
LC record available at https://lccn.loc.gov/2017002331

This book is dedicated to

My mother

Willowdeen

Without you, nothing would have been possible.

You taught me so much and was always so proud of me.

I will love you forever.

CONTENT/

Photographs follow page 100

FOREWORD

MURPHY HICKS HENRY

Barbara Martin Stephens is a brave woman and this is a brave book. A groundbreaking book. Lives of bluegrass musicians have been chronicled in biography (Bill Monroe, Lester Flatt, the Stoneman Family), autobiography (Ralph Stanley, Roni Stoneman), and memoir (Bob Black, Gene Lowinger), but never has the partner of a bluegrass musician written about what it was like to share his life and give birth to his children. *Don't Give Your Heart to a Rambler* gives us an inside look at Barbara's fourteen years with Jimmy Martin, the brilliant but unpredictable King of Bluegrass. Tagged with this appellation by Moe Lytle of King Records, Jimmy took the title and ran with it. Even the license plate on his limousine proclaimed him "King JM."

Singer and guitarist Jimmy Martin (1927–2005) was a bluegrass pioneer. Frequently mentioned in company with Bill Monroe, Lester Flatt, and Earl Scruggs, he was an early inductee into the International Bluegrass Music Association Hall of Fame. His influence on bluegrass music is enormous. Songs and tunes that he recorded have become bluegrass standards. His side musicians, having been trained in the Jimmy Martin school of music, left him to found their own trailblazing bluegrass bands: J. D. Crowe and the New South, Doyle Lawson and Quicksilver, Alan Munde and Country Gazette. Bill Emerson would anchor both the Country Gentlemen and County Current with his immaculate banjo playing. Jimmy's songs like "Rock Hearts" and "Widow Maker" would climb the country music charts and crack *Billboard*'s Top Twenty. Yet he never became a member of the Grand Ole Opry, a slight that would haunt him until his death. And because Barbara was the "last person living" who knew the reason why, she decided to write a book.

Fans and friends of Jimmy Martin may find this a difficult book to accept. No one likes to learn that their idols have feet of clay. And it is certainly not the bluegrass way to air dirty laundry in public. Less-than-flattering stories are told only in private, often late at night when the white whiskey is being passed around. As the stories reach a crescendo, someone will inevitably blurt out, "Damn, somebody should write a book!" Barbara has written that book, only most of these stories about Jimmy Martin have never been told before. These are Barbara's stories.

In the beginning the ever flamboyant Jimmy was playful and sexy and even sweet. When he found a little success in Detroit with the Osborne Brothers, however, he began to change, and a cycle of abuse, both emotional and physical, began. Barbara would leave many times, but she always came back. Why? It is a question she asks herself many times in this book. At first she didn't recognize what was happening. After all, this was the 1950s, and abuse was still hidden behind a curtain of shame and the belief among many women that it was somehow their fault. Furthermore, as Barbara readily admits, Jimmy Martin was "like an addiction" to her, and addictions are notoriously difficult to abandon.

But there is another side to Barbara's story, a side in which Barbara herself is the principal actor. In 1958, when Jimmy was a member of the Louisiana Hayride in Shreveport and the family was "starving," Barbara stepped in to do some booking herself. She was so successful that eventually she formed her own Barbara Martin Agency and continued to book Jimmy, along with other acts, until she left him. Fans of Jimmy Martin may be surprised to learn that it was Barbara who arranged for Jimmy to play at the Golden Nugget Hotel and Casino in Las Vegas for six weeks in 1962. At a time when almost no women were booking country music acts, Barbara was breaking new ground.

Barbara's path after leaving Jimmy, however, was a lonesome valley that many women before her had walked. Fortunately, Barbara and their four children survived. That in itself is a blessing, a moment of grace. *"Through many dangers, toils, and snares I have already come / 'Tis grace hath brought me safe thus far and grace will lead me home."*

As this book prepares to go to press, Barbara is eighty-two years old, eats primarily vegetables and fruit with lots of fish, and takes no medication. She has been a paralegal in Florida for the last forty years. I will soon meet her for the first time here in Winchester, Virginia, where I live. She is passing through with her son Mike (born before she met Jimmy), and together we will visit the grave of country music great Patsy Cline, who was killed in a plane crash in 1963. Barbara has never seen the grave of her friend. I will be honored to stand in the presence of these two strong women, one who died young and one who lived to write about her long journey home.

PREFACE

In the early months of 2014, I was playing around on YouTube, watching and listening to some of Jimmy Martin's early recordings that he made not too long before he died. As I watched the first half of the film, Jimmy was cussing like a sailor. Every other word started with the letter "f." This was not the man I knew. I ordered a copy of the film.

When it arrived, I watched it over and over, because I still couldn't believe what I was seeing and hearing. I was saddened by the cussing and hearing him say, "I'm not good enough for the Grand Ole Opry." It was obviously a defensive move by Jimmy to deny the mental pain he suffered daily for over fifty years because he was never asked to join the Opry. In turn, we had all suffered. As the last person living who knows the true story of why Jimmy was never made a member of the Opry, I decided it was time to write this book.

This book is not only about why Jimmy was not a member of the Opry, but it's also the story of our family, who could have been at the top of the world. We could have had the best family band ever. Our children were all musicians and good singers. I was a good booking agent and manager. But I had a client who wouldn't listen, and I didn't know enough to help him. This would lead to a world of heartaches for our family.

So much has been written about Jimmy Martin—some true and some not. In fact, I read an article one time claiming he was a Melungeon. ("Melungeon" is a term traditionally used for a person of many mixed European,

African, and Native American racial groups in the Cumberland Gap area of central Appalachia, which includes portions of east Tennessee, southwest Virginia, and eastern Kentucky.) He was not. It was rumored that his brother-in-law was a Melungeon, but that was never proven.

I hope you will understand Jimmy Martin better after reading this book. Jimmy was a kindhearted man and a father who cared deeply for his children but was unable to let them know it. He was a terrific entertainer and singer, a man who suffered humiliation and coped with it in ways that only further injured his pride and his standing in the music world. He was often misunderstood. He hid behind the "don't care" façade he built around himself. Now you will know the reason for his behavior as well as my part in it—both good and bad.

ACKNOWLEDGMENTS

I especially want to thank the following family and friends for listening to me for the past two years about my book.

Many thanks go to my good friend Jeanne Fuchs, PhD. She is an adjunct professor who works with doctoral candidates in writing their theses. Jeanne took the time out of her busy schedule to read my book, make suggestions, have three-hour lunches with me to discuss changes I had made and things I should do, and reread chapters. I will be forever grateful to her for encouraging me in sharing my dream of writing this book, or as Jeanne calls it, my "opus manuscript."

Thanks also to my editors, Andrea MacVicar and Nancy Cardwell, for the many hours they put in editing my manuscript and for keeping faith in me and my work.

My sons James Henry (Timmy) Martin Jr., Michael Hollis Morgan, and Ray Willard Martin were extremely helpful with their assistance in remembering details. I appreciate their listening to me going on and on about my manuscript and am grateful for their encouragement. Special thanks go to them for digging up old newspaper clippings and photographs and for always being there with an "I love you, Mom."

Thanks as well to my daughters-in-law, Donna Morgan and Susan Martin, for listening while I read chapters to them, for their opinions, and, most importantly, for their love. And to my granddaughters Hollie Morgan Beeson and Sarah Arnold Christopher, thank you for listening, for your phone calls, and for your love.

My good friends Carol Winters, Karen Burnham Balzanti, Helen Myers, Anna and Tony Mody, Carol and Christie Sadowski, Lynn Mahoney, Valerie Schick, Arlene Kleimeier, and Brian Arrowood were all helpful as well. They took the time to listen to my story and give me input, and they never told me, "Enough about the book." They loved me through all the days of writing, editing, and getting this book off the ground. Doris Flynn, my dear departed friend whom I loved very much, would be so proud of my book.

Two exceptional people, Vern Gilhouse and Sharon Merrill McMurdie, listened to me read out loud for hours and gave me encouragement and advice. I am especially grateful to Vern, whom I feel I have never thanked enough for helping me with my husband Chuck, who suffered from Alzheimer's. Chuck loved going to the St. Andrews golf course in Scotland with Vern. He was so gentle and kind with Chuck, and Chuck loved him very much.

To four former Sunny Mountain Boys—Bill Emerson, banjo player extraordinaire; Paul Williams; Alan Munde, another fantastic banjo player; and Tee Meroney—your input was priceless. Thank you for sharing your memories with me.

To my great-granddaughter, Reagan Brown, who chose me as the subject for her biography assignment in her fifth-grade class, I am so honored and grateful. I love you very much and am so proud of you. Your writing was superb.

Thank you to those hundreds and hundreds of people I have met over the last two years across the United States, in Poland, in France, or wherever I traveled, who listened when I told them about my book. I don't think I came across anyone I didn't tell about the book.

I would also like to thank Marty Stuart and his band, the Fabulous Superlatives, for their acknowledgment of me and their kind words when they appeared at the Parker Playhouse in Fort Lauderdale on February 11, 2016. Marty, you will never know how much that meant to me. Thank you for being you. You are fantastic and your show is terrific. Come back to Fort Lauderdale again soon.

Last, but not least, thanks to my friend, my coffee buddy, and the greatest Grand Ole Opry radio and television announcer ever, Eddie Stubbs. Without you, I couldn't have done it. You are a treasured friend and I will love you for life.

INTRODUCTION

SOMETHING ABOUT ME

My working life and my sense of business all started with my grandfather, Robert Hollis Farmer, giving me a soft drink stand to run in his mattress factory. He taught me how to determine profits and losses. I may have been only five when he started teaching me, but I was already reading and writing cursive. I paid attention to everything he told me, and I remembered it. That strong work ethic has followed me all my life.

I was the apple of my mother's eye and remained so for the rest of her life. As Mother, Willowdeen Farmer Gibson, held my face in her hands, her dying words were "You have been the best daughter anyone could ever have. I love you more than life itself."

I told her, "I love you equally as much."

She then said, "I would give my life for you." Standing by the door to her room, my granddaughters, Sarah and Chandler, heard us. She passed away early the next morning.

Mother and Daddy, George William Gibson, owned the Gibson Mattress Company and Upholstering Company in Memphis. The factory was located behind our house at the back of a vacant lot. Daddy also kept hives of bees at the back of the property close to the shop. Mother helped Daddy in the business each day, and she was an expert at tufting the mattresses and upholstering furniture. She was also one tough lady. More than once I saw her carry an innerspring mattress over her head around the factory. She never needed help lifting.

Shortly after my birth, in 1935, my parents bought a house and two extra lots at 120 Racine Street in Memphis. The extra lot on the left side of the house was filled with trees, and that is where I played. I had an imaginary friend that I named Gaga, and I didn't go anywhere without her. Today when I return to Memphis, I drive down Racine Street and always stop in front of number 120. I can see my imaginary friend under the same trees that are still standing there. The house is now gone and the property is home to a woman's club, but to me it will always be *my* home.

Mother's parents, Robert Hollis and Delma Wainwright Farmer, also owned a mattress factory in Nashville, the Hermitage Mattress Company. My grandparents, who I called Mama and DaddyHollis, lived over the mattress factory. One night, while I was visiting them, the factory caught on fire. We barely made it out with only the clothes on our back. I didn't have time nor did I think to grab the money I had saved from selling soft drinks to employees. I kept the money in a glass bank Mother bought for me at the World's Fair in Chicago. After all, I was only five years old. Mama and DaddyHollis lost everything.

A few days later the firemen found my money. It had melted. I remember it vividly because it looked like a big silver ball when the firemen gave it back to me. DaddyHollis then took me to the Broadway National Bank, where they weighed it and gave me money in exchange. I don't believe banks will do that today.

DaddyHollis rebuilt the mattress factory and ran it for many years. As I grew up, I worked there sewing mattress ticks (covers) and ginning cotton. DaddyHollis liked to have me go on the trucks to collect the money, make the bank deposits, answer the phone, take orders, or whatever other office work needed to be done. He knew he could trust me to do it right.

DaddyHollis thought I was the smartest kid ever. Later he built a bin where I could keep watermelons with lots of ice. It was located at the front of the factory, and I sold melons to employees and anyone else who stopped by. I was about nine and always busy. If I wasn't busy selling, I was working in the factory or office. Those were valuable lessons—ones that proved useful throughout my life.

Mother and Daddy had two more girls, Betty Jean in 1938 and Billie Deen in 1941. I was three years old when Betty was born and five when Billie was born. Later on, Mother suffered two miscarriages.

My daddy was a hardworking man and an excellent businessman. He also loved to shoot craps. He was good at it and he usually won. I'll never forget the night he came home and told Mother he had won a house with three apartments across the street from our house. I remember Mother saying, "Get rid of the trash that lives there." I didn't know what she was talking about, but I remembered it. Daddy later bought several more houses on the street. Mother hated his gambling, because she didn't like the time it took him away from home, but she liked the gains from the gambling.

Since Mother worked in the mattress factory in the backyard, it was easy for her to walk over to the house. She was an excellent teacher and liked spending time with me. Before I started school, I already knew the alphabet, how to write cursive, and how to read first-grade books. I started school before I was five. I never learned to print and today my printing is terrible, but my cursive writing is great.

Growing up in Memphis, I was a privileged child. I was what they now call "precocious"—spoiled rotten by both parents, grandparents, and my cousin Penny Hazel. I went round-trip alone by Greyhound bus from Memphis to Nashville when I was five years old to stay with my grandparents. Mother would put me on the bus and my grandparents would meet me at the bus station in Nashville. Mother would meet me on the return trip.

When I was a baby, Mother hired a lady named Lucy to take care of me during the day while Mother worked. One favorite memory of Lucy is when she would sometimes take me to her house whenever Mother and Daddy worked late.

Lucy lived across the railroad tracks about two blocks from our house. After we walked to her house, she would set me right in the middle of her bed, which was always white, and give me sliced bread with butter and syrup. She didn't care if I got syrup and butter all over me and all over the bed. I loved sitting on her bed and eating bread, butter, and syrup.

Mother also hired Lucy's daughter, Ruth, to do the housework, washing, and ironing. Lucy's job was to take care of me. After my sisters were born, Lucy also took care of them.

One day Mother was busy working and couldn't come to the house to play with me, and it made me mad. I was about four years old then. When Lucy told me Mother was busy and to go outside and play, I decided to go kick the bee hives. I was going to get even with Mother and make the bees swarm. They swarmed, all right—all over me! I was stung everywhere. Lucy started screaming and swatting the bees. Mother and Daddy ran out of the shop and grabbed me. But the real reason I was crying was because Lucy got stung. I loved Lucy and I didn't mean to hurt her. I promised I would never, ever make the bees mad again.

While Daddy was involved in business, Mother started running around with her sister-in-law. I think both of them were lonely. Daddy was always working, and Uncle Jeff, daddy's brother, was a ladies' man. Mother and Aunt Helon were two very beautiful women. Mother was tall, thin, and had natural, jet-black hair. She loved to dance. Her sister-in-law, Helon, was a gorgeous redhead, thin, and about five foot seven inches tall. Both women had dazzling smiles. They also had that "come hither" look. Individually or together, the two women attracted a lot of attention. They liked to flirt a bit, and they loved it when other men told them they were beautiful. After all, their husbands certainly didn't tell them how beautiful or how desirable they were.

When Mother (sometimes I called her Willowdeen) and Aunt Helon started going out together, Memphis was full of sailors from Millington Naval Air Station. This was in 1942, 1943, and early 1944. The city was booming, and Willowdeen and Helon were right in the midst of it all.

Mother was twenty-nine years old and she had never drunk liquor. When she started hanging out in bars, drinking became a lifelong habit and caused our family much misery. As a result, Mother and Daddy divorced when I was nine. Mother, Betty, Billie, and I moved in with her parents in Nashville.

Daddy continued to be a constant in my life. Every year he came to Nashville to see us. He and Mother always went shopping and bought new school clothes for us. Daddy never stopped loving my mother. He sent her cards, wrote to her, and called her. I still have a lot of those cards and letters. Before he died, he and Mother talked about getting back together. Even if they had, I don't think it would have worked. Daddy just wasn't exciting enough for Mother.

Daddy remarried, had one more daughter, Peggy, divorced, and never married again. A heavy smoker, he died of lung cancer in 1965 at the age of sixty-five. He is buried at the family cemetery in Blue Mountain, Mississippi.

Mother continued to work for her father in the mattress and uphol-stering business. That way, she could work when she wanted to. She was not a person to punch a time clock. In fact, when Daddy and Mother both worked at a tire manufacturing company in Memphis during the Second World War, Daddy punched Mother's time card in and out for her workday and she went home.

Mother was a multitalented lady. She was a good person, a gifted art-ist, an excellent seamstress, and a good decorator, but she could also be a devil. She made her own patterns for clothes, and throughout my life she continued to sew for me. I still have a spool doll she made and a toy wooden cube she made and painted for me. It is a treasure!

By the age of eleven, my cousin Rex Farmer and I were selling quarts of honey out of the back of a pickup truck. Rex's father, my grandfather's brother, was in the apiary business. In fact, he was the first man to ship live bees by air. Whenever any of our honey turned to sugar, we placed a dishpan full of water on the stove to boil. Then we would put our jars filled with honey in the boiling water. This reconstituted the honey. *Voila! Honey again.* When our supply of honey ran out, Rex drove to Cottonwood, Ala-bama, and picked up another load. On Saturdays we went to the various town squares of Springfield, Murfreesboro, Franklin, and others around Nashville to sell the honey. Once Rex got a real job, our honey business ended, because I was too young to drive.

Around that time, Roy Acuff ran for governor of Tennessee. I will never forget Rex taking me and my friend Opal Taylor, who was madly in love with Rex (he didn't know she was alive), to the front steps of the War Memorial Auditorium in Nashville to hear Roy Acuff speak. That was so exciting.

Then not too long after that, Rex took Opal and me to Murfreesboro, Tennessee. It was there we saw General Douglas MacArthur speak on the square. He had just been fired by President Truman, and I thought he was the most handsome man I had ever seen. It was wonderful seeing him speak to the crowd of around a hundred people, and we stood right in front of the podium. I'll never forget the experience.

At twelve I had a summer job babysitting for the people who lived behind our house on Delaware Street in Nashville. I took care of two babies. One was about two years old and was deaf and dumb, and the other was a baby born blind. That was a heart-wrenching job and I hated it. I also had to wash their diapers on a rub board and hang them out to dry. Ugh! I hated that job. But I didn't give up; I worked the entire summer.

I then went to work for Kuhn Brothers, a five-and-dime store, running a popcorn machine. That was a good job and I enjoyed it. I worked a ten-hour day on Saturday and made 25 cents an hour. I took home $2.25 after the Social Security was deducted. I thought I was making a fortune. That money meant I could get three yards of material for a dollar, and Mother could make me a new skirt and blouse practically every week. Other weeks, I would save my money or buy a new pair of shoes. I have always loved shoes.

To get to and from my job at Kuhn Brothers, I walked from Fifteenth and Charlotte, to where we lived at Twenty-Seventh and Charlotte. Even though that area was primarily black, I was never afraid. People knew me from Kuhn's and they watched out for me. I was twelve years old, but at five foot three, I felt tall.

From there, I was hired by McClellan's on Fifth Avenue, another five-and-dime store. At McClellan's I worked the lunch counter. That was my spot. The people there were wonderful, and my manager, Mr. Padula, was the best. Often times they sent me to the hot dog and hamburger counter to work. I loved hot dogs with coleslaw on them, and I still do. The first thing Mr. Padula would tell me was, "Don't eat. You are not allowed." But he knew I was going to be eating a hot dog before he could get back across the store. He could have fired me, but I also knew he wouldn't do that. It was like a game we both enjoyed.

I continued at McClellan's until the fall of 1951, when I started going to school a half day and working a half day at Washington Manufacturing Company. They taught me to use a keypunch machine. I had learned typing in school, and there was not much difference between typing and keypunching. You were punching holes instead of letters, and you also had to be able to read the holes in the cards. The keypunch machines were the kind where a card was fed into one side, and as you punched it, it moved to the other side. It had a mirror on the back—a dinosaur in today's world. I also learned how to use the collating machine and the sorting machine and how to wire the boards. The boards told the machines what to do, and if you wired the board wrong, you had a mess. I was very good at wiring. These skills provided me with many years of good income.

I was always known as being very pretty; I had great hair and gorgeous legs. People told me that all the time. But even though I was pretty and should have had a lot of confidence, I didn't. I was extremely shy and didn't like speaking in a classroom or in public. The only friends I ever brought to my house were Opal and Margaret Ann Taylor, Bessie Morrison, and Jean Armstrong. Their parents were all divorced and we were all in the same situation. I also didn't want anyone to know my mother drank on weekends. (Drinking only on weekends and holidays was how she justified saying she was not an alcoholic.) I never participated in any school activities, but I liked learning things and I made good grades. Studying was a breeze for me, and I rarely had to spend much time on it. I graduated from high school when I was fifteen, but I didn't come out of my shell and start talking to people until long after I hooked up with Jimmy Martin.

My mother was like a sister or a friend to me. She never abandoned us, and regardless of whom she was married to, she and her husband always lived with my grandmother and grandfather. Mother never wanted to be separated from her mother and father. As an only child, and despite her age, she was still doted on by her parents. They spoiled her, just as she and they spoiled me.

Mother liked to play jokes and was constantly doing something to try to scare me. She liked to walk outside the house to my bedroom window in the middle of the night and act like someone was trying to get into my room. Sometimes when we were sitting outside, Mother hid out in the darkened house. She always planned her jokes with my grandmother. Mama would ask me to go into the house and get something for Mother, and then when I walked into the house, Mother would jump out at me with a sheet over her head and yell, "Boo!" While I screamed and screamed, Mother was laughing her butt off. She was always thinking of one joke or another.

I kept a window in the spare bedroom unlocked so that I could go in and out after everyone was sleeping. One night I went out the window and met my two girlfriends Opal and Jean, and we went around to the drugstore and hung out. We didn't do anything, but when I climbed back in through the window, Mother was waiting. That night, she put some serious stripes on my legs with the switch. I never went in or out of that window again. Mother nailed it shut, never to be opened again.

I have had so many people ask me how my mother's drinking affected me. Remember, my mother only drank on weekends and holidays. She and each of her husbands always lived with her mother and father while they were alive. My sisters and I were happy. Mother was a loving person and wasn't afraid to show it. She was spontaneous and didn't hesitate to tell us how much she loved us, or to put her arms around us and give us a big hug. My grandmother did the same. I am a hugger, and everyone says I give great hugs.

Thinking about all that, I guess the only way her drinking affected me was that I was extremely shy in school, even though I was not like that at home. I didn't want anyone to get close to me, because I didn't want them coming to my house. In another way I desperately wanted a home with a mother and father. I didn't care what it took to get it or what it took to keep it. Those were my goals in life. I remembered very clearly my life growing up with my mother and father before they divorced, and I wanted that kind of life for my children. Off and on I had it with Jimmy, but it was impossible to keep it. If Chuck Stephens had been the father of my children, I would have had it and kept it.

Mother was a restless soul; there was never enough excitement for her. She loved the bars, and when Friday came she was out the door. The men loved her and she loved the men—she married seven times during her lifetime. She died on August 3, 2009, at the ripe old age of ninety-four. She was born on the fourth of July and was truly a firecracker! One of a kind. I always told her she was "pickled" or "preserved" by alcohol and that's why she had lived so long. She is buried directly behind Jimmy at Spring Hill Cemetery in Madison, a suburb of Nashville, alongside her mother.

My sister Billie Dean lived in Detroit and its suburbs for over thirty-five years. She subsequently married and went on to own several successful businesses. She never had children. Following her husband's death, she moved back to Tennessee. Billie died of a heat stroke in 2005 at the age of sixty-four. She is buried alongside her husband in Detroit.

My other younger sister, Betty Jean, had eleven children during her lifetime. At the time of her death, nine of them were still living. Betty Jean died in 2011 of sepsis at the age of seventy-three. Betty's children decided not to let me bury her at Spring Hill beside Mother and my grandmother, even though they knew that was what she wanted. Her children had her cremated and the whereabouts of her ashes are unknown.

Prior to meeting Jimmy Martin, I had a son, Michael Hollis Morgan, born in 1953. His father, Carl, was my first love. Carl would visit his friends next door to our house on a regular basis. I always went out on the porch and sat in the swing while I watched him go to the faucet in the backyard to brush his teeth or walk to the outhouse. The house where he stayed didn't have indoor facilities with running water.

Carl was four years older than me and already in the service. I knew his brother from school but never knew where his family lived. I also knew his sister. From the time I was fourteen years old, I idolized Carl. He took me by bus to the only school dance I ever attended. I don't know when he stopped thinking of me as a kid, but he kissed me for the first time on top of the little viaduct on Charlotte Pike just west of Twenty-Fifth Avenue as we were walking home from Centennial Park. He asked me to marry him and move to California while we were sitting in Centennial Park in front of the Parthenon by a statue we called "Corrosion" because it had turned green in the weather. He was scheduled to go overseas, and we could be married before he left. I told him I would go anywhere with him.

I was madly in love with him. He told me he loved me just as much. I remember one time when he had just come home on leave, I ran and literally jumped into his arms. Carl was over six feet tall. He swooped me up and spun me around. I was thrilled.

The day we were going to get married, Mother presented him with a pickle cake. She knew how he loved pickles and cake, so she put the two together. It was the worst cake ever but a lot of fun and typical for Mother.

Then, when the time came for us to move to Monterey, California, I was having difficulty leaving home. I was sixteen and didn't know anything about being a wife, nor did I think I wanted to know. But he was the love of my life, and at sixteen I felt grown up. I had always been thrown in with older kids from the time I was in first grade, but I had never been away from home and I was afraid. Finally, I talked to Mother and Mama about how I didn't want to leave home. They both listened to me and then explained that I had married Carl and I should go. Reluctantly, I went.

The base in California was close to Monterey, but at first we couldn't find an apartment. Finally we did find one and moved into a nice one-bedroom basement apartment in Pacific Grove across the street from the water. Shortly afterward I was hired as a waitress at the Pacific Grove Hotel. I thought, "This is the perfect job, because Carl can eat at the base and I can eat at the hotel. I won't have to learn to cook." He already did most of the house cleaning. I did dust, but I hated it. I liked to spend my spare time taking whatever book I was reading, going across the street, and sitting on the rocks to watch the seals and water. It was like being in heaven. Carl always teased me that if I died first, he would have me cremated and put my ashes in the sea at that spot. (Several years later, Chuck and I were on a trip to California. I took Chuck and showed him where I had lived, where I had worked, and where my spot near the sea had been. We got out of the car and walked around. It had not changed, and I loved it just as much.)

When Carl was killed in the service, I was devastated. My first love was gone. He never saw the baby I was expecting. I was seventeen years old with a newborn son that I didn't know how to care for. When I was growing up I had been a princess and was never asked to do anything around the house. Betty and Billie washed and dried the dishes, but I worked outside the house. I didn't like housework. We had a lady who came in and cleaned and cooked every day. All of our clothes were sent to the laundry, washed, dried, pressed, and returned to the house. We always had help, and this was how I had grown up.

There was only one thing for me to do, and that was to pack up and go home. I was still working at the hotel and had a little money saved but little else. I knew I would be getting Carl's life insurance but wasn't sure when. And I was pregnant. I knew it was going to be a hard row to hoe; then again, I felt like I was a strong person and I could do it. Fortunately, I have always been a strong person, able to think and learn quickly. So a couple of months later I flew home to Nashville.

My son Mike was born at Baptist Hospital in Nashville in 1953. When I came home from the hospital with him, Mother took over. I loved my baby, but Mike was like a toy for me. Mother did all of the feeding and changing of diapers, and I played with him and loved him. I really liked that part of being a mother. My mother, who was only thirty-seven years old, together with my grandmother and grandfather, raised Mike. (Many years later, after I met Jimmy and I knew we were going to be together, I thought Mike would come to live with us, but that was not to be. Regardless of how much I begged and pleaded, Jimmy would never allow Mike to come to live with us, because "he wasn't blood." I always thought he would change his mind, but he never did.)

After the birth of Michael, I knew I had to find a job. I was hoping to find one paying enough for the two of us to live on. I wanted to move out of my grandmother's house, but I knew that if I did, I would have to pay a babysitter and other expenses. I also was smart enough to know that I couldn't make enough money to do that. So I continued to hope for work.

Mike was such a beautiful baby, always smiling. My mother, my grand-parents, my sisters, and I all adored him. Working was going to take me away from him, and I would miss him. He was my cuddly, adorable little toy who made me laugh. The harder I laughed, the more he would laugh. I played that silly game with him every day.

Going back to work, and where I worked, would change my life drasti-cally. Without knowing it, I was about to embark on a stormy journey that would last for the next fourteen years. That journey and those decisions not only affected me for the rest of my life, but also affected my son Mike and the children I would bear in the future.

I have always been a very aggressive person, a "type A personality," as they would say today. I'm a go-getter. I freely admit that I'm more of a boss than a worker. I am one of the most loyal, down-to-earth, truthful, helpful people you will ever meet. If you are my friend, you are my friend for life.

So you may ask, Why did I make some of those decisions? Why *did* I stay with a man who was a cheater and an abuser? Very simple. I grew to love Jimmy Martin, and I wanted to have a home for our children. I also knew something was eating at him; I just didn't know what. It took me years to figure all that out.

Writing this, I am eighty-one years old. I continue to be a person who has to stay busy, who has to have a work project, and who loves life and is loyal to family and friends—one you can count on to tell you the truth. I always told my kids, "Don't lie to me, because I will catch you. And when I do, your butt is mine." If you tell me something, I will remember it, and ten years from now I can tell you verbatim what you said. My kids hate that. Fortunately, I have an excellent memory and it certainly served Jimmy and me well over the years.

How do I feel about how I have lived my life? I think I've had a damn good life. Everything that has happened to me has helped me grow into the person I am now. Did I have affairs? Absolutely! Did I do things I regret? You bet your booty! Would I have done things differently? Yes, if I had known what I know now. But, then again, I didn't know what I know now when I was sixteen, seventeen, or even thirty-five years old. It took years of living through the experiences I've had from 1953 until I'm writing these words today. And, hopefully, as long as I live, I will never stop growing as a person.

1

MEETING JIMMY MARTIN

In early May 1953, my girlfriend Jean Armstrong suggested I apply in the coffee shop where she worked as a waitress at the Tulane Hotel in Nashville. The hotel was situated on the corner of Eighth Avenue North and Church Street. It was the equivalent of a two- or three-star-rated hotel in today's market. The restaurant served breakfast, lunch, and supper—nothing fancy.

The Tulane was cheap, clean, nice, and convenient—a magnet for side-men from the Grand Ole Opry. Musicians who lived there and worked at the Opry didn't need a car. They could take their instruments, unless it was an upright bass, and walk to the Ryman Auditorium, where the Opry was held. The Ryman was located on Fifth Avenue, between Broadway and Commerce Street—about six or seven blocks.

I applied in the coffee shop at the hotel and was hired the same day. I started to work the next week. On my first day of work I met Bessie Lee Mauldin, Bill Monroe's longtime girlfriend. Bessie was a well-endowed, beautiful blonde and an immaculate dresser. I was envious of her beauty and fashion. She was easy to talk to. Maybe she needed a friend. Who knows? But she befriended me. It wasn't long before she told me she was Bill Monroe's girlfriend and had been for many years. Bessie said Bill was still married to his wife, Carolyn, and they had two children. But that didn't stop Bill and Bessie. He took her everywhere. She even appeared with Bill and his daughter, Melissa, on stage. Despite the fact I was a transplanted

Nashville girl, I had no idea who Bill Monroe was at the time, nor did I care. I did know he played on the Opry, because Bessie told me. Bessie was not only Bill's longtime girlfriend but also his bass player.

Within a week of starting work I met Rudy Lyle, L. E. White, Sonny Osborne, Charlie Cline, and into my life came Jimmy Martin. They were all sidemen for Bill. They didn't impress me, but I thought they were nice guys. I still didn't know anything about Bill Monroe. The last time I had gone to the Grand Ole Opry, I was three or four years old and it was held in the old Dixie Tabernacle. I don't remember going, but Mother told me we went.

When Jimmy first came into the restaurant and sat at one of my tables, he immediately asked me out. At the time, he was twenty-five years old and I was only seventeen, with a smart mouth. I told him, "No. If I wanted to go out with my daddy, I would go home and get him."

Even though I thought of Jimmy as old, he was still very good looking and a charmer. He had beautiful blue eyes. His hair was a dirty brown color and sort of thin, but not as thin as it was in later years. I liked him—and I didn't. I wanted to go out with him—and I didn't. I thought it would be exciting to go to the Opry with him, but I didn't want to get involved with him. Those mixed feelings would keep me with him for the next fourteen years.

Jimmy came to the restaurant every day. He was not a big tipper, but he was a big talker. He often left a penny under each plate, cup, saucer, or whatever dish he was using. That irritated me to no end. He thought he was playing a joke, but what he was doing was ripping off the waitress. In my mind, he was a typical old man trying to be cute. I didn't think he was funny. Yet he had that charisma tugging at my heart. I had to keep telling myself, "Don't get sucked in. He's too old."

A few weeks after I started work at the Tulane, Jean and I decided to go skating one Friday night. We took our skates and extra clothes to work. Jean and I had been going to the Hippodrome Skating Rink since we were in the ninth grade and considered ourselves "regulars." Our weekends were consumed with skating. Looking back now, we were kids doing kids' things while living in a grown-up world.

After work we caught the bus and went to the Hippodrome. When we got there, we put our skates on and went out onto the floor. We made a few rounds, but none of our skating partners was there, so we took off our skates, caught the bus, and went back to town.

We were standing on Union Street waiting for our bus to go home when it started pouring down rain. No umbrellas! We were soaking wet. We did have a piece of plastic covering our heads. It was Friday night, and we weren't really ready to go home.

From where we were standing, we could see the National Life and Accident Insurance Company building, where radio station WSM had its studios, and we wondered if L. E. White and Jimmy were at WSM. Jean said, "Why don't I call L. E. and maybe we can go up to the WSM studios." That sounded good. I liked L. E. but was not crazy about Jimmy Martin. I was hoping I might meet someone else at WSM I could hang out with. Jean went inside the restaurant and called L. E., and he invited us up to the studio. Neither Jean nor I had ever been in a radio studio. Our lives were to change forever with this one visit to WSM.

When we got to the studio, L. E. met us at the elevator and took us to the studio. Of course, Jimmy was there and he was thrilled that I was along. He immediately came over and took my hand and started showing me around. He introduced me to Ralph Emery and Randy Hughes. Randy and I hit it off right away.

I had never heard of Eddie Hill but later found out he was very important in the country music field. In fact, at that time in my life I was not a country music fan—and certainly not a bluegrass music fan. I didn't even know or care about what bluegrass or country music was or who was involved in those music fields. I had met one country music artist in my lifetime, and that was Carl Smith. I met Carl at a concert in Centennial Park. He later called and asked me out, but I had just washed my hair and politely refused. (That was before personal hair dryers.) Carl and I never dated, but we remained friends. Once in a while through the years, he would call me just to talk. And whenever I did see him, we always had great conversations and mutual respect for each other.

After Jimmy and L. E. finished the radio show, Jimmy said the two of them would take Jean and me home. Then I saw Jimmy's car. I wanted to turn around and go catch the bus. It was a Hudson—bright blue and yellow. A monstrosity! Jimmy asked L. E. to drive, and Jimmy and I got into the backseat. He immediately wanted to paw me. I wasn't into that and asked him to keep his hands to himself. We went to Olive's Drive Inn restaurant on Charlotte Avenue, where we sat in the car, laughing and talking for a couple of hours. We had a lot of fun. It was a nice evening and I began liking him a little more.

While sitting in the car at Olive's, two boys Jean and I knew from school, Monk Demonbreun and Jimmy White, showed up. Jean liked Monk, and I was crazy about Jimmy White, from afar. Unfortunately, I don't think either of them felt the same way about us. Jean and I were definitely not part of the "in crowd" in high school, and neither of us participated in any activities. Regardless, I wanted to talk to Jimmy and Monk. One of them had my class ring and I wanted it back. I had let them look at it, and they kept it. I never saw the ring again.

After Jean and I finished our conversation with Monk and Jimmy White, L. E. and Jimmy Martin drove us to my house. Jimmy kissed me good night and said he would see me the next day. I enjoyed the kiss, but I told myself, "Don't do that again."

Jimmy was twenty-five years old. I knew he was too old for me. I also knew he drank a lot, and I didn't like that. My mother was an alcoholic, and I couldn't tolerate a drunk. However, Jimmy was a very persuasive man, very handsome, and very talented. When he gave me that movie star smile, I melted. It was a smile that would make you want to jump his bones. Jimmy and I continued to talk every day. After a couple of weeks, he started asking me to go places with him. Once again, I kept telling myself, "Don't get sucked in." I didn't listen, and in the end I started going places with him.

Since the Tulane Hotel was in the downtown area of Nashville, Jimmy and I started walking around after I got off from work. We would look in the store windows, go in the stores if we saw something we liked, hold hands, and talk. Jimmy was extremely nice to me. During one of those walks, he bought me a beautiful pair of earrings from Harvey's, an upscale store in Nashville. (Back then we didn't use the word "upscale.") This was the very first thing I ever had from Harvey's. Regardless, Jimmy was baiting me and I didn't know it. He was nice to me, and now I was liking him more and more, despite his drinking. I kept telling myself his drinking wasn't that bad.

Soon Jean and I were joining L. E. and Jimmy in their Tulane Hotel rooms and partying with all the Blue Grass Boys (except for Sonny Osborne, who was only fifteen at the time). Partying then was not like it is today.

Sitting around in one of the musicians' rooms, usually Jimmy's, drinking beer, talking, and singing was partying. I don't think anyone in the group drank hard liquor. Sonny was only a kid, and I remember him just sitting in the window listening to everything. I don't remember any of the Blue Grass Boys living in the hotel, having a girlfriend, or bringing a girl to the rooms. Jean and I were the only females. Jean was dating L. E. and I was with Jimmy. After the party broke up, Jean and L. E. would go to L. E.'s room. Then Jimmy and I would lock the door and hit the sheets.

The Blue Grass Boys were a group of very nice, country guys. I never saw or heard any of them talking about women in a negative way or using foul language. I never saw or knew of any of them using any kind of drug. I think their drug of choice was music. That seemed to be all any of them ever thought about when they were together. This was a group of men who had grown up in the thirties and forties, most of them in the country. They were taught to respect people and things. To Jean and me, they were always very respectful. Jimmy and I were a couple and they respected that. They also respected L. E. and Jean. Personally, I thought of most of them as being uneducated and lonely. Sonny was still in school, and when school commenced he returned home.

I knew the guys working for Bill were not making much money. Jimmy told me they were paid ten dollars for each segment they played on the Opry and that they were paid for the show at the studios. They rarely went out of town on a show. So one could figure their weekly pay was about twenty-five dollars. They were barely skimming by. Jimmy was smarter than most with his money. He was a saver. He always had cash. If someone needed to borrow money, Jimmy would let them have it. I always told him he could squeeze a dime until it turned into a dollar.

Jimmy was this handsome devil of a man. I thought he was the most handsome sideman on the Opry. He had the most beautiful blue eyes and smile and was about the same height as me or maybe an inch taller. I was five foot seven and a half inches tall, with dark brown hair, green eyes, and I never weighed over 120 pounds. Despite his drinking, I thought Jimmy was a very caring person. I soon found out that he cried easily, and that made him even more special to me. He was someone with a heart.

The good times were in high gear, and I started staying away from home more and more. My mother called the Tulane and told them I was underage and to keep me out of the hotel. Her phone call did nothing but cause me to lose my job. Jimmy devised a plan where he would meet me at the back door and we would take the back stairs to his room. Several months passed before I went back through the lobby.

By now Jimmy was like an addiction to me. He and I could look at each other, and we would find a place to have sex. If we were in the hotel, we would head for Jimmy's room. If we were in the car, we would find a place to pull over and make love in the car. We didn't care where we were. Wanted it, needed it, let's get on with it. That was sort of our motto. Jimmy was an experienced lover, and in the beginning he took his time and our lovemaking was exciting and satisfying for both of us. It would be many years before that would change.

In those days Jimmy was a lot of fun. He liked to kid around. Charlie Cline played fiddle for Bill Monroe and was also living at the Tulane. I liked Charlie and thought he was a nice guy. He was funny and, I thought, a little off the wall. One day Jimmy and I were in Charlie's room playing around. Jimmy liked to tickle me, because he knew I would jump. That day, he grabbed me and started tickling. When he let go, I fell backward onto the bed, smashing Bill's prized fiddle that was on the bed. Charlie, Jimmy, and I were stunned. *What do we do now?* Charlie was afraid to tell Bill. Jimmy was yelling about the fiddle being smashed beyond repair. I didn't know what to do. But somehow or other the fiddle got repaired, though I don't remember how, and Charlie stayed out of trouble. Needless to say, we never did that again.

Our life together, such as it was, was not all about sex. We had a lot of serious moments when we would talk about what we wanted in the future. He loved family. He wanted to be a star and to be on the Grand Ole Opry. I didn't know anything about music, but I was willing to help him. We talked about education. Jimmy was embarrassed that he didn't have even a grammar-school education or the opportunity to get one. When I first met him, he could barely write his name. We practiced for hours. He wanted to learn to write his name in a flamboyant way (not actually what he said, because "flamboyant" was not a word he used). Because the capital *M* in his last name was difficult for him to write, he started making it square at the top. He liked that. He thought it looked good. But at times he would revert back to the way the *M* is supposed to be written. I think in his mind he was trying to determine what looked best when he signed autographs.

We talked about many things, including his family and my family. Those were the best times, just sitting on the bed and talking.

Times and things were changing, and we all knew that. Jean was no longer going with L. E. and was now dating Don "Suds" Slayman, who played fiddle for Marty Robbins. (Don and Jean were madly in love with each other and would later marry. They were together until Don's death in 2006. Jean passed away in 2013.)

One night, after I'd had words with Jimmy about his drinking, Jean asked me if I would like to go with her, Don Slayman, and Marty Robbins to the Starlite. The Starlite was a club on Dickerson Road where everyone went to dance. Of course I said yes. Who wouldn't want to be in the company of Marty Robbins? I went and we were having a wonderful time. Marty and I had just finished a dance and walked back to our table. As we sat back down, who shows up at our table but Jimmy Martin. Jimmy said, "Let's go." I said, "No." Marty said, "Leave her alone; she's with me." Jimmy was getting madder by the minute. I knew Marty was a former fighter and I didn't want to see Jimmy hurt. I asked Marty to let it go and said I would go with Jimmy. (Little did I know that it would be twenty years before Marty spoke to me again. Whenever he saw Jimmy and me at shows throughout those years, he turned his head and walked away. Then, in 1972, I was walking up Fifth Avenue from Broad Street on my way back to work. Marty was standing in front of the Ryman—just standing there. As I started by, he said, "Don't you speak to old friends?" I was taken aback. We hugged each other, sat down on the front steps of the Ryman, and just talked. I kissed him goodbye, not knowing it would be the last time I would see him alive.)

That night as I left the Starlite with Jimmy, I was livid. Johnny Seibert was driving the car. Johnny was a steel guitar player on the Opry with Carl Smith. When we got to Eighth Avenue and Church Street, the corner where the Tulane Hotel was located, Jimmy wanted to get out of the car. I didn't want out and I didn't want any confrontations. I asked Johnny to take me home. We let Jimmy out of the car, thinking he would go into the hotel. The last thing I saw was Jimmy sitting cross-legged in the middle of the intersection and cars going around him. I am sure that he got up as soon as we were out of sight. It was an attention-getter. The traffic was slow at that time of night, and he knew the cars weren't going to hit him—or at least he hoped they wouldn't.

The next day when I saw Jimmy, he didn't apologize for his antics. I was really upset with him and let him know he didn't own me. That did not go over well with Jimmy. It would be several days before we talked again.

During this time, one of Jimmy's favorite activities was to grab a beer and go walking down Church Street in the evening. There was an old black man who sat outside the Bennie Dillon Building and played music every night. Jimmy had made friends with him and always stopped to sing as loudly as he could with the old man. Being a generous person, Jimmy never failed to leave a quarter in the old guy's tip hat. In those days a quarter was like a dollar today. You could buy a hamburger, a Coke, and an ice cream cone with a quarter.

Jimmy liked attention and would do anything to get it. One of his stunts was to jump the parking meters on Church Street. Jimmy's legs were short, not long like mine. I often wondered how he could jump the parking meters or kick so high. He and Rudy Lyle used to play "who can kick the highest." I have some original photos showing them kicking. Anyhow, I was mortified whenever he would jump the meters. I thought people were looking at me and wondering what I was doing with him, a crazy man. Sometimes I wondered the same thing. But he was still my drug of choice. I wanted to leave him and yet I didn't.

I should have noticed that Jimmy was becoming more aggressive and possessive of me. It was more than just wanting to know where I was going, when I was coming back, and who I was going with. I didn't mind that too much, because I would ask him the same things. I told him the truth, but I don't think he told me the truth when he would say where he was going. But I was still a kid, and the only experience I'd had with men was with Mike's father, Carl. I had had a very loving relationship with Carl, and that would probably have lasted a lifetime, but then he had gone to Korea, never to return. So I didn't know what to look for as far as people's habits and personalities. I thought Jimmy was just a temperamental entertainer. At that time, he never hit me and never threatened me despite our sometimes heated words about his drinking. His major problem was infidelity. He just couldn't be true to any one woman.

After a few months of partying, Jimmy and I were growing tired of it. We both liked each other a lot and knew that we were going to be together. We decided to talk to my grandparents about moving in with them.

I will never forget the day Jimmy and I went to talk to Mama and DaddyHollis. My grandfather liked to play the fiddle. He wasn't very good at it but he tried. Jimmy and I went into the house and sat down. DaddyHollis brought the fiddle out, and Jimmy immediately started talking to him about the fiddle. DaddyHollis asked Jimmy what his plans were, and Jimmy told him we had gotten married. I think my jaw hit the floor, because that wasn't in the plan. Jimmy and I had never talked about marriage. We did talk about the future, mostly his. I liked him a lot but didn't think I was in love with him. I wanted to be with him but didn't know if I was ready to be a wife. That was not in my plan at the time. I enjoyed being his girlfriend and hanging out with him. But Mama was thrilled thinking we were married. To my knowledge, they never learned the difference.

2

MOVING ON

Jimmy moved out of the hotel in the early part of November 1953 and moved into my grandparents' house on Charlotte Avenue. His blue and yellow Hudson, an eyesore, stayed in our driveway.

He commuted to the WSM studios for his early morning program with Bill Monroe. Jimmy was not a good driver and would normally have someone else drive him. But living on Charlotte Pike, there was no one around to drive him. He *had* to drive. About the second or third time he commuted, he had an accident on his way home. It happened on Charlotte across the park from Cohn High School. The blue and yellow Hudson was totaled, but Jimmy was okay. Yeah! I was thrilled that the Hudson was gone. The only problem was that we were supposed to go to Jimmy's mother's house in Sneedville, Tennessee, for Thanksgiving. Now we had no vehicle.

My aunt Jessie lived next door to our house. She had a nice car and rarely went anywhere. Aunt Jessie liked Jimmy and trusted him, so when he asked her to loan us the car so that we could go home for Thanksgiving, she did, and we went off to Sneedville.

I had never been to the country in my life. Here was this girl born in Memphis who had moved to Nashville when she was ten and now was going to stay in a house with no indoor plumbing—no place inside to take a bath or go to the bathroom. There was only a path and an outhouse. Desperately afraid of snakes and critters, I was like a lost puppy.

I was welcomed into Sarah Johnson's home with open arms. I didn't know what, if anything, Jimmy had told them about me. Jimmy's mother didn't have a phone, and I didn't know how Jimmy could have gotten in touch with her. I knew he didn't write a letter. Nevertheless, I liked Jimmy's mother, Sarah, and stepfather, Ellis. And I loved his sisters Evelyn, Edria, and Erma. We were all about the same age, so we got along great. Erma was already married and had children, but she only lived down the road in the main part of Sneedville. She would either come by Sarah's house or we would stop there almost every day. Jimmy's older sisters, Hazel and Euna, and brothers, John and Roy, were all married and had families of their own.

Sarah's house had a big front porch. There were two rooms at the front of the house, a bedroom on the right as you entered, and the living room you walked into. Then you walked into the dining room. Off the dining room to your right was another bedroom, and the kitchen was on the left. The front bedroom had three beds in it. When I first saw it, I asked Jimmy, "Are we going to have to sleep with other people in the room?" He told me no. I was worried about having to get up in the middle of the night and use the "slop" jar to pee with someone else in the room. One thing for sure, I wasn't going to go down that path to the outhouse. I would pee in the bed first.

That night, I couldn't believe the quilts and blankets that were on the bed. They felt like they weighed a ton, but Jimmy and I snuggled down inside all the covers and giggled and played and had a wonderful time. We tried to be quiet, because Sarah, Ellis, Edria, and Evelyn were sleeping on the other side of the thin wall.

Edria and I often sat on the front porch and talked. One day we were sitting there and I noticed two chickens that looked like they were fighting. I asked Edria if she wasn't going to stop them. She said, "No, they are not fighting." I asked her what they were doing and she looked at me and said, "You *know* what they are doing." I can still see the way she looked when she said that. I felt like an idiot but laughed my butt off. I never forgot that or trying to milk the cow. A "milker" I was not and still am not. I pulled and pulled and never could get any milk. Edria was standing there watching me and laughing. I knew living in the country would never be the place for me.

Jimmy's sister Euna and her husband, Clyde, were two of my favorite people in Sneedville. They were so good to me the first time I was there and every time after. They risked Jimmy's wrath over the years whenever they tried to protect me from him. Even long after I was no longer part of the family, they continued to treat me like family.

The first time we were in Sneedville, Jimmy started drinking moonshine with homemade tomato juice. I drank the tomato juice but couldn't get the moonshine past my nose to my mouth. That was the same way beer has been all my life. And it still is. So I drank the tomato juice, which was very good. I am the type of person who never needed drugs or alcohol to have fun or love life. To this day, I wake up every morning thanking God for giving me another day. I live life to the fullest each and every day. I am not a total prude, and I do enjoy a nice glass of wine with dinner, but one or two is my limit. Wine wasn't fashionable in those days. People (at least the ones I knew) thought that if you drank wine, you were a "wino." It was either beer or hard liquor.

Jimmy and I rode around the back country roads of Sneedville every night. I usually drove and Jimmy drank moonshine. He would sing to me, grab my boob or my crotch, just playing around, or pointing out who lived where. Thinking back, it was like he wanted me to know everyone in Sneedville and where they lived.

Jimmy and I had one thing going for us from the very beginning, and that was a great sex life. He was one of the most handsome men I had ever known. He was also the oldest man I had ever been with. He liked to play and so did I. One of us would start grabbing at the other's parts, and then we would both be doing it. We would play for an hour, sometimes laughing the entire time. Even though Jimmy was old, he was still fun.

One night while riding around on the back roads of Sneedville, we pulled up alongside a barn and made a little love. It was probably a whole lot of love, because nine months later, almost to the day, we had Jimmy Martin Jr., known as Timmy. We spent most of the night alongside the barn just talking and making love. I think that was when I realized for the first time that I had fallen in love. Our relationship was no longer just about sex but was much deeper than that. It was a fantastic night. If all of the nights over the next fourteen years had been like that one, I still would have been with Jimmy.

We returned Aunt Jessie's car to her when we got back to Nashville, and Jimmy bought another car. He wanted to go back to Sneedville for Christmas. I think he wanted to show off his new car. I didn't want to go but went anyway. There was nothing to do in Sneedville, and I was bored. I liked the city lights. I also hated the outdoor toilet.

Nonetheless, we went back to Sneedville to spend a couple of days with Jimmy's mother. Then we went to his sister Hazel's in Morristown to spend a week. I liked it so much better at Hazel and her husband Jake's house. Hazel and I could talk forever. She was such a good person and a good mother to their four kids. Those kids were lots of fun. They reminded me of my son, Mike, and the fun I had playing with him. Hazel and Jake had a bathroom and running water. The house was small, but there was so much joy in it. I always felt at home there. Jimmy seemed to be much more at ease with Hazel and Jake than at his mother's house. Hazel and Jake's house was alive with laughter, the smell of good food cooking, and happiness.

The one good thing about going to the homes of any of Jimmy's brothers and sisters or aunts was that all of the women, including the younger ones, were and are excellent cooks. I had never tasted food that good in my life. The only thing I didn't like was the milk. I just couldn't drink milk that came straight from the cows and not in a bottle from the store. I had already tried milking the cows, and it gagged me to think about drinking it. I freely admit that I was a spoiled city girl, and I still am. Give me the bright lights of the city anytime.

When we returned to Nashville after Christmas, Jimmy decided we were going back to the Tulane Hotel. I was working on Charlotte Pike at a drive-in restaurant and making pretty good tips. (At the time, making ten dollars a day was considered "good" tips.) I didn't want to leave my job but knew it was too far to travel every day to and from the hotel.

At the Tulane we had our own room and we weren't involved with the partying. The partying had quieted down. Everything had changed. Rudy Lyle, Bill's banjo player, was running around with Connie Dickens. At the time, Connie was married to Little Jimmy Dickens. Little Jimmy didn't know about the ongoing affair. In fact, he didn't find out until after Rudy quit Bill Monroe. Then Connie and Rudy went away to an unknown place. I liked Connie and Rudy, and I was sorry that I never saw them again. Jean was involved with Don Slayman. L. E. was dating someone else, and Charlie Cline and Sonny Osborne had left Bill.

After we returned to the hotel, Jimmy started leaving and going off to unknown places. He would never let me know where he was going. He would just take off. I had become good friends with Hillous Butrum (who was one

of the original Drifting Cowboys for Hank Snow and now played for Hank),
Ray Price, Doyle Wilburn, and Hubert Long, and several others. We were
just friends, never romantically involved. They would often take me home,
but a lot of times I would go with Hubert to his house. Doyle would stop
by. My girlfriend Jean would go with us, and we would all sit around and
talk. With them, it was an interesting, innocent good time. There was no
sex involved and no pairing up. We were all just good friends. Even though
Doyle would usually have a drink, the rest of us would drink Coca-Cola.

One night Ray Price and I were sitting and talking at Mom's, a beer
joint across the alley from the Ryman Auditorium, which housed the
Grand Ole Opry. Everyone from the Opry went to Mom's, sidemen and
stars alike. "Mom" Upchurch sold Mom's in 1960 and it became Tootsie's
Orchid Lounge. She also had a rooming house in East Nashville where a
lot of the sidemen, and sometimes stars, rented rooms. As the place was
closing, Jimmy was nowhere to be found. I didn't have a ride home, so Ray
volunteered. We had just turned onto Broad Street and were having a nice
conversation when Ray remembered he had to let his dog out. He had a
big German shepherd. Ray lived off Murfreesboro Pike and what is now
called Briley Parkway, close to the old Avco plant. Ray asked me if I would
mind riding to his house with him and I said no. We immediately turned
around and went to Ray's house. He had just gotten out of a relationship
with a woman he had lived with for years. He was hurting and we talked
about that. We also talked about my relationship with Jimmy, which he
couldn't understand. I told him I was a couple of months pregnant. Then
he understood as we discussed it. Ray's house was small. I don't remember
the exact house, but the same style houses are still sitting and occupied in
that development today. We let the dog out and sat down on the sofa. We
were having a great conversation when Ray kissed me. It was a night to be
remembered. I think we were consoling each other. I never found out where
Jimmy was that night. Frankly, I didn't care. He had disappeared and I had
had a wonderful evening.

A couple of nights after that, I wanted to go skating at the Hippodrome
Roller Skating Rink, so I called Jean. She said she couldn't go. I thought
that was rather strange, because I knew she didn't have any other plans,
or at least I thought she didn't. We both loved to skate and we hadn't been
for a while.

A little while later I couldn't find Jimmy. He wasn't in any of the other musicians' rooms. I became suspicious—Jimmy had vanished and Jean didn't want to go skating. I called Mama and asked if I could use the car. She didn't have a problem with that. I asked L. E. to give me a ride to my grandmother's house. By now it was around 7:30 p.m. The minute I got home, I grabbed the car keys and drove to the skating rink. I parked the car across the street and sat there. It wasn't long until Jimmy's car pulled up and Jean walked out of the skating rink and got in. They were laughing as they drove off. My best friend and my boyfriend were going to shack up. My heart broke.

The next day, I saw Jean. I told her that I had seen her getting into Jimmy's car and the two of them laughing as they drove away. She knew not to deny it. I told her, "Do *not* ever walk on the same side of the street as me, or I will *stomp* you. I never want to see or speak to you again." It would be forty-five years before I would talk to her again. (By then she had been married for years to Don Slayman. Don was in the early stages of Alzheimer's when I went to their house. Jean had just recovered from cancer of the tongue and mouth.)

Jimmy had been caught again and he knew it. I had also found out that some of the times he went missing, he was with Melissa Monroe, Bill's daughter. I found this out only because she had torn up an eight-by-ten-inch photo of me. When I discovered it, I went home to my mother and stayed a few days until Jimmy pestered me to death—calling to get me back. It's so easy now to see the pattern that was starting to develop.

I should have left him then and never looked back. But at the time, I was blinded not only by our relationship but by ignorance as well. I was eighteen years old, pregnant, and knew nothing. I had no one to guide me or talk to, and even if I had, I wouldn't have listened. They say love is blind. Well, so is lust and ignorance. I was ignorant and in lust. I was also in love with him. Terrible combination!

During these years, Jimmy was never threatening to me. His only problem was that he desperately needed attention from women—the more women, the better. One wasn't enough, even though he wanted that one to be loyal to him at all times. But he couldn't return that loyalty. It's easy to see now that he was seeking the attention he should have received from his mother. He never did. Because she had so many children and worked so hard on the farm, she simply didn't have time. If he could have let the past go, he would have been much happier. He would often shed tears over his childhood. Nothing or no one could relieve his loneliness.

When I returned to the hotel, Jimmy told me that he had dated Melissa Monroe before he met me. What he didn't tell me was that he had continued to see her after he met me. Melissa was a year younger than me. I had just turned eighteen when all of this took place. Jimmy told me that Melissa didn't mean anything to him. I believed him. I didn't think that was the case with her and I was right. (Melissa never married and died relatively young.)

Jimmy and I talked about his leaving Bill Monroe. I agreed that he should do what he wanted to do. He wanted to be a star. We both felt that together we could make him a star, even though I would have to learn the music business. I was a fast learner, and I believed I could do my share.

Jimmy gave his notice to Bill. But Bill was a man who didn't like losing a good musician—or anything else for that matter. Bill called and wanted to talk to me. I don't remember where Jimmy was (I think rehearsing) when Bill came by our room. I will never forget Bill sitting on the bed and asking me to get Jimmy to change his mind about leaving the Blue Grass Boys. We talked for a good hour about it. In the end I told him that I wanted Jimmy to do whatever was necessary to see if he could become a star on his own. I refused to talk Jimmy into staying. I think Bill liked me better for that honesty, because throughout the many years I knew Bill, he was always friendly to me. He never saw me that he didn't stop to talk.

I liked Bill even though sometimes he could make cutting remarks. Like the time I saw him at a telethon many years later in Nashville. He said to me, "You've gained a little weight there, Barbara." I said, "Yes, Bill, that's what happens when you become affluent." Both of us laughed at my comment. Lisa, my daughter, was just a baby-in-arms and was looking at us laughing like "What's going on?"

In March 1954 Jimmy and I packed the car and left Nashville. We didn't have much except for a few clothes and his guitar. I think I had more clothes than he did, but everything fit into a couple of suitcases. I was now almost four months pregnant without showing. We were driving to Middletown, Ohio, where Jimmy had a job with radio station WPFB.

On the way, Jimmy heard a young banjo player on the radio. We stopped and he called the radio station and found out how to get in touch with him. I don't remember the name of the program or the station call letters. Anyhow, Jimmy called the banjo player, who turned out to be J. D. Crowe. He invited us to his house. We went there and I believe Jimmy and Crowe played a couple of songs together. Knowing Jimmy, that was what he always did whenever he got around musicians. I do know Jimmy talked to Crowe's parents about him working for Jimmy after school was out.

I liked Mr. and Mrs. Crowe, and I especially liked his sister, Rosa. I remember Crowe's father, Orville, talking to me about his job with IBM. I thought that was so cool to be working around computers. I had worked around computers, such as they were then, at Washington Manufacturing Company while in high school, so I knew a little bit about them.

Mr. and Mrs. Crowe told Jimmy they would let J. D. work with him when school was out. Jimmy was very happy about that. We left their house and headed to Middletown.

We arrived and got a motel room. The following day we found a room in which to live. It was large with a private bathroom. It was downtown, too, so it would be easy for me to find a job nearby where I could walk to work.

After we moved in, Jimmy went to WPFB to see Smoky Ward, and I went to look for a job. The first place I applied hired me. It was a bar called Sonny's and was practically across the street from our room. I started work the following day. I thought it was a good job; the people were nice and the tips were good. I liked it there, but Jimmy became a problem. I worked the evening shift from three to eleven. Every afternoon, around five or six, Jimmy would come in and sit at the bar on the end stool, where he could talk to me. This was okay at first; the manager didn't say anything, because Jimmy was buying beer. But after about two months of Jimmy sitting around night after night while I worked, it got old with the manager. One day the manager told me he was letting me go. I asked him why, and he said, "Your husband cannot sit here every night watching you work." That was my last paying job in Middletown.

We had lived in the one room for about a month when Johnny Dacus came to play fiddle with Jimmy. Johnny would be staying in our room. For privacy, Jimmy and I hung a curtain between our bed and the pallet we had made for Johnny. After they both woke up each morning, I then got up to get ready for work. These were hard times, but things began looking up.

For the life of me, I have tried to remember the names of the two local musicians who were playing mandolin and banjo with Jimmy. They played on the radio show and at occasional beer joints with him. I keep thinking it was Noah Crase on the banjo and Earl Taylor on the mandolin. The problem is they are both dead, so I can't verify this as true.

When school was out, Jimmy drove to Lexington, Kentucky, and picked up J. D. Crowe. I don't remember going, but I wasn't working, so it's very possible I went with him and drove, since Jimmy did not like to drive. Crowe was going to work with Jimmy over the summer months. Johnny Dacus had gone home to Cumberland Gap. By then we had moved into a two-room apartment. The main room had a double bed and a sofa that made into an extra bed. The small kitchen had a stove, refrigerator, sink, and a small table and chairs. We brushed our teeth in the sink, since we didn't have a bathroom. We took a shower or bath in the main house and, when needed, followed a path that led to an outhouse. I had never cooked in my life and didn't even know how to boil water. Thinking about it now, we should have moved the sofa into the kitchen for Crowe. But then we would have missed all those good times.

Crowe slept on the sofa and Jimmy and I slept in the bed. Crowe and I were both very young. He was sixteen and I was eighteen. Jimmy liked to go to bed early. So of course when he wanted to go to bed, we had to go to bed too. Crowe and I would start giggling. He would then start with some phrases from Chuck Berry, or Little Richard's songs, or other old sayings. When he started that, I would laugh so hard the bed would shake. Jimmy would yell at us, "Cut it out and go to sleep." We didn't and couldn't. We would be quiet for a while and then start again until Jimmy really got mad, and then we would quit. One of Crowe's sayings that I remember was "Around the curve lickety-split. It was a nice car, wasn't it?"

We had been living in the apartment for about a month. I was pregnant and bored. So one day I decided I was going to cook. How hard could it be? I knew that pork chops are fried and you mashed potatoes. The cornbread, I was not sure of. But regardless, I decided to make my favorite meal: pork chops, mashed potatoes, green peas, and cornbread. Jimmy took me to the store, and I got all the stuff I thought I needed, including a box of cornbread mix. We went back to the apartment, unloaded the groceries, and Crowe and Jimmy left for the station.

I didn't have a cookbook, so I was going to do all of this from memory from watching my mother cook (which was seldom). I took all my food out of the refrigerator and first peeled the potatoes. I put them on the stove to boil. Then I mixed the cornbread and put it in the oven. I was doing great. I decided I was going to make gravy for the mashed potatoes, too. I had a little sack of flour I had bought to use to batter the pork chops. (Mother used to do this.) Then I fried the pork chops and opened the can of peas. I was *really* proud of myself. I had a great meal going for the guys.

I had the table set with the food on the table when Jimmy and Crowe came back. Jimmy took a pork chop but couldn't cut it. The potatoes were so lumpy and pasty you could barely get them out of the bowl. And the gravy you couldn't cut with a knife, it was so thick. No one told me that I needed to salt and pepper the pork chops, potatoes, gravy, and peas. We didn't even have salt and pepper or butter. The meal was so bad, a dog wouldn't have eaten it. Jimmy threw everything in the garbage and was mad about spending the money and not being able to eat the food. He yelled at me and told me never to cook again.

Jimmy became more and more demanding. I thought it was because I was not working and helping with the expenses. I soon found out that was not the problem. Normally I went with Jimmy when he was playing a club so that I could pass the hat and collect tips. One night he decided he didn't want me to go, but I had nothing to do and insisted on going. The club was in Hamilton, Ohio, a few miles from Middletown. I went along, and all night he made nasty remarks about me. "Pregnant bitch!" "Lazy-ass-whore!" Things like that. I ignored his remarks and just passed the hat. I had no idea what was going on. Jimmy had never talked to me like that before. We had argued many times and he never used language like that. He had never hit me. I didn't like the way he was behaving but chalked it up to alcohol. How wrong I was!

When it came time to go home, Jimmy wouldn't let me into the car. I had no idea how to get home. I had no money and knew no one there in the club. So I jumped onto the hood thinking that he wouldn't drive off. Boy, was I wrong! He pulled out of that parking lot like a bat out of hell. I hung on to the hood ornament and the windshield wipers for dear life. I was scared to death. I knew if I fell off, I would die. He drove about two miles like that, hoping I would fall off. When I didn't, he stopped the car and let me get in.

Why didn't I leave him then? Who knows? I certainly don't. I do know that I was in love with him. I thought his tantrum was a one-time thing. He had never done anything like that before. I did know he ran around on me with Jean and Melissa. But I couldn't understand his reason behind his actions that night. Later I did find out. And the truth was he had another woman waiting for him. When I insisted on getting in the car with him, I spoiled his fun and fling.

In the summer of 1954, Crowe went back home. I was sorry to see him go. In my mind, I felt like he was my buddy. Now I wouldn't have anyone to laugh and cut up with at night. I don't think Crowe felt the same way about me.

3

HAVING BABIES

I first met Bob Osborne backstage, actually in the back alley, at the Grand Ole Opry when Bob got out of the marines. Jimmy was still with Bill Monroe and he introduced Bob to me. I already knew Bob's brother, Sonny, from the time he played with Bill Monroe.

Jimmy reconnected with Bob and Sonny Osborne over the summer in 1954. Jimmy had previously worked with Bob in the Lonesome Pine Fiddlers, a popular bluegrass music band, before he joined the marines. He and Sonny played together with Bill Monroe. They all decided to form a band called Jimmy Martin and the Osborne Brothers.

Sonny and Bob's parents lived in Dayton, Ohio. Middletown is halfway between Cincinnati and Dayton, and it's fifty miles between the two. Jimmy and I went to visit them. There I met Pat Osborne, Bob's wife. I also met their parents and their sister, Louise. I liked the Osborne family and was happy that Bob, Sonny, and Jimmy were going to be together as a group.

At the time, Pat and Bob were living in a trailer just outside Middletown. Pat was eight months pregnant with their oldest son, Robbie. None of us had any money or insurance, so Pat went home to stay with her family in Kentucky to have Robbie. Pat's father was Ezra Cline of the Lonesome Pine Fiddlers. When Pat left, Bob moved back home with his parents, and Jimmy and I moved into the trailer.

Sometime toward the end of July, Jimmy, Bob, and I went to Nashville. Jimmy and Bob were meeting with Steve Shoals at RCA Victor, hoping to sign a recording contract. Jimmy and I stayed with my mother. It was fantastic to see Mike again and play with him. He was a year and a half old, walking and all over the house. I believe Bob stayed with Mother as well. I know we didn't have any money for hotels, so it makes sense that Bob would have stayed with Mother. I also remember Gordon Terry coming by Mother's house to rehearse with Jimmy and Bob. I also remember Bob, Jimmy, and Gordon standing in the living room picking and singing. I believe Jimmy and Bob were interested in hiring Gordon, who was a terrific fiddle player and one of the most handsome men I had ever seen. Today the younger people would call him "eye candy." They rehearsed together, but Gordon never worked with them.

Jimmy and Bob signed the contract with RCA and a recording session was scheduled. I remember the time clearly, because after they concluded their business with RCA, we were going to Mayfield, Kentucky, to visit a radio station. It took us forever to find the place. Bob was driving, I was in the passenger seat, and Jimmy was sleeping in the back. During this time, we heard Elvis Presley on the radio singing "Blue Moon of Kentucky." None of us could get over someone singing "Blue Moon of Kentucky" as a rock 'n roll song. Jimmy didn't like Bill Monroe's song being sung like Elvis sang it, but Bob and I liked it and thought it would be a hit. (A couple of years passed and Jimmy learned that Elvis liked his music. After that, it was a different story with Jimmy. He started liking Elvis. Later we began receiving Christmas cards from Elvis every Christmas. I wonder what happened to those cards. Knowing Jimmy, he didn't throw them away.) When Bob and Jimmy concluded their business at the radio station, we drove back to Middletown.

Jimmy and I knew it wasn't going to be long before I was going to be giving birth. I was tired of being pregnant. I had already tried castor oil to induce labor, and that didn't do any good. It just wasn't time.

By now we were in mid-August. Jimmy had been in negotiations with Casey Clark and the WJR Barn Dance in Detroit, Michigan. Jimmy had signed a contract, so we were going to be moving. Jimmy, Bob, and Sonny were going to Detroit. They would find a place for all of us to live. Pat was already in Kentucky with her parents, and I went home to Nashville to have the baby.

The trip on the Greyhound was a long eight hours, and when I arrived, I was worn out. Mother picked me up at the bus station. I had one suitcase—just what I had left home with. I had no baby clothes, or much money, or anything else. But I was welcomed back home by Mother, my sister Billie, and my grandparents. And, of course, there was my sweet baby, Mike. I couldn't get over how much he had grown.

Mother and her husband, Clem, had moved in with my grandmother (Mama) who was fighting cancer of the esophagus. Mama's house was located between Sixteenth and Seventeenth Avenues on McGavock Street. Aunt Jessie lived next door. Both houses have now been torn down, but the steps leading from the sidewalk to Mama's house are still there. I have been known to sit on those steps for an hour just reminiscing.

Saturday morning I decided I would walk downtown and do some shopping. I picked up a couple of things for the baby; then I went to lunch at Walgreen's. I had a pimento cheese sandwich, potato salad, and a Coke and walked back home. When I got home, I sat down in the big comfy chair in the living room, threw my legs over the arm, and started watching television. I had a halter-neck sundress on, since I was barely showing. I hadn't sat there too long when my water broke, and I started yelling for my mother. She came running and said, "We have to get you to the hospital." She took me to Vanderbilt Hospital. I was immediately put to sleep, and when I awoke around 11: 00 p.m. I had a healthy baby boy who weighed seven pounds, ten ounces. And I was starving. Before Mother left to go and get me a sandwich, she called Jimmy. He was thrilled it was a boy and said he wanted the baby named after him. So we made him a junior. Me, all I cared about then was eating.

Jimmy Jr. was born with a skin condition on his cheeks and a blood blister on his scrotum. The blood blister was removed with dry ice when we got back to Detroit. But he has fought the skin condition all of his life. I will always believe those things happened as a result of the stress I was under during my pregnancy.

One week to the day after Jimmy Jr. was born, we were on a Greyhound bus headed to Detroit. This time we had two suitcases. My grandmother had given me some money to use and some to keep for when I needed it. She knew I would need it. The bus ride to Detroit was far worse than the bus trip from Middletown to Nashville. This one took about twelve hours, and I had a newborn baby to feed, change, and try to keep quiet. I was dead on my feet when Jimmy picked us up at the bus station and took us to our new home in Michigan.

On the way to the apartment, Jimmy and I started talking about what to call the baby. Jimmy wanted to call him Junebug. I said, "No way will he grow up with a name like Junebug." Jimmy said, "We can't call him Jimmy, because we won't know who is being called, me or him." We then settled on "Timmy." We both liked that name. Now you know why he has always been called Timmy.

Jimmy couldn't get over looking at Timmy as he was driving and telling me about the apartment. He was so proud of his first-born child. Sonny, Bob and Pat, and their son, Robbie, were all going to be living with us at 1203 Glover Street. Sonny had his room in the back of the apartment; Bob and his wife and son were in the front bedroom; and Jimmy, Timmy, and I had the second bedroom. We had a big living room with a royal blue and yellow eat-in kitchen. (I couldn't get away from those colors. Ugh! Remember, Jimmy's old Hudson was royal blue and yellow.) But we had a nice bathroom and a laundry in the basement with the furnace.

There were four apartments in the building—two upstairs and two downstairs. We didn't have a phone, but we met the people upstairs across the hall from us, Ray and Willard (I have forgotten their last names), who lived with their mom and sister. They had a telephone and didn't mind us using it. We didn't know the people downstairs except to say hello.

I applied for a job in the offices of Chrysler Corporation, located a few blocks from where we lived. I was hired immediately and started working there when Timmy was less than three weeks old. Jimmy would babysit him during the day.

Pat and Bob Osborne's baby, Robbie, who was twenty days older than Timmy, was in the house as well. When one baby cried, the other one cried. It was bedlam. The good thing was that as the only one with a day job, I didn't have to listen to all the crying. By the time I came home from work, Jimmy had already fed Timmy, and if I wanted something to eat, I fixed it. Normally I didn't eat. Then Jimmy would take off for the clubs to shoot pool and drink. (This habit started in Detroit. The drinking would continue, but the pool playing ended with Detroit, as far as I know.)

Diapers were laundered every day. Jimmy took care of washing diapers, feeding Timmy, and everything. For this I was very thankful. I didn't have to wash diapers. I was still that spoiled eighteen-year-old kid with two babies, although Mike was still living with Mother in Nashville. I missed him like crazy, but Jimmy still refused to come to terms with Mike living with us.

Jimmy Martin and the Osborne Brothers were the top act on Casey Clark's Barn Dance. I had never seen Jimmy on stage in an actual show until I went to the Barn Dance for the first time. Of course, I had seen him playing in the bars and with Bill Monroe, but this was different. Jimmy and the Osbornes hit that stage and the crowd went wild. Jimmy was the emcee and lead singer. He literally took over the stage. I had never dreamed he was that good. Jimmy, Sonny, and Bob were the best ever. Their harmony was flawless; their music and instrumentals were incredible. They received standing ovations at every appearance. The audience loved them. And I was so proud of them, I was bursting at the seams. After that first night, I told Jimmy, "I didn't know how good you were. The three of you together are wonderful."

Every Saturday night, I took Timmy and sat in the front row with Pat and Robbie. Sometimes I would get up and dance. Pat would watch Timmy for me while I danced. Jimmy didn't seem to mind my dancing with other people, so anytime anyone asked me to dance, I would. I was not a very good dancer, but because I enjoyed it, and still do, I was not ashamed to try. Bob and Pat and Jimmy and I started a new tradition of going out to eat after the Barn Dance. We always had Robbie and Timmy with us. They would sit in their highchairs and have fun with us. Saturday was our big night out.

Detroit in the fifties was exciting. The automobile factories were booming. The neighborhoods were running over with people from Kentucky, Tennessee, Alabama, Georgia, and West Virginia. They were the country music crowd. The bars were packed every night. Everyone was making good money. Things were happening, and we were in the middle of it.

Shortly after they began at the Barn Dance, Bob said to Jimmy, "Let's go to Indian Village and get some pizza pie." The Indian Village was an Italian restaurant on Jefferson Avenue near East Grand Boulevard, and it had a teepee on top of the restaurant. Jimmy told Bob, "We can go there, but I never did like peach pie." Bob told Jimmy, "It's not peach pie; it's pizza pie." Jimmy said, "I don't know what that is, but I'll try it." We did and he loved it. From then on, we were regulars at the Indian Village.

Another place we all liked to go was a Chinese restaurant on Jefferson near St. Jean Street. Neither Jimmy nor I had ever eaten Chinese food. Once we had it, we loved it. Pat, Bob, Jimmy, and I used to go to that restaurant at least once a week. Timmy and Robbie seemed to enjoy going to the restaurants even though they were just babies. They never created a fuss. Maybe it was because they had each other as company. It was so much fun eating, talking, and laughing. When we all laughed, the babies would laugh too. Then, the grown-ups would just crack up. Those are great memories.

It was 1954 and RCA Victor had released Jimmy and the Osborne Brothers' songs "20/20 Vision" and "Save It, Save It." During this time, I was still working at Chrysler. As soon as I got off work in the afternoon and got home, I immediately started writing letters to disc jockeys all across the country. They were all written by hand. At that time we didn't have a phone, so we couldn't call the disc jockeys. Telephone calls were expensive. So once in a while we would call a disc jockey or two from either a pay phone or a neighbor's phone. We then packed the records, put a note in each of the envelopes, and sent them out the following morning. That is when I started getting involved in the music business. We never had a typewriter throughout the fifties, and computers were unheard of then. Besides that, we made each note personal. I started doing this with "20/20 Vision" and continued for as long as I was with Jimmy.

Casey Clark sometimes had a guest act on Saturday night, usually with stars like Faron Young, Skeeter Davis, Webb Pierce, Kitty Wells, Johnnie (Wright) and Jack (Anglin), and many others from the Grand Ole Opry. It was in Detroit where I became friends with Kitty and Johnnie and Webb. I already knew Faron from our days in Shreveport. Regardless of how many top performers appeared on the Barn Dance, Jimmy and the Osbornes always got the standing ovations and the loudest applause. The audiences seemed to never tire of them. Jimmy was the ever ready showman. He was fantastic and he knew it. As a group, they were perfection. Now they had a record on the radio. We all felt it wouldn't be long before they would be number one in their field.

Bob and Jimmy's portion of the show featured an act where Bob would dress up as a woman wearing a dress and high heels. Sometimes he would wear a ladies' hat. Bob was not a skinny man. I always thought of him as being sort of round, not fat. He was hysterical in the dress, hat and purse, and heels. He and Jimmy performed comedy routines where Jimmy, playing the straight guy, asked Bob questions. Bob responded to Jimmy's questions in a high-pitched voice, sounding exactly like a woman. The audience would howl. Even though I knew the routine, sometimes I laughed until I was doubled over.

Not long after starting at Casey Clark's, Casey contracted for a television show on CKLW-TV out of Windsor, Ontario, Canada. Casey had Jimmy and the Osbornes do guest appearances. Now they were on television! It was thrilling! We were all thankful for the extra money and we were moving on up in the music world. None of us—except Bob, when he was in the service—had ever been outside the United States, and now we were going to Canada—a foreign country. Exciting was not the word for it. It was beyond that. Just the trip through the tunnel from Detroit to Windsor was awesome.

There was nothing to compare with being in the television studio and watching how they did everything. Of course, there was no way to record the show. Our little twelve-inch Motorola TV set didn't have a recorder. Recorders were unheard of. But Pat and I would sit there on the sidelines every week watching our husbands perform. Jimmy Martin and the Osborne Brothers were flawless. The sad part is they couldn't stay together. If they had, they would have been the number one group in the country.

Their record was being played on all the radio stations. It was one of the top requested songs on the radio stations where it was being played, especially in Detroit. They were on television, and they were the star act on Casey Clark's Barn Dance. I was continuing to promote their records by writing letters to disc jockeys across the country. We were moving on, but it felt like it was the calm before the storm. Something out of the ordinary had to happen. Everything was going too smoothly!

We and the Osbornes continued to live together. Pat made frequent trips with Robbie to see her parents in Kentucky. One of the times when Pat was gone, the rest of us were sitting in the living room talking. I had just finished getting Timmy ready for bed, and Jimmy was playing with him. It was in the winter and it was cold. Bob said, "I am going down and fire the furnace." Jimmy said, "No, I will do it." Neither Bob nor I thought too much about it. While Jimmy went down to the basement to stoke the fire in the furnace, I put Timmy to bed. When Jimmy didn't come back, I knew he had left through the basement door.

That night I really got to know Bob. He was playing his mandolin for me and singing some songs he had written. We talked a lot. I think Bob's objective was to keep my mind off Jimmy's leaving. I liked Bob and thought he was a nice guy. He treated Pat with respect. That made him a special person to me. I also liked Pat, despite the fact that I didn't feel like she paid much attention to her husband. She was constantly going to Kentucky to visit her parents. Whether she was gone or at home, I never saw Bob even look at another woman.

The next time we saw Jimmy was three days later. I had missed two days of work before I was able to get someone to care for Timmy. Jimmy came home wearing a baseball cap. The minute I saw it, I remembered a girl at the Barn Dance that past Saturday night wearing it. I also remembered her talking to Jimmy. This was the fourth time I knew for a fact that he had cheated on me and with whom. I can tell you in no uncertain terms, it wasn't the last time. And over the next few years, he became more and more brazen about his cheating. But this time, shit hit the fan! I packed Timmy's and my clothes and called my mother for a plane ticket—I was going to leave. But he talked me out of it. And I stayed. I unpacked, called Mother, and told her to forget the ticket.

You may be wondering why I continued to put up with Jimmy's infidelity. At that time in my life, it was only the infidelity that was a problem in our life together. There was no fighting or arguing. I chalked it up to my being a creature of habit. I have always gotten up at the same time in the morning, taken my shower, put on my makeup, gotten dressed, and made my bed before I came out of the bedroom. I always stayed with a job, even if I knew I should have left for a better job. I'm still that way. Thinking back now, I see that Jimmy was like one of my habits. I couldn't let him go, despite what he did or didn't do. It was my nature to stay with him until I could no longer tolerate it.

While living on Glover, I started getting sick. I went to the doctor. He told me I had a tumor and wanted to give me x-ray treatments. I told him, "No, I think I am pregnant." He said, "You are not pregnant." I told him, "In nine months, I will bring the tumor in and show you." I never went back to see that doctor. I knew he didn't know what he was doing.

When I got home, I told Jimmy I was pregnant. We couldn't believe it. We had been using protection every time we had sex. We weren't ready for another child, either financially or otherwise. Then in the middle of our talking about it, Jimmy said, "Timmy needs a little brother to play with." I almost cried, because I didn't want another baby. But I was happy that Jimmy was okay with it. I was working all day and writing letters all night.

I was tired. I felt more like a fifty-year-old than a nineteen-year-old. Even though Jimmy and the Osbornes were now stars, we were still skimming by on my salary, or so I thought. Jimmy cried "poor-mouth" all the time, but I now know he wasn't as destitute as he let on. We had limited expenses. We paid just a third of the rent and bought our own food. We didn't have to pay utilities, since they were included in the rent. Jimmy babysat, so we didn't have child-care expenses. And I was making a good salary at Chrysler.

I had no idea of finances back then. I didn't have a checking account. I didn't pay any bills. Jimmy gave me money to go to work. So dumb me believed everything he said when he told me we didn't have any money. Today I would have been adding things up.

Jimmy was great at playing snooker. In fact, many times he made our portion of the rent by playing. He would come home with his pockets loaded with money. I don't know where he learned to play, because until we moved to Detroit, I never knew him to play pool. But I thought between the snooker money and sharing expenses we were making a decent living. So where was the money going? I didn't dare ask, because that would end up leading to a war.

A few months into my pregnancy, Jimmy's brother Roy and his wife, Norma; their daughter, Kaye; and Jimmy's mother, Sarah, came to see us. Timmy and I were thrilled they were there. Norma was pregnant with their second child and I was pregnant with Ray. Roy and Norma lived in Anderson, Indiana, not very far from Detroit. We had such a good time while they were there. We all went swimming at Belle Isle, an island in the middle of the Detroit River, and ate pizza at the Indian Village. I had always been friends with Norma and still love her like a sister. To have her for a fun weekend in Detroit was great. I was always overjoyed whenever I had more company; it meant I had people to talk to.

Mr. and Mrs. Osborne and Louise came to Detroit to see the show with Bob and Sonny. While they were there, Louise and I went to the movies on Jefferson Street to see *Gone with the Wind*. I had not been to a movie since I had met Jimmy. I used to go to the movies all the time with my friends Jean Armstrong and Opal Taylor and my sisters, Betty and Billie. In fact, DaddyHollis used to load Jean; Opal and her sister, Margaret Ann; Helen Dickens; and my sisters and me in the back of the truck and drive us to the movies out on Charlotte Pike in Nashville. To get to go to the movies again was ecstasy, and *Gone with the Wind* was my favorite.

Shortly after Mr. and Mrs. Osborne and Louise's visit and Jimmy's three-day escapade, Bob and Pat moved out with Robbie. They moved to an apartment just a couple of blocks away at 1203 Fairview. Sonny stayed with us, but we rarely saw him. In the morning he would take his bath or whatever else he had to do and leave. When he did come home and go to bed, we didn't know it. He was certainly a good roommate.

A few weeks after Bob and Pat moved to their new apartment, Jimmy Martin and the Osborne Brothers parted ways. I had not noticed any dissension among them, but if their talks occurred during the day, I was at work and could not have known. Recently I asked my son Ray if Jimmy had ever said anything about why he and the Osbornes split up. He said, "No, but Sonny hated Jimmy." I don't know if Sonny really did, or if Jimmy just thought he did, and said as much to Ray. When I started to think about it, it occurred to me that Jimmy and I never discussed the reason for Bob and Sonny leaving. It came as a shock to me that we didn't talk about it. Now, I will never know.

When Sonny moved out, Jimmy moved the electric guitar player from the Barn Dance, Hoppy (I can't remember his last name), into the room formerly occupied by Bob and Pat. Hoppy's wife was pregnant, and their little boy was about three years old. Jimmy was always looking for some way to make extra money with the least amount of effort. Renting a room was one of the ways to cut down on expenses.

About a month after Hoppy and his wife moved in, Jimmy woke me up and said, "Hoppy's wife is having a problem. You need to get up and see what's going on." I got up and asked her, "What is happening?" She said, "I am having pains." I told her, "You probably have gas. Why don't you go to the bathroom?" She said, "Okay." By now Jimmy was up, dressed, and out in the hallway.

She was in the bathroom with the door closed when I heard her scream. I ran and opened the door. She had had the baby in the commode! I knew the water was freezing. I yelled for Jimmy and he came running. Immediately he told me to get some towels and to lay Hoppy's wife down on the floor. Then he told me to pick the baby up out of the toilet water. That's when I started backing up. Jimmy said, "What are you doing?" I said, "I am going to get help." He said, "Get back here and get this baby out." I said, "No!" and ran out the door. We didn't have a phone, so I went across the hall to the neighbors and told them what was happening. They called the police. I went back to the bathroom. Again Jimmy said, "Pick up the baby." But I was afraid to touch it, because I thought it might be dead. He could see I was afraid. He told me to come over and he would pick up the baby. I did and he picked the baby up. We laid her down and we wrapped a towel around the most beautiful little girl I had ever seen. She had two front teeth, not completely cut through, but visible, and the most beautiful black hair.

The police and ambulance arrived. They picked up Hoppy's wife from the floor, put her on the bed, cut the cord, and removed the placenta. They put the placenta and afterbirth in a pan and asked me to take it down to the furnace and burn it. By now Pat and Bob were there. Being the kid I was, I said to Pat, "Let's go down to the basement and operate on it." We did. We were trying to see what the placenta was made of. It was like a tough muscle (which I thought it was), and we couldn't cut it. It was also bloody and we didn't like that. After about twenty minutes of trying to dissect it, we gave up and burned it. That was our foray into playing doctor.

After the ambulance attendants finished with Hoppy's wife and the baby, they took the baby to the hospital. She was put in an incubator but developed pneumonia. She was only about a week old when she died. I cried and cried. I really loved that little girl and thought if only I had picked her up right away, she might not have gotten pneumonia. I still think about that. But being so young and scared at the time, I hadn't thought of those things.

Seeing Jimmy's assistance at the delivery and how calm he was after the birth, while we were waiting for the ambulance, we all started calling him "Dr. Martin." He wore the title proudly.

After Hoppy's baby was born, it was not too long until Jimmy and I moved out of the big apartment with Timmy and into a two-room apartment at 1203 Fairview Street. This was the same apartment building Bob and Pat had moved into before they left town. The living room had a Murphy bed with room for Timmy's crib, a sofa, a table for our small TV, and a very small coffee table. The bed pushed up into the wall during the day, so Timmy had plenty of room to play. We also had a nice eat-in kitchen and bath. The kitchen table sat in front of a big window that looked out onto the alley. I liked sitting at the table drinking coffee.

The best part was that we were finally able to live by ourselves. This was the first time we had done that since Middletown. I thought things would be different—that Jimmy would spend more time with me after I came home from work. But it didn't matter where we lived, who we lived with, or whether or not we lived alone. Jimmy continued to be friends with the neighbors Ray and Willard, drinking beer and running around.

Timmy loved the little apartment. He could crawl everywhere and pull himself up. He was just learning to walk. He was the most beautiful baby—and mischievous. I had a small table and I put a couple of whatnots on it. I didn't have much in the way of things to decorate the apartment. Timmy wanted those little trinkets, and when I would tell him no, he would back up and start inching his finger toward whatever was on the table. It became the cutest game and we played it every day—me with the stern face and him as the touchy one. It was so much fun.

Another one of my favorite memories in that little apartment happened one morning when Jimmy and I woke up and Timmy was playing in his crib. Jimmy said, "Shoo, let's go back to sleep for a little while." We did. Then we woke up to the most god-awful smell in the world. Timmy's bowels had moved, and what he wasn't trying to eat, he was playing with. He had thrown it all over the wall. Jimmy and I were both gagging and laughing at the same time. He said, "I will pick up Timmy and put him in the bathtub. You get the sheets and take them down to the washer." That's what we did. I put the sheets and Timmy's pajamas in the washer. By the time I got back upstairs, Timmy was clean and Jimmy had washed the walls. That was the last time we left Timmy in the crib while we slept in. When he woke up, we got up.

My pregnancy with Ray was a breeze. I didn't have any problems except for starving all the time. The one thing I craved was Krystal hamburgers. We didn't have a Krystal restaurant nearby, but several times during my pregnancy Jimmy would get up in the middle of the night, drive across town, buy me two dozen Krystals, and bring them back. I ate every one. After Ray was born, I never ate another Krystal.

Even though I was pregnant with Ray, I was still working. Now I was working at US Rubber in the office as a keypunch operator. I never forgot how to keypunch after being taught in high school. I enjoyed being around the computers (such as they were in those days). I really liked my job but knew I was coming up on a time when I would have to leave. In 1955 there was no such thing as maternity leave, and they wouldn't let you work after seven months. Fortunately for me, my pregnancy never showed much, so I could work almost up to the time of giving birth. And we certainly needed the money.

While working at US Rubber, a favorite memory of mine had to do with a freight elevator. One morning, several people in my department and I were riding it up to go to work, and it got stuck between the sixth and seventh floors. Several of us had our lunch, someone had cards, so we all sat on the floor and enjoyed ourselves. We were finally rescued around three in the afternoon.

The last time I was in Detroit I drove past the old US Rubber plant. It is empty now and the windows are all broken. The big stove is gone. I almost cried when I remembered what a lively place it had been in 1955. The restaurants across the street were all busy at lunchtime. I had my very first rice pudding in one of those restaurants and fell in love with it. The houses on East Grand Boulevard were magnificent. I wanted to live in one of them so badly. Now there is devastation everywhere—it's very sad.

4

BACK AND FORTH

While we were living in Detroit, Jimmy made friends with a family who lived on the west side, quite a long way from where we lived on the east side. I didn't know where Jimmy had met them—probably a nightclub. Jimmy told me one day, "We are going out to see Fred and Mary Smith." (Since I can't remember their names, I have made them up.) We went to their house and visited for about four hours. Timmy was just a baby, so they gave me a dresser drawer to lay him in. They had a twelve-year-old son named Zak. They also had a big white rabbit in a cage in the kitchen. I felt so out of place in their house, but I was friendly. When they invited Jimmy and me to come back for dinner the following day, Jimmy proudly accepted.

The next day, Mary had the table set beautifully. But before we could sit down to dinner, it started snowing buckets. At the table they passed the meat to Jimmy, who took a big piece, and I passed it on to the person sitting beside me. Then I filled my plate with veggies and mashed potatoes. After Jimmy took a big bite of the meat, he said, "Fred, what did you do with your pet rabbit?" Fred said, "You are eating it." I thought Jimmy was going to spit the rabbit all the way to the east side. Instead he gagged and spit the piece out on the plate. I wanted to laugh so badly I had to cross my legs. I will never forget the look on Jimmy's face. That was one rabbit he never finished. His look was priceless.

The snow continued to fall heavily. We couldn't drive home, because our car was stuck. Fred and Mary kindly extended an invitation for us to spend the night. Timmy could sleep in the drawer, and Jimmy and I would sleep on the sofa that made into a bed. But the sofa bed was not like a sofa bed of today. This one folded in the middle; one side was let down to make the bed. It had no innerspring mattress and no cushions. That was okay until Zak kept appearing and talking to himself. Every time he came into the room, Jimmy and I both sat up. Zak would say to himself out loud, "Zak, where is your sock?" Then, he would answer himself: "You know where your sock is." This continued all night long. Around noon, the plows had been down the street and we could go home. We were so eager to get out of that house, I think we half ran and half slid to the car. That was the last time we ever went to Fred and Mary's house, but we did often see them at the Barn Dance. We were friendly, but not overly, to them. After all, they were still fans.

Jimmy worked at Casey Clark's Barn Dance from 1954 to 1958. Following the breakup with the Osbornes in the early to the mid-part of 1955, I saw Jimmy's at-home personality start to deteriorate. It was like he no longer trusted anyone or anything. He became more agitated when he didn't get what he wanted. He was afraid of people leaving him, whether it was a banjo player, a mandolin player, or me. During this time, he never hit me, but he did yell and threaten. (In fact, the only time in our relationship I had ever been fearful of Jimmy was in Hamilton, Ohio, when he'd cussed me out and driven around with me on top of the hood of the car.) But I loved him and I thought his insecurity would pass.

Jimmy then hired Earl Taylor on mandolin and Sam Hutchins on banjo. I remembered Earl from the Middletown days. In 1957 Earl and the banjo player were replaced by Paul Williams and J. D. Crowe. Jimmy now had J. D. on the banjo and Paul on the mandolin. They made a good team, and the people at Casey Clark's Barn Dance loved them.

Jimmy and the Osbornes had recorded six songs together for RCA. All did well and all were promoted by my writing notes to the disc jockeys and packing and mailing the records. Sometimes we called some of the better-known disc jockeys. We could have called many more of them, but we still didn't have a phone. The songs included "Chalk Up Another One," backed with "I Pulled a Boo"; "They Didn't Know the Difference," backed with "That's

How I Can Count on You"; and, of course, "20/20 Vision" backed with "Save It, Save It."

Jimmy and the Osbornes rarely played a show other than on television and the Barn Dance. They never went out of town, and I don't remember any bookings or if they even had an agent other than Casey Clark. With their songs played constantly on the radio, they could have been playing lots of shows. We never talked about them playing shows, and "booking shows" was not in my vocabulary at that time. They did play some of the bars around Detroit. Most of the time, I went and passed around the hat to collect tips. The neighbor girl across the hall would watch Timmy, so we didn't have to be in a hurry to get home.

Despite Jimmy's infidelities, Detroit was a happy place for us. We went out to eat on Saturday nights, had friends, and went boating and fishing on Sundays. I learned to water ski and ride what they called a surfboard. I was very good at both. From all outward appearances, we were a happy family having a good time. Timmy was growing like a weed. Jimmy and I adored him. Whenever Jimmy sang, Timmy would start singing. He wasn't old enough to know the words, but he would sing just the same. We couldn't get enough of his singing.

Jimmy's aunt Thelma and uncle Oscar Fields lived in Flint, Michigan. They had a son, Michael. They both worked at General Motors (GM), so they often came down to see us on Saturday or Sunday, or we would go up to see them on Sunday. Thelma was teaching me to cook. She taught me how to make biscuits and cornbread first. She also taught me other basics, like the mashed potatoes and pork chops I had tried to cook once in Middletown. She taught me how to make gravy. She was a person I really loved and looked up to. I still cook the way she taught me.

Thelma and Oscar worked for GM for over twenty-five years. Upon their retirement, they moved back home to Tennessee. Jimmy loved to stop by their house or meet them at the truck stop near their house when traveling from Nashville to the East Coast for shows.

In May 2015 I visited Thelma and spent two nights with her in her home in Bean Station, Tennessee. On that visit Thelma had an appointment in Sneedville to get her hair done. I went with her and we drove around town looking at all the changes. Jimmy's grandfather's house had been torn down as well as the house where Jimmy had grown up. There were so many changes, it made my heart ache. Of course, Jimmy's sister Euna and Clyde are both gone, but their house is still there. It looks exactly the same. Since my return to Florida, I continue to talk to Thelma periodically on the phone. She is now in her nineties and lives alone. Her husband is deceased, but I am friends with Michael on Facebook. Her daughter, Tammy, lives close by and keeps a watchful eye on Thelma.

Whenever Thelma and Oscar would come to Detroit to visit us, we would go hear Jimmy play. They always stayed at our house for the weekend. Jimmy and Oscar were big buddies and liked to go out drinking together. Only they knew where they went—probably to all the country bars on Jefferson Street or the country music bars in Flint. Thelma and I stayed home with the kids. If they didn't return by 10:00 p.m., we went to bed.

One morning in Flint, while Thelma and I were making breakfast after the boys had been out drinking the night before, Jimmy came into the kitchen and said, "We really liked that potted meat you had in the refrigerator. Buy that same kind the next time." Thelma and I almost fell on the floor laughing. They had eaten dog food and liked it. When we told them, they were nonchalant and said, "It was good."

By now I had become a good cook with Thelma's help. On the afternoon before Ray was born, I had made cabbage, cornbread, and mashed potatoes for our supper. The cabbage was so good that Jimmy, Timmy, and I ate the entire thing. After I gave Timmy a bath, we watched TV and went to bed. Jimmy was now going out only once or twice a week, and I was happy about that.

Around 5:30 a.m. Jimmy woke me up with stomach pains. I was pissed. I told him, "Take some Alka-Seltzer. You probably have gas." He said, "It doesn't feel like gas. Maybe I am having a heart attack." I said, "I'll get up and get you something to take." Well, by the time my feet hit the floor, I was crying—doubled over with pain. Jimmy saw that I wasn't faking and his own pain disappeared. He jumped out of bed and helped me to a chair at the kitchen table. I told him what to put in my bag. After Ray was born I always told Jimmy that he was the one who suffered the first pains of childbirth with Ray.

Jimmy went and asked a neighbor to watch Timmy. He helped me to the car to take me to the hospital. We had a 1951 Cadillac, pale green with "Jimmy Martin and the Sunny Mountain Boys" painted in big letters on both sides. I always called it a "circus car." As we were driving down Jefferson Avenue in the circus car, I was in serious pain. Morning rush-hour traffic was just starting. I was crying and Jimmy kept telling me, "Hold it, hold it. Don't have the baby in the car. It will ruin the car." I was crying, "I don't care about the car! I want this pain to stop!"

Other than that, Jimmy was so caring during this time. He was very worried. And when we reached the Evangelical Deaconess Hospital, he went running in and telling everyone, "My wife is having a baby. Please help her." They came out to the car, lifted me onto a stretcher, and immediately gave me a shot to help with the pain. That was the last pain I had. I don't remember when they gave me the "happy gas" to put me out. The next thing I knew Jimmy was standing by my bed holding my hand and saying, "We have a beautiful little boy." It was on October 13, 1955.

We talked about a name for the baby. Jimmy wanted to name him after his two drunk friends, Willard and Ray, from across the hall on Glover Street. Jimmy was still hanging out with them. I objected, but my objections fell on deaf ears. Jimmy was determined to name him after his friends. So we named him "Ray Willard Martin." Ray was such a beautiful little boy. The nurses kept blue bows in his blond curly hair while he was in the hospital. They thought he should have been a girl, since he was so pretty.

Ray couldn't come home right away. He had breathing difficulties and didn't weigh enough. He weighed only four pounds, despite all the Krystal hamburgers I had eaten while I was pregnant. He had to weigh five pounds before he could go home. Jimmy and I made daily trips to the hospital to see him. In those days we weren't allowed to hold him while he was in the incubator, but we could see him through the nursery window. He was so tiny but so amazing.

Once he weighed five pounds, he came home. Jimmy watched Ray and Timmy while I worked. Two or three days a week after I got home, he would leave to go shoot pool and drink. He was like a caged animal. He had to get out. That was okay with me, because two or three nights were better than every night.

Even though we took excellent care of Ray, he developed pneumonia numerous times in the first few months of his life. We rushed him to the hospital each time he started coughing and became feverish. After several emergency visits, the doctors told us we had to get him out of the Detroit climate if we wanted him to live. Since we couldn't move because of Jimmy's job, we called Jimmy's mother to see if she would keep him for us until we moved somewhere else. My mother was already taking care of Mike. That's why we took Ray to Sneedville. It never dawned on me that Jimmy would never let me bring him home until after his mother died. It would be nine long years before I got him back. If I had known this, Ray would never have gone to Sneedville. My intention in letting Ray go to Sneedville was for him to heal and give us time to get another job. I would never have voluntarily given up my child. When I left Mike with Mother, I had always intended to go back and get him. But just as with Ray, that didn't happen.

We were still living on Fairview the night Elvis Presley made his third and final appearance on the *Ed Sullivan Show*, January 6, 1957. I loved Elvis and his music! I liked to jitterbug and this was good music for that. Jimmy and I both remembered him singing "Blue Moon of Kentucky" when we were in Mayfield, Kentucky.

That night when Elvis was singing, Jimmy and I began playing—kissing and rolling around. We did this often. But this time both of us were fully clothed—biting and grabbing at each other. He was holding me down playing when he bit my left breast through my blouse and bra. The pain was sharp and fleeting. I saw the blood seep through and yelled, "Stop!" Jimmy looked at my breast. He couldn't believe he had bitten me that hard. I looked at him and said, "I didn't bite myself." I thought I would lose my nipple, so I told Jimmy, "Get Timmy up and let's go to the hospital."

The doctor in the emergency room at the hospital wanted to know what happened. He looked at my breast, trying to decide what to do. Jimmy and I were looking at each other sheepishly. Finally, Jimmy said, "We were just playing around." The doctor put a butterfly bandage over the wound. He then said, "Don't bite so hard next time." After we left the hospital, both of us were laughing like hyenas. I said to Jimmy, "Did you see the doctor's face when he looked at my breast?" Jimmy said, "Yes, he couldn't figure out how it happened." We laughed all the way home. That night is embedded in my mind and on my body. To prove it, I have the scar that will go to my grave with me. It was one fantastic night.

In the summer of 1957, J. D. Crowe came back to work with Jimmy. I don't remember where he lived—probably with us, sleeping on our sofa. The reason I think he lived with us is because one day I came home from work to find Crowe and Jimmy gone with a note saying they were taking Timmy to live with Jimmy's mother. I was livid. I had never been so mad or felt so betrayed in my life. In my fury I grabbed a pair of scissors and cut up all of Crowe's clothes and most all of Jimmy's. I packed my things and left.

I flew to Nashville and Mother picked me up. I had some money but no car. I called Hillous Butrum, who played for Hank Snow. Hillous was a friend of mine from the days when Jimmy worked for Bill Monroe and Hillous had worked for Hank. I asked Hillous if I could borrow his car to go to Sneedville to get my kids back. I told him what Jimmy had done and he was appalled. He told me I could have one of his cars and to keep it as long as I needed.

The following morning, I headed to Sneedville. I didn't know what I was going to run into, but I was determined my kids were going to come home with me. Mother didn't want me to go by myself. She was worried I might get hurt. But I was not afraid and didn't want Mother to go with me. I knew if she went with me, there would be trouble. Mother could hit a person too quickly to talk about it, and I didn't want any of that.

When I pulled up in the yard, Sarah, Jimmy's mother, came out onto the porch and told me to leave. I told her I was not leaving without my kids. She told me to get out of there or she would shoot me. I stood my ground and told her I was not going. About that time, Timmy ran out of the house, yelling, "Mudder!" (He couldn't say "Mother" yet.) I put him in the car. Sarah told him to get out of the car, but I told him to stay. And he stayed. Finally she let me leave with Timmy. Ray was only a baby and couldn't come outside or I would have put him in the car with Timmy. I asked Sarah to bring Ray outside to me. She wouldn't give him to me. It would be several months before I would see Ray again. I drove back to Nashville with Timmy. I didn't have any clothes for him except what he had on.

When I got back to Nashville, I knew that I was not going back to Detroit—at least not at that time. Mother wanted Timmy and me to stay with her. Mike was thrilled to have Timmy to play with. There was only nineteen months difference between them, so Timmy could wear Mike's hand-me-downs. Mother had kept a lot of things that Mike had outgrown, so that eased my mind about clothes. The two boys shared the toys. They loved each other, even though they had not been together very much. Seeing them play together just seemed natural for me. I was wishing Ray could be with them. Today, Timmy, Ray, Buddy, and Lisa love Mike and enjoy his company.

Things were going well for us in Nashville. I had returned Hillous's car even though he told me I could keep it. I didn't really need it for driving around town, because my grandmother, Mama, let me use her car. My grandfather, DaddyHollis, still owned the mattress factory, so I worked there for the time being. I figured I could make enough money to get whatever necessities I needed for Timmy and me.

I was steadily getting information from people I knew in Detroit. They told me that when Jimmy and Crowe had returned to our apartment there after taking Timmy to Sneedville, they were furious when they walked in. Can't say I blamed them. I had done a damn good job of destroying everything, and I figured I had good reason to do so. At that point in time, I was sick of Jimmy Martin and the entire crew. But it wouldn't be long before I would hear from him. First he called to cuss me out. I hung up the phone. I didn't care what he thought or said. I was finished. He had done the unthinkable! He had stolen my children. I didn't know it wouldn't be the last time he would do that.

A couple of weeks went by and Jimmy started calling again. The calls were just wondering how Timmy and I were doing. I said, "We're fine." Then he started with "It's not the same without you here. I wish you were here. When are you coming home?" To tell the truth, I wanted to go back, but I didn't want to go back to the same old thing. After many, many phone calls, he finally convinced me to return to Detroit. I still loved Jimmy and remembered that we'd had a lot of fun together. I didn't like his drinking and carousing, but when I weighed everything in my mind, I knew I was going back to him.

After I first got back to Detroit, things were fine between Jimmy and me—at least for a while. Then he started demanding that I give him my paycheck each week. I didn't like his demanding or the way he spoke to me. I wanted to get along with him, but I also wanted my own money. But that was not to be. Jimmy became very assertive and insisted I give him the money. I was working every day at Bauer Roller Bearing and making one hundred dollars a week. For 1957 that was very good money. He would give me bus fare and lunch money each day. I felt like a child taking school money from her parent. Even with the piddly amounts he gave me, I was able to save a little money. I had to hide it for when I needed it. The good thing was that now he was staying home.

We moved to a two-bedroom apartment on Parkview Street. It was a carriage house behind a mansion. You could walk out the front door down to the Detroit River, and the boatyards were on one side. We had a small front porch where we could sit and look at the water and boats. The mansion rented rooms, so Jimmy's boys could rent their own rooms there. This was the best apartment we had ever had. No more musicians living with us. Yeah!

I thought now that Crowe and Paul Williams had returned to work for Jimmy, his confidence would return and he wouldn't worry about people leaving him. I could now see that was constantly on his mind, even though he didn't talk about it. He showed it in his actions, and sometimes I would catch him just staring into space. I felt sorry for him, but I never mentioned it. I knew if I tried to talk to him, he would say he wasn't thinking about anything like that. Besides, I really didn't know how to help him.

After I returned to Detroit and we moved to Fairview, we rarely went out after the Barn Dance. That all stopped after the Osbornes left. We continued to go out on Jimmy's friends' boats whenever they asked. We also continued to go the Indian Lodge for pizza; rarely did we go out for Chinese food. My life revolved around Jimmy and Timmy and my job. I continued to work at Bauer Roller Bearing and I really liked it there. Thinking about it now, going to work was sort of an escape from my realities. Work was a place I could talk to other women and have lunch with them. Even though I didn't have any close friends at work, I did like everyone.

On my way back and forth to work, I began noticing this cute little dress shop about a block from where I got off the bus. Now that summer was coming, the shop had their summer dresses out. The one I loved was a tan, printed, halter-back dress. I felt like it was the cutest dress ever! I watched this little dress for about two weeks. When I couldn't stand it anymore, I got off the bus, went into the bank, and cashed my check. I tried the dress on, thought it looked beautiful, and bought it. At $19.99, it was mine. That was a lot of money in 1957.

As soon as I got home, I immediately put the dress on. I was so proud of it and thought it looked terrific on me. I went in to show Jimmy. He said, "Where the hell did you get that?" I said, "I bought it." He went ballistic, jumped up from his chair, grabbed the front of the dress, and ripped it off. He was mad because I had spent money without his permission. Timmy began crying at the top of his lungs. I was scared to death and crying, too, afraid Jimmy was going to hit me. He told me to never put that dress on again. There was no way I could wear it ripped down the front. But I saved the dress. When I went home to Nashville, Mother sewed the rip and I did wear it again—just not in front of him.

I knew after that episode with the dress, our time together was coming to a close. I couldn't live like this. I also didn't want Timmy around violence. Up to that time, Jimmy had never hit me. The only violent incident had been when I was pregnant with Timmy. I didn't know whether to leave or to stay, because Jimmy was in negotiations with the Louisiana Hayride in Shreveport.

Also, I loved living on Parkview. The entire area was so pretty and so convenient. I liked walking down the street to the river, or walking in the opposite direction to the grocery store or drugstore. Timmy loved going for walks, and sometimes Jimmy would walk with us. It was easy for me to catch the bus to go back and forth to work. But the most special thing about Parkview was that we didn't have any musicians living with us. They were in the mansion.

While we lived on Parkview, Jimmy started experimenting with cooking. He had long been making breakfast and lunch with eggs and hot dogs for Timmy. Now he wanted to cook supper. One night as he was frying potatoes, he decided to add onions and a can of salmon. The dish looked and smelled so bad, I couldn't eat it. He was angry, but I didn't care. I wasn't eating it and I told him so.

I don't like a lot of foods mixed together. Plus, if anything has a smell to it, I can't get it past my nose, so Jimmy's dish just wasn't for me. He continued to experiment, and although some of the things were good, others were god-awful. Strange, but our sons Timmy and Ray both love to cook. Ray is always sending me pictures of what he's cooked. Timmy does the same. They are both proud of the dishes they make.

I also liked the carriage house apartment because Timmy had his own room. He could either sleep with us or on the sofa, which he did whenever Mother came to see us. Mother would stay a week, and I was happy to have her. At that time she had been off of the booze for about six months and was between husbands. Jimmy went out a few nights while she was there. I really didn't mind him going out. It gave me a great opportunity to just sit and talk to my mother.

I loved my mother dearly. The older I was, the more I loved her—though I didn't like her drinking. When I was growing up, she had been a weekend drunk. Fortunately, she never drank at home. As she grew older, the drinking times didn't wait for Friday. When she was sober, she was great. She was funny, loving, talented, calm and human. When she was drinking, she was like a tiger getting ready to pounce. And she would. She could be foul-mouthed. In the 1980s she would call me up drunk and say, "I am going to come to see you." I would say, "Mother, don't come here. Go the other way." Fortunately for all of us, she quit drinking when she was about seventy years old.

The morning of January 11, 1958, I awoke around 5:30 a.m. and sat straight up in the bed. Jimmy asked, "What's wrong?" I said, "Mama just died." He said, "You don't know what you are talking about. You had a dream. Lay back down." The phone rang. It was Mother telling me that Mama had just died. I cried my eyes out. Immediately I started packing. Jimmy kept Timmy, and I flew that same morning to Nashville. Mother picked me up at the airport and we went straight to Pettus-Owen & Wood Funeral Home on Charlotte Pike. I was devastated and I had to see Mama.

My grandmother was buried at Spring Hill Cemetery in the Madison area of Nashville. This is the same place Jimmy would later be buried, as well as our grandson, Michael James Martin; my mother; and my daughter-in-law Susan's mother, Jimmie Dean Browning. After Mother died, I moved my grandmother from the far side of the cemetery and reinterred her next to Mother. Now the two of them are together again.

After my grandmother's funeral, I helped my mother sort out my grandmother's belongings. She had a 1949 Ford and my grandfather told me I could have it. That was great. But because we were going to be moving to Shreveport, I couldn't take it right then. I told him I would get it when we got settled. I returned to Detroit, and within a couple of weeks Jimmy, Timmy, and I were on our way to Shreveport, Louisiana.

From the time we rolled into Shreveport, I loved it. After coming from Detroit, I thought it was the prettiest city I had ever been in. Little did I know that I wouldn't be there long.

We found an apartment and moved in. The apartment had floor vents for heat. It was winter, and the heat blasted out of those vents. One night after I got Timmy ready for bed, he jumped down and ran to find his daddy. In doing so, he ran across the vent and burned his feet. Shit hit the fan once again. Jimmy came after me with a vengeance for letting Timmy burn his feet. He pounded me in the face. I had two black eyes and bruises all over. I called the police and they arrested him. But before he could get out of jail, I took Timmy and left. I went back to Nashville.

5

UP AND DOWN

Once Timmy and I were in Nashville, I took my grandmother's Ford and traded it in for a 1954 Oldsmobile 98. It had low miles and was in great shape. My grandfather paid the difference on the trade-in, so I wouldn't have any payments. My dream car was forest green and vanilla, and it was mine.

I had a little money that my grandmother left me. I decided to take Timmy and go back to Detroit. There, I could find a job. I called our landlady on Fairview Drive to find out if our old apartment was still available. It was. I asked her to hold it for me.

At that time, my mother was married to Clement J. Lusky, a catering manager for hotels and country clubs. Clem was a fantastic man from Massachusetts with a resume a mile long, including a position at the Waldorf Astoria in New York City. My sister Billie, Mike, Timmy, and I all adored and respected him. He was the best husband Mother ever had. Clem didn't drink, which was a good thing. He had recently acquired a new job at the General Shelby Hotel in Bristol, Tennessee, and he and Mother would have an apartment in the hotel. Mother suggested that I let Timmy go with her, Mike, Billie, and Clem. Timmy would stay with them until I could get settled. I agreed.

I packed up my new Oldsmobile and headed to Detroit. Once there, I moved into the apartment and got a job quickly. I was happy. I had my own money, my own car, a good job paying me $150 a week—and I had a new boyfriend, Laney Cobbolino. He was a tall, good-looking guy. He made my heart go pitter-patter. We talked about my kids, Jimmy Martin, Mother and her many husbands, Mike's father, and just everything. Laney couldn't wait for Timmy to come to Detroit. He was from a good Italian family and he loved kids. I thought I had found my soul mate again.

Within a couple of months I was situated so I could have Timmy come back home. Billie and Timmy arrived on a Greyhound bus, and I picked them up. Before we went home, we stopped at a restaurant to get something to eat. Timmy was four years old and quite beautiful for a boy. He had long black eyelashes and just a lovely face. We ordered, and when the salads arrived, Timmy asked for a salad fork. I was amazed at the good table manners he had learned while living at the General Shelby Hotel. Today when he eats, I ask him where those manners went. (Just joking—Timmy is still very polite and mannerly.)

After our meal, we went to my apartment, where all three of us would live for another month. The apartment was small, so I checked on the place where we'd lived on Parkview and found that it was for rent. Immediately I rented it.

At this time, Billie was dating Louie Abdul, a friend of Laney's. Louie was the finest. He treated Billie like a queen, and I thought Billie was falling in love with him. They dated for several months. I don't know what happened between them. I know that after Billie passed away in 2005, I found Louie's picture in her wallet. She had carried it all those years. Even though she had been married for thirty-five years to Woody (Francis Witalec), she never forgot Louie.

Billie applied for a job and was hired at the Fiesta Market on Jefferson Street, a couple of blocks from the house. Our rent was twenty dollars a week and Billie paid ten. I was thrilled. We made good roommates and Timmy was very happy. He always loved Aunt Billie.

Laney and I continued to be a couple. He treated me like a lady. One of my favorite dates with him was going to an elegant restaurant for dinner by candlelight with a strolling violinist. The food was superb and so was the service. I was falling in love with Laney, and Timmy thought he was the best person ever. Laney would come over to play with Timmy for hours. Timmy was overjoyed he had someone to play with him; he missed Mike. Jimmy had never played with him like Laney did. Jimmy was all about the music, even with his own son.

Then, in the latter part of September 1958, Jimmy came to Detroit. He called and asked me to come over to where he was staying and to bring Timmy. I didn't want to do it, but I did. Looking back now, I should have listened to myself. Once we were there, he wined and dined Timmy and me, begging and pleading for me to return to Shreveport with him. I spent two nights with him. He went home and sent me telegrams. After much persuasion, I decided to pack up and go back to him in Shreveport.

I had to tell Billie that I was leaving. I didn't know if she would want to go back home to Nashville or stay in Detroit. Once I told her, she decided to stay. She said she would be able to afford the rent by herself for a while and then she would find a cheaper place. She ended up staying in Detroit for the next thirty-five years. She would marry and own many successful businesses.

The hardest part of returning to Jimmy was telling Laney. I was very much in love with him. I knew my decision was going to break his heart, and it did. It also broke mine. I was no longer in love with Jimmy. I was returning because of Timmy and Ray. At least that is what I told myself.

I don't think I ever got over Laney. To this day I remember him holding me in his arms while we were dancing. Our favorite songs were "It's All in the Game," "Who's Sorry Now?," "One Night with You," "What Am I Living For?," and "You Are My Destiny." I will never forget the way he looked at me or how he kissed me at the end of every dance. Every time I hear Conway Twitty singing "Fifteen Years Ago," I always think of fifty years ago. During the writing of this book, I learned that Laney died in Florida in 2013. I only wish I had known.

In those days Jimmy never looked at me kindly or like he cared for me. I think about that and all those years I threw away trying to make something out of nothing. I believe now that I was with Jimmy for reasons I have only recently been able to figure out. I know that I desperately wanted my children to be together. I wanted to give them a home with a mother and father. I had once loved Jimmy, but he couldn't give me the kind of love I needed. He didn't give me hugs and kisses, or just walk up and put his arms around me, or hold my hand. If I tried to hold his hand or put my arm around him, he would say, "What the hell are you doing?" When Laney gave me that kind of love, I realized that was what I needed. Sadly, I never experienced that with Jimmy. It would take years before I would have that kind of love again.

I now understand that Jimmy was incapable of showing love to others because he had never been shown that kind of love growing up. I also believe he was afraid to show love; he thought he would lose control if people knew he loved them. His father had died when Jimmy was just a baby, so in his mind his father had left him. Just a year or so after his father's death, his mother had remarried and had three more children. She had no time for hugging or kissing or pampering her children.

I had grown up in a semi-stable home. My grandparents were very loving and good providers. My mother was home all week, but when the weekend came, she was off to party. When she was home and sober, though, she was great. And despite her problem with alcohol, I never blamed her. It was like Mother went on a vacation Friday night and came home Sunday.

Shortly after we moved to Shreveport in 1958, Decca Records released "Ocean of Diamonds" backed with "Sophronie." The crowd at the Louisiana Hayride would go wild whenever the band went on stage and sang those two songs.

Back in Shreveport, we moved into a house at 552 Egan Street. The owners of the house were Helen and Bill "Son" Kirkpatrick. They became our very close friends. The house was large and we had the entire downstairs—the front large bedroom for Jimmy and me, a big bedroom for four-year-old Timmy, a huge living room, a good-size kitchen, plus front and back porches.

After we were settled, Jimmy went and checked in at KWKH with Tillman Franks. This was a daily affair with him. Tillman was in charge of the talent for the Louisiana Hayride, as it was affectionately known. He booked Jimmy and all the other members.

I will never forget my first night at the Hayride (Jimmy had been there for several months already). I was so thrilled. I even remember what we wore. I was dressed in a pale green jersey-type dress and black high heels; Jimmy wore his white jacket and looked so handsome; and Timmy had on his khaki pants, a bow tie, and a little striped blazer. Mother had bought the clothes for Timmy when they were living at the hotel. We were all three dressed to the nines and I was so proud of us.

That night, I met Johnny Horton and his wife, Billie, who had been married to Hank Williams. (I never told Billie, but Hank Williams Sr. was in love with my cousin Swanee Wainwright. He would come by our house in Nashville when I was just a kid to pick up Swanee when she came up from Montgomery.) Johnny was one of the nicest men I had ever met.

A pure gentleman, he reminded me a lot of Jim Reeves. I also met Carl Belew, Johnny Mathis, Donny Lytle (who later became known as Johnny Paycheck), Merle Kilgore, the Browns (Bonnie, Maxine, and Jim Ed), Bill Black, Scotty Moore, and D. J. Fontana. Bill, Scotty, and D. J. all worked with Elvis and stayed at the Hayride while Elvis was in the army.

A few years ago I was on a Southwest Airlines flight from Nashville to Fort Lauderdale and D. J. Fontana was on the same flight. When we landed in Fort Lauderdale, I went over and asked him if he had been at the Louisiana Hayride in 1958. Startled, he said yes. I introduced myself, and then he remembered me. He told me he was in town playing at the Hard Rock Hotel, which was not too far from my house in Plantation, Florida. Seeing him after the flight, I thought, "What a really small world." I had just recently been talking to Timmy on the phone. He told me he was heading over to D. J. Fontana's house to look at some old pictures D. J. had of the Hayride and himself. D. J. lives very near the Hermitage area of Nashville, where Timmy lives. It seemed like D. J.'s name kept popping up in my life.

Getting back to my first night at the Hayride, I was really excited. When Jimmy and the Sunny Mountain Boys hit the stage, the crowd went wild. After the Hayride, we went to Harry's Barbeque in Bossier City, which would become a regular Saturday night outing, usually with Merle Kilgore and his wife, Dorothy; Carl Belew; Margie and Shelby Singleton; and several more. Depending on who was playing the Hayride, that's who went. It was always a lot of fun. During those Saturday night get-togethers, I made friends with Merle and Carl as well as Faron Young, George Jones, and Webb Pierce. I continued to see Merle, Faron, and Webb off and on throughout their lifetimes.

Shreveport was wild in those days. The Starlight Lounge in Bossier City across from the air force base was going strong. Johnny Mathis, Faron Young, and Donny Lytle used to hang out there. I remember one time when we were there, Faron was inebriated. He wanted to fight some guy. The guys would put Faron in the car on one side, and then he would get out on the other side to go after the guy. Finally they got him to stay in the car long enough to get him to go home. That was so funny. Everyone around the Hayride talked about it for quite some time.

Wages were low in Shreveport—nothing like Detroit. I got a job at Reliable Investments, which was located in the same building as KWKH. I made thirty dollars a week. My office was on the ground floor and had lots of glass windows. Anyone going to KWKH had to pass by my office. At the time, Tillman Franks was promoting Johnny Horton's song "The Battle of New Orleans," so Johnny was in the building every day. He always stopped by to say hello. As a hobby, Johnny was making metal ashtrays, each with a big mosquito on top. He brought me one. It was orange, yellow, and black. I had it up until the time I left Jimmy. I don't know what happened to it after that. I have asked Ray and Timmy. They remember the ashtray but don't know who has it. They also didn't know that Johnny Horton had made it. I guess neither Jimmy nor I told them.

Regardless, Tillman was so immersed in promoting Johnny and "The Battle of New Orleans," he had no time for the rest of the entertainers. We were all starving. I was one of the more fortunate wives, because I had a job.

After a long dry spell of Jimmy not having any show dates, the only money coming in, *other* than my paycheck, was from the Saturday night show, which was not much. I had watched Tillman during the times I had been in his office. I watched him on the telephone as he booked shows for Johnny Horton. I told Jimmy, "*I* can do that." He said, "If you think you can, do it." I knew I needed some contracts, so I asked Jimmy to go to the musicians union to see if he could get some blank ones. Jimmy was able to get the blank contracts. Now I could book shows.

It was election time in Louisiana. One of the people running for governor was the incumbent, Earl K. Long. I told Jimmy I was going to contact Mr. Long's headquarters and see if they had considered having a band on their campaign trail. The person I spoke to was very much interested in having Jimmy on the tour with them for one week. After we discussed the price, they were going to get back to me. But before they could, Long was committed to a mental institution. That deal was off, but I still believed I could get some dates for Jimmy with the other candidate who was running against country-western singer Jimmie Davis for governor, DeLesseps Story Morrison.

Morrison was then the sitting mayor of New Orleans. I contacted his office and spoke with his campaign manager, who was very much interested. I think part of his interest was because Jimmie Davis was a country music singer and had Grand Ole Opry people coming out to vote on his behalf. I negotiated a price for the band, signed the contracts, and we had a week's work. I was thrilled. I sent records, brochures, and pictures to Morrison's promotion office. I was strutting like a bantam rooster. I had booked my first shows. I *knew* I could do this! Tillman was *not* thrilled. He told Jimmy to tell me "not to do that anymore." Fortunately for us, I didn't listen.

I loved Shreveport. I liked my job. I liked the people. I loved fishing and skiing on Lake Bistineau and Lake Caddo. Even Jimmy and I seemed to be getting along better. We weren't fighting or arguing. He was staying home most nights, so things were good.

But accidents do happen. One day Jimmy, Paul Williams, and Joe Stuart were rehearsing while I was ironing in the living room. Timmy ran in through the back door, crying his eyes out with blood spewing everywhere. Jimmy threw his guitar across the room and grabbed Timmy. His tongue had been cut almost completely off. Jimmy held Timmy while I drove us all to the hospital. Once there, they rushed Timmy into the emergency room. One of us had to stay with him and Jimmy said he couldn't do it. So I stayed with Timmy and held him while the doctors sewed his tongue together. We later found out that he had been playing house with the little girl who lived behind us when he fell through a windowpane, severely cutting his tongue. The pane was standing up on the ground by the garage. I never found out why Timmy had his mouth open and his tongue hanging out while he was running.

While we were living in Shreveport on Egan Street, I had a little Chihuahua named Lady. Jimmy and Timmy called her Little Bit. She was the first dog I ever had that was supposed to be all mine. She was so cute. Then she came into heat. Jimmy wanted puppies and he got the biggest dog ever and mated her on our enclosed porch. I was furious. I knew that it would kill her when she gave birth to the puppies, and it almost did. She had nine of them, and Jimmy gave all of them away. Then he and Timmy took Little Bit and gave her away too. Timmy remembers that to this day. I cried and cried over my little dog. Jimmy called me stupid for crying over a dog and told me to shut up.

We were having some rough times, but we were also having some good times. Jimmy went hunting for ducks and deer with our landlord, Bill Kirkpatrick. Because he loved hunting so much, I bought him a sixteen-gauge Remington automatic shotgun for his birthday. Now he could go hunting in style. Everyone teased me about the gun, saying, "I hope you don't shoot each other."

I had never cooked duck or venison but started asking around for help. One of the tips someone gave me was to use a whole orange with any wild meat. It takes some of the gamey taste out. I experimented and finally learned how to cook duck and venison. Not ever being much of a meat eater, I just couldn't bring myself to eat either one. That was a real sore spot for Jimmy.

Jimmy, Timmy, and I would go fishing together practically every day. We always had fresh fish. Jimmy cleaned the fish and we froze it in large pans of water. When the fish thawed, they were the same as fresh. While out fishing, and if we had time before the sun went down, I would go water skiing. Skiing was my sport.

Most times when we went to the lake, the Kirkpatricks were with us. It was special having friends to do things with. We also had friends who worked on the Hayride: Dot and Merle Kilgore and Carl and Kate Belew. Carl and Kate had a son who was Timmy's age. It was a bright spot in Timmy's day to get to go see Carl and Kate and play with their son. I have tried to remember his name, but I can't. And I keep forgetting to ask Timmy if he remembers.

One day, Jimmy, Timmy, and I were all on the lake in one boat and Helen and Bill Kirkpatrick were in another. They had gone over to the other side of Lake Bistineau to fish. Jimmy, Timmy, and I were looking for a good place for crappie when our boat began to drift up under a tree. I could see a wad of snakes in the tree. I was so scared, I was about to pee in my pants. I said, "Get me out from under this tree!" Jimmy said, "Shut up, the snakes are not going to bother you." I again asked him, "Please, get me out from under this tree." By now he was mad. He yelled, "Shut up, you are scaring the fish." About that time, the boat was next to the tree and the snakes were right above me. I took my paddle, put it against the tree, and shoved as hard as I could. Jimmy's end of the boat went into some bushes that held a wasp nest. The wasps covered him. He was swatting and cussing as loud as he could. I was laughing and Timmy was afraid Jimmy was going to kill me. Across the lake Helen and Bill heard Jimmy yelling and immediately headed in our direction. Jimmy said, "What did you do that for?" I told him, "I asked you to get me out from under the snakes and you wouldn't." Although he later scared me numerous times with snakes, he didn't do that to me again whenever we were in the boat.

Another time when we were on Lake Bistineau we had our fish strung up and hanging off the side of the boat to keep them fresh. We were catching fish as fast as we could put our poles in the water. We would catch several before we stopped to string them up. After a while we had quite a few fish to add to our string. We stopped, pulled up our fish, and—surprise—no fish. But there was a huge gar fish chomping down on the remainder of our catch. The only fish we had left were the ones we had kept in the boat.

One time I was skiing on Lake Bistineau and I fell off the skis. Jimmy was driving the boat and yelling for me to hurry. I was swimming toward it as fast as I could. When I climbed into the boat, he showed me a big water moccasin that had been swimming right behind me. That knocked my socks off. If I had known about it, I probably would have frozen up and been unable to swim. While Jimmy was yelling, I just thought he wanted me to hurry up because he had to go to the bathroom or something. We had so many good times on the lakes around Shreveport, it would be impossible to tell about all of them.

Sarah, Jimmy's sister Erma, and Ray all came to visit us in Shreveport. Timmy loved having his brother there. I was nice to Sarah, but I could never forget how she had treated me when I went to get my kids back. I loved Erma and her children. She was such a good person. They only stayed a couple of days with us, but it was a terribly difficult couple of days for me. Every time I looked at Sarah, all I could still see was her standing on her front porch telling me to leave or she was going to shoot me. If I had not held my ground, Timmy would still be in Sneedville. That memory was still too fresh in my mind. Even though I had agreed to Ray's going to live with her because of his health, I had never agreed to his remaining there. I thought he would come back to us in a few months. Well, it took nine years.

In the summer of 1958, I had my ironing board set up in the living room. In those days I ironed practically everything. It was early evening and Jimmy was planning on going out, so I was mad. He had been out practically every night for a week until the wee hours of the morning. I was sitting on the side of the bed, and when I looked up, he threw the iron and it came straight at my head. I ducked, and it hit the headboard and created a hole the size of the iron. Had it hit me, I would have been dead. At that point I knew he was going to meet someone, and I was interrupting his plans again. He figured I would shut up, and I did. Jimmy's throwing the iron had scared me to death.

I got up and walked toward the kitchen. He was furious and followed me. He grabbed me from behind and threw me at the kitchen sink. He had his fist drawn back when I found a small paring knife in the sink. I grabbed the knife and rammed it into his neck. He quickly let go of me and grabbed his neck. The knife had also cut the tendon of my little finger in half. Blood was flying from both Jimmy and me. The only saving grace was that by this time he was more concerned with his neck than he was with me. I ran out of the house and didn't come back until he left.

When I returned, I packed Timmy's and my things, got into my Olds, and fled with my son. By the time Jimmy got home, I knew I would be in Memphis at my aunt's house. I stayed at my aunt Billie Turner's house for a couple of days, drove on to Nashville, and then after thinking about it, decided to return to Detroit, where I knew I could find work. I found out later that Jimmy had been having an ongoing affair with a young college girl for a couple of weeks. That was who he had planned to meet.

Back in Detroit at my sister Billie's apartment on Parkview, I applied with Kelly Employment Services. Billie worked primarily afternoons in a grocery store on Jefferson Street, a couple of blocks away. With Kelly Services I could pick and choose my jobs. The money was good, so I didn't have to put Timmy in daycare. He would stay with Billie while I was working and with me when I was off.

Billie and I got along great. We made good roommates, and it was such a pleasure not to be afraid of anything. We each paid our share of the expenses, which left us with more money for ourselves. We were both very happy. I became even happier when Laney stopped by one day. Timmy loved Laney and called him "the football player," because he was over six feet tall and a big man. Recently I asked Timmy if he remembered my boyfriend Laney. He said, "Oh, yes, he was the football player."

I could say Laney and I took up where we left off, but we didn't. We did date and go dancing together, but things were never the same. He told me he thought I would eventually return to Jimmy. He was right.

Even though Laney and I continued to date, I met a new man by the name of Frank, who owned a cocktail lounge in downtown Detroit. He had a large boat and we would meet at the Rooster Tail restaurant, go out on the boat, and come back to the restaurant for dinner. Some days we went skiing on the Detroit River. I was still skiing at every opportunity. But even though I liked the life I was living, I was still addicted to Jimmy Martin. I couldn't seem to get him off my mind. Besides that, Frank was just more of a friend and playmate.

I hadn't been in Detroit long when Jimmy started calling again. By this time Billie and I had a phone. My life *was* coming together. I told myself, "I don't want anything to do with Jimmy. And I'm only talking to him because Timmy loves talking to his daddy." But I knew in my heart that wasn't true. I was like a drunk—not wanting to take that drink but reaching for it all the time. I still wanted to be with Jimmy. So his manipulations began. I know that now, but at the time I didn't. It wasn't long before I was crying and promising him that I would return. It was during this time in 1958 that Jimmy and Paul Williams wrote "She's Left Me Again" and "It's Not Like Home." Jimmy recorded both songs.

Shortly after I returned to Shreveport, Jimmy asked me to marry him. He bought me a beautiful set of rings. I don't know why I couldn't do it. At one point in time, I would have loved to marry him, but things had never been as bad as they had been in Shreveport. I knew I didn't want to marry him. He didn't like my "no" at all. I told him things were fine the way they were and that I would think about it.

We never got around to the subject again, but I wore the rings until I left him in 1966. Then one day after being in court with him over the kids, and losing again, I was walking across the Woodland Street Bridge back to my car when a lightbulb went off in my head. I stopped in the middle of the bridge, took off the rings, and threw them as far as I could into the Cumberland River. It was like I was now free.

Soon after I returned, Jimmy started taking my car on the few show dates he had. Of course, he would never leave the keys to *his* car, so I couldn't drive. He also started leaving me with very little money to use for groceries, cigarettes, and other things while he was gone. I chalked this up to the idea that maybe we didn't have much money.

Once he began using my car on the road, it started needing maintenance. This was the perfect excuse for him to tell me I needed to get rid of it. I wanted to get it repaired, but he refused to spend the money. Knowing what I know now about cars, it probably just needed an oil change, but Jimmy insisted that the car be sold. He was getting rid of my transportation, so I couldn't leave. As I look back, I can now see what he was doing. At that time I would never have thought him capable of doing something like that. But this would not be the last time he would take my car.

We were in Shreveport for only two years, and I left Jimmy twice during that time. After Jimmy and the Osbornes had split up in Detroit, I had never been friends with anyone else or their wives until we had moved to Shreveport. I felt alone. Jimmy was never a person who would sit down and carry on a conversation, unless it was about his music, other singers or musicians, hunting, or bluegrass. There were no other topics. When Bob and Sonny had lived with us, I had someone to talk to about other things and other types of music.

Not too long after I returned, both Paul Williams and J. D. Crowe left Jimmy. I had no idea what had happened or why they had left. Following Paul and J. D.'s departure, Buck White came to visit us. He brought his daughters, Sharon, who was around six, and Cheryl, who was around three. I was thrilled to have those little girls at my house. They were so beautiful. Timmy, who was four or five at the time, was in love with Cheryl. He and the girls played all afternoon while I watched. I had a great time watching them. I thought Buck was an excellent father, and I would have liked to meet his wife. They were just the nicest family. I wanted my family to be like that. Buck and his family lived in Texas at the time. He had come to pitch some songs he had written to Jimmy and I believe to apply for the job playing mandolin. Jimmy wound up recording "Home Run Man," written by Buck.

Jimmy's liaisons with other women were becoming more and more frequent. It seemed like whenever Jimmy had a date with a new lady, he would pick a fight with me. He was a star on the Louisiana Hayride. Women swarmed around him like flies on honey. One night we were at Harry's Barbecue when he started picking on me. The Kilgores, the Belews, and, I believe, Margie Singleton and Shelby, and Timmy were there. I had asked Jimmy several times to stop, but he continued on. After he grabbed me, I grabbed an ashtray and hit him on the back of his neck as hard as I could. The blood poured. I was embarrassed, but I was not sorry. Needless to say, he didn't make his date that night. Instead he went to the hospital and got stitches. After we got home, he slept in the bed while I slept on the couch—with one eye open. I didn't know if he would seek revenge while I was sleeping. He never did.

In January 1960, Jimmy signed a contract with WWVA Jamboree in Wheeling, West Virginia. He would be booked by Gene Johnson, who was in charge of the talent. We were leaving the Hayride and going to the Jamboree.

Our years in Shreveport had been a very volatile time for me, but I was still very sad to be leaving. It had also been filled with good times and good friends. Unfortunately, I would never again see Helen and Bill Kirkpatrick.

6

BOOKING JIMMY MARTIN

As we came into Bridgeport, Ohio, across the Ohio River from Wheeling, West Virginia, the weather was nasty with snow on the ground. And I started crying. I couldn't believe I was going to live in this godforsaken place. It was nothing like Shreveport, which was warm and green. Here, the houses were built on stilts. I called them "stilt houses" because they were so high off the ground. We spent the first couple of days in a hotel while looking for a place to live.

Jimmy wanted to be close to the radio station. The first place we started looking for an apartment was on Wheeling Island. I needed to be close to a bus stop so that I could get to work when I found a job. It didn't take long before we found a small apartment on the second floor above a store. The people on the other side of the street had regular houses on stilts. I hated how those houses looked and couldn't imagine living in one.

Our apartment had two bedrooms, a small kitchen, small bath, and a small living room. The whole place was small, and the living room had windows looking out onto the street. Next door was a Lions Club or something similar. The bus stop was at the corner about two houses away.

After we paid the rent and got our few things moved in, Jimmy, Timmy, and I went to see Gene Johnson, who was in charge of the WWVA Jamboree talent. His office was in the Hawley Building along with WWVA radio. Gene mentioned he was looking for a secretary, so I applied and he hired me. He wanted me to start work the next day. I would now be working for a booking agent, and I intended to learn everything he knew.

The next morning, I walked over to the bus stop to go to work. Several people were standing there. I said, "Good morning." They looked at me like I was crazy. No one spoke a word. I couldn't figure out what was wrong with me. I looked to see if my slip was showing or something. Later I would learn that you didn't just walk up to strangers and start talking in Wheeling. It was not like Shreveport, where everyone talked to each other.

I now had my ideal job, working for Gene Johnson, a good-looking man in his late forties. He was very good at his job, friendly, and extremely helpful. Within a week I had met most of the entertainers from the Jamboree and all of the announcers. Singer Donna Darlene would become my good friend. At that time she was dating Doug Kershaw.

Every week or two the Jamboree would have special guests. Some of those included Wilma Lee and Stoney Cooper (I had known Wilma and Stoney since 1953), Grandpa Jones and Ramona, and Hawkshaw Hawkins and Jean Shepard. Hawk, Jean, and I would develop a friendship that would last many years beyond Wheeling. Jean continued to be my friend even after I was no longer in the business.

Jimmy and I soon discovered that Wheeling Island had a horse race track. Since neither of us had ever been to a horse race (or any other kind of race, for that matter), we decided to check it out. Once we went, we really liked it. We liked betting on the horses and watching them run. At first we knew nothing about the races or how to bet, and we were too stupid to ask. We did learn that if a horse came in across the finish line first, second, or third, it was called "show." We had no idea, though, that if one came in first or second and we had placed bets for our horse to show, we could collect. We thought the horse had to come in *third*. We threw all those tickets away. But we were having a lot of fun yelling and screaming for our horse.

One night we went to the races with Wilma Lee and Stoney. The horse we had bet on to come in third came in first. Jimmy said, "We did it again. We bet he would come in third." As he started to throw the ticket away, Wilma Lee yelled, "Don't throw that ticket away. You won!" We couldn't believe it. We told her we had bet on it to come in third. Then she explained it to us. Oh, were we sick because we had been throwing all that money away. From then on, we knew how to bet. We had to laugh about it because it was so comical.

A few months after we moved to Wheeling, Gene Johnson bought a radio station in Pittsburgh. He talked to me a long time letting me know he was going to leave. He told me I was good at his job and I should continue on. It was going to be a few more months before he left for good. He had to wait for all the FCC licenses and permits before he could open the new station. He told me he would teach me everything he knew and would let me start booking the shows while he watched. There are no words to describe how thrilled I was about it. By now I had gotten my foot in the door working for Gene, and I knew I could do it on my own.

But just about when you think everything is going great, crap hits the fan. I woke up one morning sicker than a dog. While I was in the bathroom vomiting, Jimmy was standing there asking, "What's wrong with you?" Then I knew. I hadn't had a period. I was devastated. I didn't want any more kids. Jimmy said, "Let's just get rid of it." I asked him, "How?" He said, "I will find someone." I know that sounds callous, but at that time we couldn't handle having another child. The only income we had was what Jimmy made from the Saturday night show and my salary. He and Timmy and I were living above a store, and we had enough other children scattered. We didn't need more.

Jimmy found a regular doctor in Steubenville, about twenty-five miles from Wheeling, who did abortions after his office closed for the day. Jimmy made arrangements for me to go to be examined. I talked to Donna Darlene, and she agreed to go with me. A couple of days later, Donna and I went to the doctor's office and sat in the reception area until everyone had left. The doctor called us in and examined me. We scheduled an appointment to come back for the abortion. It would cost five hundred dollars.

I went home and told Jimmy. He said okay. A couple of afternoons later, Donna and I took another trip to Steubenville with the five hundred dollars. We waited once again until everyone left the office. When the doctor called me in, I was so scared, I asked Donna to stay with me during the surgery. Donna went in with me and held my hand. I could not have made it without her. She drove us back to Wheeling and I spent the night with her at her hotel.

The following day, I returned to our apartment. Jimmy was very caring and tender with me, because he knew I had been through a lot, not only mentally but physically as well. We both were fully aware of what we had done. We also knew that we could not afford another child. We never discussed the abortion, not that day nor during the remaining years I was with him. We knew it was never going to be a subject we could talk about. It was too sensitive. I could now focus on learning the booking business, a good opportunity for our family.

Working for Gene was great. I liked talking to people on the phone and booking the talent at WWVA. Suddenly I liked myself, and my self-esteem was improving. I had never had any self-esteem and always blamed it on Mother's alcoholism. But now I don't think it was Mother's drinking that caused my low self-esteem. I think it was feeling inadequate and never doing the best I could do. Things started changing when I saw I could have a career.

At that time, other people on the Jamboree were Lee Moore; Doc Williams and his wife, Chickie, with their daughters; Donna Darlene; Rusty and Doug Kershaw; Kathy Dee; Lois Johnson (who was gorgeous); Kirk Hansard; Dottie Swan, part of the old radio duet of Radio Dot and Smoky; and Jimmy and the Sunny Mountain Boys. Lois and Kirk were married but had separate acts. They would also work with Jimmy and his band. Lee Moore had a late-night show on WWVA. John Corrigan and Lee Sutton were announcers. When Gene left, I would have an agency to book shows for all of them. The Barbara Martin Agency would be promoted over the air waves every night for booking talent. I couldn't wait.

When we first arrived, the live-audience broadcast was being made from the Virginia Theatre in Wheeling. Then after the Virginia was demolished, in 1962, the show moved to the Rex Theatre; eventually it was moved to the Capitol Theatre. Following the live show at the theatre, a radio program was broadcast from the studios of WWVA in the Hawley Building. A different artist would perform each Saturday night. Once when it came time for Jimmy to host the program, he said, "Well, boys, what are we going to do tonight with all that time?" Timmy popped up and said, "I'll sing, Daddy." And sing he did! He sang "Hang Down Your Head, Tom Dooley" just like a grown-up, with Jimmy and the band playing. He was five years old. Jimmy and I were so proud of him, we were beaming. We still have the audio tape from the live show.

That same night, Doug Kershaw was sitting at the piano with Donna and me, playing "Louisiana Man." He had just written it and was getting ready to record it. He said, "This is going to be a hit." Donna and I agreed. Now I look back and think about how I was in the right place and at the right time to witness two smash hits in the making: "The Battle of New Orleans" and "Louisiana Man." How lucky could I be?

By the end of 1960, Gene Johnson told me he was leaving and moving to Pittsburgh. He asked me to go to dinner with him. Jimmy was out of town and I accepted. I got a babysitter for Timmy before Gene took me to dinner. It was wonderful. It was my first and last dinner out in Wheeling.

Gene took me to a very nice restaurant. We had such a good time, laughing and talking. I really got to know him as a person, not just as a booking agent and boss. Before the night was over, he kissed me. I was starving for affection, and Jimmy certainly wasn't paying any attention to me. He was too busy with his music and his groupies. I wound up spending the night with Gene. It was the most romantic night I had had since Laney. And it was the only time I would cheat on Jimmy while living with him. (When we were separated, it was a different story.) I've never had any regrets about it nor felt any guilt. We both knew it was just for one night, and we made the most of it. The next day we were back to normal business.

I woke up one morning to find that a flood had hit Wheeling Island. When I looked out the window, I could see water everywhere. Jimmy was still sleeping. I shook him and said, "Get up; we have a problem. The water is up to the running boards on the car. The island is flooded." Jimmy jumped out of bed, looked out the window, and said, "Pack; we are going to the hotel." We checked into the Wheeling Hotel. When the water went down and we were able to go back home, we immediately started looking for a new place. We later learned that flooding was almost an annual event, especially on Wheeling Island—that was the reason for the stilt houses.

We bought a house on Euclid Avenue in Martins Ferry, Ohio. It was just north of Bridgeport and across the river from Wheeling. The house cost fifty-eight hundred dollars. We put down five thousand dollars and financed the rest. Within a couple of months, we paid off the eight hundred. That was a lot of money. The house had two bedrooms, a living room, one bathroom, and a small kitchen. Timmy and Paul Williams, who had returned to play for Jimmy, would share the one bedroom and Jimmy and I the other. The house was across the street from the school where Timmy would be starting in September. We all loved that little house. We bought it furnished. Once we bought it, I couldn't wait to start decorating. The first thing I did before we moved in was hang wallpaper in the living room and paint the rest of the house.

While I was hanging the wallpaper, Timmy was watching me. There were bugs flying around, and Timmy said, "Mudder, what are those bugs?" I jokingly told him they were termites. Those words would later come back to haunt me.

After Timmy started school, Jimmy and I were talking about kids getting colds. Jimmy said his mother used to make sassafras tea when they had colds. He bragged about how good it was. The next thing I knew, he came home with some sassafras roots and wanted me to make the tea. I went into our tiny kitchen, put the kettle on, and then set the cups on the table. I made the tea. It was horrible! Neither of us could drink it. We were laughing like hyenas and gagging at the same time. Timmy was looking at us like we had lost our minds. He did that a lot whenever Jimmy and I got tickled about something.

I cleaned up the mess and put the kettle back on the stove to make a cup of regular tea. The kitchen was very narrow, and the stove and table were across from each other. There was a narrow aisle between the stove and table. As I turned toward the table with the kettle of boiling water in my hand, Timmy came flying through the kitchen and knocked my hand. To keep the boiling water from hitting him, I jerked the kettle straight down toward the floor. The water went into the sock on my right foot, scalding the complete back of my leg. I was taken to the hospital, where I was treated for first-, second-, and third-degree burns. Afterward I was told to keep my foot elevated, and I was given crutches and medication.

One day while I was recuperating, Timmy came home from school through the back door. That was very unusual. I was sitting in a chair with my foot up on a stool. I asked Timmy why had he come in the back door, and he said, "I brought you a present, Mudder." I said, "That's good. What is my present?" He said, "I brought you a snake, Mudder." I said, "You better *not*." He said, "I did." He was so proud of it. I asked him, "Where is the snake?" He said, "I put it in a cup on the back porch." I got up, looked out the door, and sure enough, there was a dead snake in a little white plastic cup on the back porch. I then explained to Timmy that Mudder was afraid of snakes and asked him to throw it away. He did, and he never brought Mudder another snake. He was so cute, I couldn't get mad at him. He had brought it to me out of love.

Timmy was such a good little boy. He was loving and just a pleasure to be around. We would talk and talk and talk. He was my pride and joy. He liked school and he was smart; he also liked having other kids to play with. I started giving him tap dancing lessons in Wheeling, although at that time not many boys were taking tap dancing. He was in the class for about two months and didn't want to go anymore, so I let him stop. But he remembers those lessons to this day.

J. D. Crowe left Jimmy in 1960. Fortunately for me, Timmy has a great memory. He was only six or seven at the time, but he remembers Crowe selling his car and leaving Wheeling. Timmy remembers the car and how Crowe loved it. After Crowe left, Paul Craft joined the Sunny Mountain Boys, playing banjo.

One of my favorite memories—and Timmy remembers this—was when Timmy had the mumps. Paul Craft lived across the street and behind the school, but he was at our house every day. Paul had never had the mumps. Well, he has had them now. He got them from Timmy.

The doctor came out to see Paul to give him a shot. The doctor told me that I would need to give him another shot the next day. When I went to give Paul the shot, he didn't want me to see his behind. I said, "Paul, how can I give you a shot without seeing it? I can't close my eyes. I might stick you someplace else." We both argued back and forth, and finally I said to Paul, "Just cover up all but one little spot. I will give you the shot in that one spot." He did. And I did.

Timmy and I were talking about this just recently, and he told me about seeing Paul at the Station Inn about a year before he died. He sneaked up on Paul and whispered in his ear, "Do you want the mumps?" Timmy said, "Paul jumped like he was shot." Then he looked around and said, "Timmy!" They both laughed about it. Paul Craft was a wonderful person and a good songwriter. I was sorry to hear of his passing in 2014 at the young age of seventy-six.

My work as a booking agent kept me going. I hated Wheeling. I would have been bored to tears without my work. I probably would have left and never returned.

After we moved from Wheeling Island, Jimmy and I never went out together unless it was about business. There were no more races. It was all work. Not for Jimmy, of course. He took off every night and went drinking or God knows where. I knew he was running around with other women. I just didn't know the extent. My work and my child were what I cared about, and I was going to learn everything I could about the booking business.

Gene was very patient in teaching me how to book shows. The last few days we were at the office together, we went through his list of contacts—people who booked shows, clubs, parks, and other venues—and he told me a little about each one of them. I was like a sponge soaking up this information. He told me how to price an act, whether it was a soloist or a group, and how to determine the price for the venue accordingly. He went through the fair associations and let me speak to various buyers on the phone. He would listen to my conversations and critique my performance after the call. Sometimes he thought I could do better; I corrected those areas and did do better. By the time Gene was ready to move to Pennsylvania, I was already booking all the shows. Gene gave me all the supplies and the typewriter in the office, and I took those things home.

Booking shows was a lot more difficult than one would imagine. It took negotiating skill and personality on the phone with the buyers. I also learned very quickly that the buyer was the happiest when you asked about his wife or kids, or sometimes his girlfriend. When you did this, he was on your side. That was one of the first things I learned. You also had to be good with follow-up. You had to make sure your letters, promotional pictures, records, and brochures went out on time. I had to make sure Jimmy's records continued to be played on the air by calling the disc jockeys and writing them little personal notes from Jimmy. And as soon as I booked a show, I immediately typed up the contract and got it in the mail. If I didn't receive it back within a week, I called the buyer. It was repetitive but stimulating work.

I continued to book all the people at WWVA, and my name went out on the nightly radio shows promoting the Barbara Martin Agency. I was getting enough calls and booking shows that I decided to join the fair associations, where I could book the fire carnivals and fairs. Fire carnivals are little carnivals in various small towns usually promoted by the fire departments to raise funds. I also booked county and state fairs, which were larger and you could get a better price for your act. At the state fairs, I would usually book a package show and use talent from the Grand Ole Opry as well as the Jamboree people.

The first association I joined was the Pennsylvania Fair Association. I went to their exhibition, where their vendors, fair managers, and fire carnival managers were booking shows for the coming season. I was fortunate, booking ninety dates that year in Pennsylvania. They were not all for Jimmy, but a good chunk of them were. I was even able to add dates for

Wilma Lee and Stoney, Hawksaw Hawkins, and Grandpa Jones, who had all previously been members of the Jamboree. I was walking on air.

I was booking Jimmy and the band on lots of show dates, and we were making money. At the time, I was getting three hundred to five hundred dollars per show for him. That was good, decent money in 1960 and 1961. We felt like we were rolling in money, and Jimmy's records were doing extremely well. Gas was cheap, and he didn't have to pay the 15 percent booking agent commission on the money he was making. Our house was paid for and our living expenses were minimal. I was making 15 percent on shows I booked for other entertainers. We were pleased, because most of the dates were only a day trip from Wheeling.

By now I had joined the fair associations in Michigan, Ohio, Illinois, Kentucky, Pennsylvania, West Virginia, and New York. At each association meeting, Jimmy and I would set up my table with the brochures, photos, and albums. The brochures included Jimmy and all the various other artists from Nashville and Wheeling. My abilities as a good booking agent and manager were becoming well known. The primary object at the fair conventions was to book package shows using not only Jimmy and his band but stars from Nashville as well. It was fairly easy to do that with the large fairs, but the smaller ones and the fire carnivals could afford to book only one act a day.

I was getting calls from other artists to book them, including Dottie West. Dottie worked out of Nashville with her agent, Lucky Moeller, and wanted me to use her. I would be buying her from Lucky, but that was the way all of the artists in Nashville were booked if they had an agent. I was constantly in contact with Bob Neal, Hubert Long, Buddy Lee, Lucky Moeller—all of the top booking agents in Nashville. If an act didn't have a booking agent, I just called them directly.

I liked Dottie, and we became friends and remained so for the rest of her life. I was literally sick to my stomach when I learned she had been killed in a car accident in 1991. I cried for what seemed like days. What a loss. She was such a beautiful and talented lady.

I had also made friends with several different disc jockeys at the conventions who booked talent, including Tom Reeder from North Carolina and Bobby Brown from Baltimore, Maryland. Both were top disc jockeys in their area who booked shows. Bobby Brown's wife, Sally, was a terrific singer. I tried booking her, but she didn't have the name recognition for her talent outside the Baltimore area.

Despite the fact that Jimmy had his groupies in Wheeling, we had a very good home life. He treated me well, with the exception of the trip to Nashville, when he had a hidden agenda to meet Melissa Monroe and didn't want me to go. We didn't fight like we did in Shreveport. Life was different, calmer. I liked that. I think the reason I didn't care about his women was that I was no longer in love with Jimmy. I loved my child and my job. I loved our little house. At the time, that was enough for me. But that would change.

One night during the show at the Rex Theatre in Wheeling, I went to the ladies room. As I was sitting on the commode in one of the stalls, I heard two girls talking. One said, "Jimmy is going to take her and the kid home, and then he will meet us at the bar." I sat there for about ten minutes listening to them talk about me. I knew what I was going to do.

On the way home, Jimmy never said a word and neither did I. After he took Timmy and me home, he went into the bedroom and changed clothes. He then left. I took Timmy across the street to a neighbor's house and asked her to babysit him because I had someplace to go. I called a cab and went to the bar. Sure enough, outside the bar sat Jimmy's car. I walked in and saw him sitting all hugged up with the girl I had heard talking in the ladies room. I walked over to the table, stood there, turned around, and went back out to the cab to go home. You have never seen anyone getting out of anywhere as fast in your life as Jimmy Martin. I didn't speak to him for a week. No yelling, no cursing, no threatening. I just wanted him to know that I knew what he was doing. I really didn't care.

In November 1961 Jimmy and I were going to the annual Disc Jockey Convention in Nashville. Problems arose when we were getting ready. Jimmy decided he didn't want me to go, but I insisted. I was the booking agent, and I needed to be at the convention to meet people and make friends. I was also the person who did all of the publicity for the records. I was mad as hell that he didn't want me to go. I didn't care. I got in the car with my bag and wouldn't get out. Timmy was staying with Janet, a girl who lived across the street and often babysat so that he could continue to go to school.

Jimmy was livid with me on the trip. Before we even got out of Ohio, he threatened to hold my head out the car door until it hit the pavement. He had already jerked the curlers out of my hair, hair and all. I was scared but didn't let on. Bill Yates was driving and he was trying to get Jimmy to stop. Jimmy was yelling at Bill to shut up. I didn't know what all of his anger was about. I would think that he would want me to go, meet people, possibly book some shows, and talk to the disc jockeys about his records.

When we arrived in Nashville, we were supposed to be staying at the James Robertson Hotel, but Jimmy wouldn't let me stay in the room. I had no money or car. I called Mother. She gave me my stepfather Clem's number at the country club to call him. He told me to get a cab to the Hillwood Country Club, where he was working, and I could use his car. Once I got to the country club, Clem paid for the cab and then gave me some money and his car keys. He also bought me lunch. I was starving. Jimmy would not pay for anything for me all the way to Nashville. When he and Bill stopped to eat, I couldn't, because I had no money. I just went to the bathroom and then got back in the car. I hurried in the bathroom, too, because I was afraid he would leave me there in some town or gas station with no money.

After the Hillwood Country Club, I went back to town to the Andrew Jackson Hotel, where the convention was being held. There I ran into Judy Steinberg and her mother. Judy was the president of the Jimmy Martin Fan Club. They asked where we were staying, and I told them Jimmy was staying at the James Robertson Hotel but I didn't have a place to stay. Mrs. Steinberg said, "You do now. You will stay with us in our room."

Judy Steinberg was a fantastic person. She was blind but maneuvered around like a sighted person. She was very intelligent and her mother was adorable. I could not have asked for better people to be my roommates.

The following day I ran into the western swing singer Hank Thompson. I had known Hank for many years. He told me he was staying at the Hermitage Hotel and asked me to stop by his suite, so he could introduce me to Bill Greene. Bill Greene owned the Golden Nugget in Las Vegas, and he and Hank were staying at the Hermitage Hotel.

Shortly after seeing Hank, I went by their suite, where they were holding an open house. Hank immediately saw me, came over, and took me to meet Bill. Bill and I talked at length about booking Jimmy and the band into the Golden Nugget. He told me he would want at least six pieces in the band, including a girl singer, and I said that was not a problem. My thoughts ran to Kirk Hansard and Lois Johnson. Kirk and Lois had played dates with Jimmy previously. Bill and I discussed prices and dates, and he told me to send him a contract for six weeks. The dates would be in the spring of 1962. He gave me his personal phone numbers and address.

A couple of nights later I ran into Bill Monroe in the lobby of the Andrew Jackson. Bill said, "Barbara, where is Jimmy?" I told him, "I don't know. I have not seen him since we got here." Bill said, "I will tell you where he has been, and that is with my daughter!" Bill was mad as a wet hen. I had never seen him like that. Now I knew why Jimmy didn't want me to go to the convention. He had plans all along to meet up with Melissa Monroe for the weekend.

Jimmy had dated Melissa Monroe before he met me, but that had supposedly ended when he and I met. He showed her my picture and she tore it up. I don't know when he got back in touch with her, or if she got in touch with him first. They probably had been in touch with each other all along, but this was the first time I had heard about them being together again. It would prove to be another of his many downfalls with Bill Monroe.

One day at the convention I ran into Dottie West and her friend Kathy Dee, whom I knew from the Jamboree. They were both friends of mine, and I told them what was happening with Jimmy. They, as well as Judy and Mrs. Steinberg, were very supportive of me.

I continued to do my business at the convention. I didn't let Jimmy Martin and his antics interrupt me. I was basically trying to make a name for myself. And even though I was booking other artists who paid me a commission, I didn't get to keep that money. Jimmy always took it and doled out whatever he wanted me to have to go to the store or for whatever I needed.

Jimmy barely spoke a word to me during that entire convention. I really didn't care, because I wasn't interested in talking to him either. He had treated me like a piece of shit and I was mad. In the end, he told me if I was going back to Wheeling to be at his hotel by 7:00 a.m. or they would leave without me. I was there and waiting. I would be going home to my child and my business. To hell with him! The ride back to Wheeling was silent.

It took weeks for life to get back to normal. By now Jimmy knew that I had booked him for six weeks at the Golden Nugget in the spring. On the day I wrote those contracts for the Nugget, I wanted to say to Jimmy, "Motherfucker, if I had not gone to the convention, you would not be playing the Nugget." I didn't, though, because at that time I didn't use that kind of language. I only learned to do that later when I worked for lawyers. Like musicians, lawyers will get to you every time.

Jimmy and the Sunny Mountain Boys with Paul Williams, Lois Johnson, Kirk Hansard, and Zeb Collins left Wheeling and traveled to Las Vegas. But before Jimmy played the Nugget, Paul Craft left and Bill Emerson came to Wheeling to play banjo. The day they were getting ready to pull away from the house and head to Las Vegas, I wanted to go out front and hold up a sign in big capital letters that said, "You are going to Las Vegas because of me!" I never forgot the hell I had gone through to go to the Disc Jockey Convention that November.

Jimmy and the band played six shows a day, forty minutes on and twenty off every day for six weeks. While they enjoyed being in Las Vegas at the Nugget, they said it was their toughest gig ever. Quite honestly, when Jimmy told me about the hours they had to work at the Nugget, I felt sorry for the band. I didn't feel sorry for Jimmy. I thought he should have worked twice as hard and earned the privilege of going to Vegas. I would have been a dead duck if he had known what I thought about the work he had to do in Vegas.

Bill Emerson started playing banjo with Jimmy in 1962. He and his wife and twin boys moved into an apartment just a few blocks from our house. When Timmy found out Bill had two boys, he was overjoyed. He had someone to play with. Unfortunately they were only babies, so they were too young for Timmy to play with.

I liked Bill immediately. He was tall, good-looking, and polite. He was also educated, and one could talk to him about any subject. His wife was beautiful and I liked her very much, too, even though I never got to know her very well. Jimmy liked working with Bill, who was always a gentleman. He was there to play the Golden Nugget with Jimmy and then go to play in Thule, Greenland, and Goose Bay, Labrador.

Bill stayed with Jimmy until early 1964 when he left to go to work with Red Allen. He would return in mid-1965 and stay until 1967. When Bill left, Doyle Lawson came to work for Jimmy. When Doyle left in 1965, Bill returned. Sort of like a merry-go-round of good banjo players. Bill went on to be with the US Navy band and was an original partner in the Country Gentlemen Band. Later he became a star in his own right.

Doyle Lawson went on to form his own band and continues to appear with his award-winning band at festivals and shows. I will never forget meeting Doyle. He was from around Sneedville. Jimmy and I were at his mother's for Christmas when Doyle came over to see Jimmy. He brought his banjo and played some with Jimmy. He was good and he was looking for a job.

During that time Jimmy's mother and sisters Erma and Edria came to Wheeling. While Edria was there, she and Paul Williams started getting together. You could tell they really liked each other. When Edria went home, they stayed in touch and a real romance developed. I was so happy for the two of them.

November 1962 rolled around and Paul told me he was going to marry Edria. Now we had to devise a plan to get Paul away from Jimmy. It was once again time for the Disc Jockey Convention in Nashville. I told Paul this would be an ideal time to go to Sneedville, get married, and be back by the time we returned from Nashville. I assumed that I would be going despite what had happened the year before. Our plan went off without a hitch. Paul went to Sneedville, and he and Edria got married.

After we returned home, Jimmy found out and went ballistic. He blamed me and the fact that I knew what was going on and didn't tell him. He was outraged, but I didn't care. I didn't want him trying to break up Paul and Edria, because I knew the way his mind worked—break them up. It wasn't about their getting married; it was because Jimmy thought that Paul would quit playing music and move to Sneedville with Edria. That did happen, but not just then. Paul and Edria are still married—fifty-four years and counting, as Edria says. And they still play music in the summertime at festivals. Edria has always been a terrific singer, as is her sister Evelyn. I am still in touch with Paul and Edria and love them both. I have always thought of them as my family.

I was booking shows left and right. I had booked Jimmy and the band with Lois Johnson and Kirk Hansard in Labrador and Greenland. To get to the air force bases for both dates, they would fly on Military Air Transport Service, or MATS. I was becoming well known as a good booking agent. It was magic for me. I had found a profession that I was very good at, and it gave me a tremendous boost of self-esteem. I was beginning to feel like an adult and not a kid.

My home life was a different story. Timmy was thriving. He loved having me at home after school. At the same time, though, Jimmy continued to run around with other women, and I continued to ignore it, unless I was slapped in the face with it. Then I would raise hell. But I never left him while we were in Wheeling. I was so involved in my booking business that I didn't much care what he did.

One time I really did care. I had been itching in my crotch so badly, I couldn't stand it. I thought I had gotten lice but couldn't imagine how that could be. The only place I ever went to was the Jamboree and to the studio afterward. I asked Jimmy what was wrong, and he said, "You have been out with someone that gave you crabs." I said, "You are crazy. I have not been out with anyone. The only person I have been around is you." I didn't know what crabs were. He went to the drugstore, and when he returned he told me to get completely undressed and to stand in the bathtub. I will never forget how terribly humiliating that was and how much the medicine burned. We then had to strip all of the bedding and wash and spray all the furniture to kill all of the crabs. The next time I went to the drugstore alone, I asked the pharmacist how you get them. He told me, "You get them from sleeping with someone who has them." When I got home, I lit into Jimmy. I told him, "If this ever happens to me again, I am out the door for good."

Jimmy and I went to the November 1962 Disc Jockey Convention in Nashville. This time there was no fighting, because he didn't have any hidden agendas, like meeting Melissa Monroe. We saw a lot of old friends and made a lot of new ones.

It was during this visit that we decided to move to Nashville. Jimmy couldn't be a regular on the Grand Ole Opry, but he could make guest appearances. We had met Bob Neal, who was a booking agent for Wil-Helm, an agency owned by the Wilburn Brothers and Don Helms. Bob said he would take over Jimmy's management and booking, and then I could become an agent with Wil-Helm. That really sounded great to both Jimmy and me. Bob had been Elvis's first manager before Colonel Parker, so I figured he knew what he was doing. We agreed, and we set a date for February when we would move to Nashville and I would start working at Wil-Helm.

Back at the convention, I ran into Bill Monroe and we stopped to talk. I was proud of the fact that we were moving back to Nashville, so I said to Bill, "Jimmy and I are moving back to Nashville." He said, "Barbara, don't do it." I asked, "Why?" Bill said—and I quote—"Jimmy will never be on the Grand Ole Opry as long as I live." I didn't want to believe it, but I knew why. Bill was still angry about Jimmy going out with his daughter and spending all weekend with her the year before. I found Jimmy and told him what Bill had said. His words were "Fuck Bill Monroe." I thought Bill would get over it. He never did. But the one thing I admired about Bill was that despite his anger toward Jimmy, he never held it against me. Bill was friendly to me every time I saw him. He always, without fail, stopped and talked to me *unless* I was with Jimmy.

Back in Wheeling, Jimmy and I started making preparations to move to Nashville. We put the house up for sale furnished. Shortly after the house went on the market, a nice couple came by to see it. Timmy was out of school that day. As I was showing the house, Timmy, proud as he could be, and with his chest out, said to the potential buyers, "You know what we have?" The buyers said, "No, what do you have?" Timmy replied, "Termites." I almost fell through the floor. I immediately said, "I told him the flies were termites." We sold the house, termites and all.

We probably looked like the Beverly Hillbillies moving. We rented a small trailer, loaded up our few things like dishes, linens, pots and pans, clothes, instruments, and Timmy's toys, and set off for Nashville, the Cadillac plastered on both sides with JIMMY MARTIN AND THE SUNNY MOUNTAIN BOYS, DECCA RECORDS.

When we arrived, we stayed with my mother and Clem. Jimmy and I had talked about where we wanted to live in Nashville. I had always dreamed of having a brick house on Murphy Road. Jimmy wanted a brick house, too. As we drove down Murphy Road, it wasn't the same as I had remembered from high school. It was now looking run down. We knew we were on the wrong side of town and started looking at other places.

By now we were in touch with Bob Neal, who was with the Wil-Helm Agency, where I would be working. He lived in an area called Hermitage Hills. We went to visit Bob, and the area was just beautiful, with new houses and a school right in the development that Timmy could walk to. We looked at a house at 224 Jacksonian Drive, about a half block from Bob's house. It was a beautiful three-bedroom, bath-and-a-half, tan brick house. The yard was almost an acre, and the house and land together cost ten thousand dollars. That was a lot of money, but we paid cash and bought it.

After we moved we took Timmy to Hermitage Hills Elementary and enrolled him. He had started third grade in Martin's Ferry that year, but we transferred him. After settling in, we decided to go see Bob Neal at the Wil-Helm Agency. It was located on Sixteenth Avenue South next door to Decca Records. I needed to find out when I would be starting work. We met with Bob Neal and Lester Wilburn. During our meeting, Bob told Jimmy they were not going to be able to book him, but they would still like for me to come to work for the agency. I was shocked. I told them if they wouldn't represent Jimmy, then I couldn't work there. I looked at Jimmy and said, "Let's go home. I will set up my office today." I was back in business, but Jimmy was devastated that they had treated him like that. I will always believe that Bill Monroe had spoken to Lester Wilburn about not booking Jimmy. Bill had nothing against me, and that was the reason they wanted me to stay and book talent. Given my situation with Jimmy, I probably should have done that. But if I had become a booking agent with Wil-Helm, Jimmy would have had no one to book him. I couldn't do that to him.

After our visit to the Wil-Helm Agency, we went next door and talked to Harry Silverstein and Owen Bradley at Decca to let them know what was happening. I liked Owen. He was such a regular guy, one would never know he was a legend. He always smiled and stopped whatever he was doing to talk to you. He never changed during all the years I knew him. I liked Harry, too. He was a down-to-earth type of gentleman, who in 1998 died way too soon. I cried, standing by his casket. I just couldn't believe he was gone. I had lost another friend.

After we moved to Hermitage, we became friends with Mooney and Loretta Lynn. Loretta had been in Nashville only a short time. She, Mooney, and their four kids—Betty Sue, Cissy, Ernest Ray, and Jack Benny—lived not too far from us in Tulip Grove. Loretta was getting ready to start filming a TV show with Doyle Wilburn and the Wilburn Brothers. She asked me to go with her to a luncheon about the new TV show, at the Irish pub on Twenty-First Avenue South. Doyle Wilburn was there. He and I had been friends since I had worked at the Tulane Hotel, and he was part owner of the Wil-Helm Agency. When he saw me, he immediately came over and hugged me. He apologized for not being able to book Jimmy but told me, "The door is open for you." I told him that what had happened was probably for the best.

After the luncheon, which lasted about three hours, I went with Loretta to pick up a stage dress she had had custom made. If I remember correctly, it was her first custom-made stage dress. It had blue checks and looked terrific on her.

Loretta, Mooney, Jimmy, and I continued to be friends. There were always people at Loretta's house. Her sister Peggy Sue; her brother Jay Lee (Jack) and his wife, Shirley; and her mother were there quite often as was her sister Brenda Gail, who was about twelve years old at the time. Brenda is now known as Crystal Gayle.

I became bosom buddies with Loretta's sister-in-law Shirley and Loretta's brother Jack Webb. Shirley and I would talk almost every day. She and Jack didn't have any children. They were a great couple, and they lived down Lebanon Road in a mobile home park. Jack was a straightlaced guy and he was also a good singer. I saw Peggy and Jack only a few times after I left Jimmy.

Loretta's husband, Mooney, was quite a character. He had this red face that always looked a little sunburned. He liked to drink and carouse. I used to tell Jimmy that he and Mooney were probably born twins and just didn't know it. They were just alike. They liked to hunt together, both animals and women. Still, I liked Mooney. He was what he was.

Timmy loved going to Loretta's house to play with Jack Benny and Ernest Ray. The girls, Betty Sue and Cissy, were not into playing with the boys. Betty Sue was always my favorite. She and I talked and talked whenever we were together. She is the reason I wanted a girl of my own so badly.

In early 1970 Betty Sue and her kids came to my apartment. She was looking for a place for herself, her two children, and her boyfriend, Dan. I went with her to the office at the Madison Square Apartments, where I lived, and she rented the place across the hall from me. From that point on, she and I spent every day together. I was on medical leave from Metro at the time, having just had a hysterectomy.

Betty Sue was a singer and a very good one. She told me she felt like her family had pushed her to the back burner as a singer. She never said it, but she indicated by the way she talked about her family that she had some jealousy of her twin sisters. She was very happy living in her little apartment with Dan. She told me she was going to marry him and asked me to go with them. My friend Wayne Johnson and I drove them to Georgia and stood up for them when they got married.

Betty Sue and Dan continued to live in the apartment for several months. A couple of nights a week they would come to my house for dinner. I loved to cook and still do. Betty Sue and Dan, Wayne, and I went out almost every Friday and Saturday night, either to the Dusty Road or a place on Gallatin Road and Trinity Lane that played music. Sometimes we would hit both places. Betty Sue and Wayne sang whenever we went out. Both were excellent singers and could really get a crowd dancing.

I saw Betty Sue one time after she moved back to Loretta's house. I was married to Chuck Stephens then and we went to Hurricane Mills and spent the afternoon with her. Loretta and Mooney were out of town, but her mom was there. I had always loved Loretta's mother. We all had a wonderful afternoon. Shortly after seeing them, Chuck and I moved to Orlando.

But back to 1962: Timmy and I also became friends with Jeanne Pruett. She was married to Jack Pruett, who was the guitarist for Marty Robbins, and they had two children, Jack Jr. and Jael. Jeanne recorded "Satin Sheets." They lived just a couple of blocks from us in Hermitage Hills, and Timmy went to school with Jack Jr. and Jael. A lot of afternoons he went to play at their house after school. In those days the kids were free to roam the streets to visit and play with their friends. Kids were always at our house. It was the same for all the parents in Hermitage Hills.

At the time, few musicians in Nashville were making money. Jimmy was one of those few, and that was because I was booking him. If he didn't work, our family didn't eat. I had my typewriter and my telephone set up in the living room. I worked every day and loved it. We had settled in to an everyday routine.

Part of Jimmy's daily routine was to go to the bank in Donelson. I never saw any of the mail, so I didn't know what he was depositing or why he was going to the bank. He was out of the house and I had time for myself. I loved it. I also loved the gifts he received from the bank every day. Back then whenever you made a deposit, the bank gave you a gift—a toaster, hand-held mixer, small gifts like that.

I adored our little house. It was perfect for our family. We used one of the bedrooms as a den to watch TV. I had new living room furniture. I was so proud of it, I didn't want anyone touching it. Jimmy and I had gone to Farrar Furniture Company in Donelson to purchase our living room furniture and a bedroom suite, which he still had when he died. The furniture for Timmy's room and the den and a new table and chairs for the kitchen were also purchased there. I was so happy. We finally had a beautiful home, and it even had hardwood floors throughout. We were both very proud of it. Those floors were so much fun for the boys and me. We made a game of waxing and shining them. Ray, Timmy, and I would put our socks on and run and slide all over the floors.

With our big backyard, Jimmy could have some hunting dogs. He built a pen in the lower part of the yard and then bought two beagles and named them Bessie and Becky. They were prize beagles. Jimmy was very protective of those dogs. We were not allowed to play with them. When Jimmy was gone, Timmy and I could feed them, but that was it—nothing else.

One day Jimmy was on the road and Timmy and I were sitting in the den when I heard Bessie barking. I looked out the window and saw Bob Neal's big collie mating with Becky right under the window. I grabbed the broom and ran out of the house. I tried to get them apart, but I couldn't until they were ready. When I got them separated, I grabbed Bessie and put her back in the pen. Well, it wasn't long until she climbed over the fence to get to Bob's collie, who was still lurking around. I figured, "Well, it can't hurt anything now. They have already done their bit." Finally, Timmy went out and put Bessie's chain on her so she couldn't get out again. When Jimmy returned, he put a wire roof over the pen to keep them from climbing out.

Well, when we found out Bessie was pregnant, a mountain of shit hit the fan. To hear Jimmy shouting and yelling about my letting Bessie get with Bob's collie, you would have thought the world was ending. Turned out, Bessie had seven or eight pups. Jimmy could not tolerate them and said they were not staying at our house. I begged him to take them to the pound, but he wouldn't. Instead he put them in a tow sack and took them to Stone's River and threw them in. I cried for days about that. Timmy remembers it well.

For Christmas 1962 we went to Sneedville to Jimmy's mother's house. This was never a fun trip for me. I couldn't help but remember what had happened when I went to retrieve Timmy after Jimmy took him to Sarah's without my knowledge when we were living in Detroit. Ray was six years old now, and I wanted him to come home with us, but Jimmy didn't want to ever talk or hear about taking him away from his grandmother. I was sick to my stomach over it, but what could I do? I also wanted my son Mike to come live with us. But that wasn't happening either. Even though I was working every day, I had no money, other than what Jimmy wanted to give me, and no car. I didn't realize it at the time, but I was virtually a prisoner.

In 1963 Jimmy and I seemed to be getting along better. The fighting had calmed down, and Jimmy had become more loving. He was not going out at five o'clock every afternoon, we were doing more things as a family, I was booking shows, and life was good. We started talking about having another child. I wanted a girl desperately. Everyone told me if I just waited until Jimmy turned forty, we could have a girl. But I didn't want to wait four more years. I was going to be twenty-eight in October. We decided we were going to try for that girl but would wait a few more months.

7

FUNERAL/

The morning of March 5, 1963, is embedded in my memory. I was sitting on the yellow hassock, having a cup of coffee. Timmy had gone to school and Jimmy was in the bedroom getting dressed. I had the TV on and the announcer said that Patsy Cline, Hawkshaw Hawkins, Randy Hughes, and Cowboy Copas had been killed in a plane crash. I screamed at the top of my voice. Jimmy came running into the room and said, "What happened?" I was crying so badly, I could barely say the words: "Patsy, Hawk, Copas, and Randy Hughes have been killed in a plane crash." We were stunned. I called Loretta and she told me that Mooney had gone to find Charlie Dick, Patsy's husband. No one had been able to reach him. By the end of that day, either Jimmy or I had been on the phone with at least one person from each of the families.

I just couldn't get my mind off Hawk. I called his wife, Jean Shepard, and went over to their house. I remember walking up on the back porch. Jean was pregnant at the time. When she opened the door, I started crying. I felt so sorry for her. I put my arms around her and we hugged and cried. I wanted to take her mind off why I was there, so I started talking about how much I liked the back porch. She said they had killed a rattlesnake on it a few days before. I said, "I am scared to death of snakes." But I knew going to other subjects was useless when all I could really think about was how this beautiful man had brought me candy at the office in Wheeling and how much he loved Jean and their unborn son. He would never be around to share with Jean the happiness of watching his child grow up. Even now I am sad and almost in tears just remembering that day.

I had been friends with Randy Hughes, Patsy Cline's manager, since the first night Jean Armstrong and I went to the studios at WSM to meet up with Jimmy and L. E. White. You know how when you meet someone, you either click or don't. With Randy, we were friends from the start. Not boyfriend and girlfriend, but real friends. I knew his secret about being in love with Patsy. I also knew both of them were married—Randy to Kathy Copas and Patsy to Charlie Dick. But how could anyone not help but love Patsy? She was giving and loved her children. And, although it was not generally known, she loved Jimmy Martin's music. She had Jimmy's album covers on the wall of her den in the basement. Best of all, she was flamboyant, and I admired that. I remember one night Jimmy and I were sitting in Tootsie's when Patsy came flying in. She was wearing this swinging, white wool coat trimmed in white fox fur. I thought she was the cock that walked. Fantastic! I wanted to look, walk, and talk just like her. I can see her to this day coming through the door and saying, "How the hell are you?"

A joint funeral service for Patsy, Randy, Hawk, and Copas was held at the Phillips-Robinson Funeral Home in Nashville. It was a very solemn affair. Four very talented and nice people were dead. I remember standing with Kitty Wells and, I believe, Jean Shepard and Loretta Lynn in the foyer at the funeral home when someone came in and said, "Jack Anglin has just been killed in a one-car accident on Due West in Madison." I thought Kitty was going to drop to the floor. I grabbed her and we all burst into tears. Jack had been part of the duo of "Johnnie and Jack" on the Opry, and he was the brother-in-law of Kitty's husband, Johnnie Wright. Now five were gone.

After the funeral, Jimmy and I, Loretta, and Mooney all went to Patsy Cline's house. Johnny Cash and June Carter Cash were already there. June was in the kitchen, so I stored my purse and stuff and went to help her out. After we finished cleaning the kitchen, but before I could sit down, I noticed that Patsy's daughter, Julie, was having trouble getting the sash tied on her dress. I went into the bedroom, hugged her, and asked if I could help. I tied her sash and told her how beautiful she looked. It was all I could do to keep from crying.

8

LIVING WITH JIMMY MARTIN

When all the funerals were behind us, we tried to get back to a normal life. I spent the rest of the year booking Jimmy and others from the Opry. Timmy continued in school and started singing at hootenannies. He was having a good time, and people liked him.

Summer came and Timmy sang at Centennial Park at one of the open-air concerts with the Boys from Shiloh. He was photographed and they were featured in the Nashville *Tennessean*. Timmy loved music so much that Jimmy and I decided we would get him a snare drum for his eighth birthday. From the minute he took the drum out of its box, he knew how to play it. Jimmy started rehearsing with Timmy on the drums. It wasn't long before Timmy was one of the Sunny Mountain Boys. I made him a little red vest to wear, which I still have in my cedar chest. He didn't appear on all of the shows because of school, but he went out with the band whenever he could. That meant I was going more often as well.

At that time I was quite a good seamstress. Jimmy wanted all the boys to have vests to wear on stage. He said, "Can you make them where they are two-sided?" I said yes. Now I was not only the booking agent but the seamstress, too. I made black brocade vests for all the band members, including Timmy. The vests were reversible, so they could wear them either as the solid black side or the brocade side with gold running through it. I also made Jimmy a suit. He wore that suit forever. After making that one suit, I quit. I said to him, "That was the most difficult thing I have ever tried and I am not doing that again." And I didn't.

When Timmy was ten years old and not in school, he traveled with Jimmy. He was a regular Sunny Mountain Boy. The band loved to tease him; he was a kid in a grown-up world, and they thought it was funny. One time Jimmy and the band had played Kansas City. It was a packaged show with Tex Ritter. Everyone stayed at the same hotel. After the show Vernon Derrick, Bill Emerson, and Bill Yates held Timmy down, stripped his clothes off of him, tied him up naked, and put him in the elevator. They pressed all the buttons so that the elevator would stop at every floor. Tex Ritter was waiting for the elevator. When the door opened, Tex saw Timmy sitting on the floor. He looked at Timmy and said, "Like father, like son." He didn't get on the elevator. The guys eventually got Timmy off the elevator and untied him. Timmy never told me where Jimmy was that night, but he loves to tell the story of how they put him in the elevator.

My booking business was going well. Jimmy had show dates, and I was also booking shows for other people. Lois Johnson and Kirk Hansard had left Jimmy and were trying to get work on their own. I also booked shows for them individually and together.

Jimmy talked to Dolly Parton about coming to work for him. She was graduating from high school in May. I don't know if he was talking directly to Dolly or to her agent. He always said he was talking to Dolly. Of course, she wasn't a star at that time. In 1967 Porter Wagoner had his television show. Dolly auditioned and Porter hired her. The rest is history. That was the end of her coming to work for Jimmy.

Jimmy met Penny Jay in the latter part of 1963 or early 1964. I don't know where he met her. She lived in West Nashville and we never discussed where or how they met. Penny had written a song called "Widow Maker." Jimmy was madly in love with that song and so was I. Penny also played bass and sang. Jimmy recorded "Widow Maker" and the song made the charts. We had a hit! I started working on it immediately to make it an even bigger hit. Penny started going on the road with Jimmy and continued to work for him for a year or so. I really liked Penny. She was a nice lady and easy to talk to.

Jimmy was on the road a lot. We didn't live close to a grocery store or a post office, which I had to go to almost daily. Jimmy's brother Roy had a small Renault for sale. The car was cheap and in good shape. Jimmy, Timmy, and I headed to Anderson, Indiana, to look at the Renault. Once there, I fell in love with the car. We spent the weekend with Roy and his wife, Norma, and I drove the car home. I was overjoyed—I now had a car!

Once I had the car, Timmy and I visited Mother or Aunt Jessie regularly. Aunt Jessie owned a restaurant/beer joint type of place on Dickerson Road, and Mother owned a café on Porter Road. Whenever Timmy and I went to see Mother or Aunt Jessie, they would make Timmy a hamburger and me a bacon, lettuce, and tomato sandwich. Our basic diet was made up of hot dogs (we could get a lot of hot dogs for one dollar), eggs, beans, rabbit, squirrel, and fish. Never beef! Rarely pork! But I really didn't care. I didn't like meat, and I didn't know how to cook beef. I also never ate rabbit or squirrel. It was a sore point with Jimmy that I wouldn't eat either one. Even if I cooked a piece of meat, I never picked it up with my hands—only with tongs.

When we visited Mother, Timmy and Mike played cowboys and Indians together. Mike always told Timmy, "I am going to take care of you when you get big." It was very difficult seeing Timmy and Mike play together, because I wanted Mike living with us—always a sore spot with Jimmy and me. I knew Jimmy didn't want me to go visit my mother or Aunt Jessie, but I went, regardless. Sometimes he raised hell; other times he didn't. He probably figured it wasn't going to change a thing.

Paul Williams returned to work for Jimmy. He and Edria bought a small house in Donelson, about five miles from Hermitage Hills. They came over to our house almost every day. When they were on the road, Edria stayed with me if she didn't go home to Sneedville. I always loved Edria, and we had a lot of fun together.

In early November 1963 we found out that Jimmy and Edria's mother, Sarah, was in the hospital in serious condition. Jimmy and the Sunny Mountain Boys were heading to Vermont and New Hampshire for show dates. They planned to drop off Edria at the hospital where Sarah was a patient. Jimmy also wanted go up to her room and spend some time with her.

A few days later I received a phone call advising me that Sarah had passed away. I don't remember who called, but it was someone in the family. I *had* to get in touch with Jimmy. I knew where they were playing, so I called and told him that his mother had passed away. He was devastated. I told him I had canceled the remaining bookings, taken Timmy out of school, and would meet him in Sneedville. I stayed at Jimmy's sister Euna's house. I was always comfortable with Euna and her husband, Clyde.

I was already at the funeral home when Jimmy arrived. I met him as he entered the door, put my arms around him, and walked with him up to the casket. Starting with the first time he took me to Sneedville, Jimmy and I had talked about his hatred of Ellis, Sarah's husband. He had never gotten over Ellis making him and Roy work in the fields. Because Jimmy worked in the fields, he wasn't able to go to school, and when Ellis would let him go, he wasn't allowed to turn the lights on to do his homework. He also resented his mother for letting Ellis treat them like he did. Jimmy believed that Ellis's kids were the only ones that mattered to either Ellis or Sarah. Yet he still loved his mother unconditionally. He just wanted her to love him back. I knew she loved him, but I believe she had difficulty showing it. In turn, Jimmy treated his own children as harshly as Ellis had treated him and Roy. But he never mistreated the boys or our daughter, Lisa, when I was around. If he had attempted to mistreat them, I would have gone after him, tooth and nail. I think Jimmy took my leaving him out on the kids. After all, Timmy looked like me and that was something he had to look at every day. Sometimes I think Jimmy was harder on our kids than Ellis had been on him. Jimmy's scars were all mental, while Ray and Timmy carry both mental and physical scars from the abuse. Timmy says he has quit blaming his dad for the abuse he received. I don't believe he has fully come to terms with it, but I am hopeful that one day he will.

Personally, I liked Ellis. He had always been very kind to me. I never heard Ellis say a bad word about anyone. In fact, years later my husband, Chuck, and I visited him in Sneedville. Euna made dinner for us, and afterward we spent a very enjoyable hour or two with him.

Our son Ray was eight years old when Sarah died. For all of those years, Jimmy wouldn't let me take him away from Sarah. Now he was coming home. Timmy was thrilled that Ray was going to be living with us. And now Ray was going to meet Mike. Now if only we could get Mike.

Ray had grown up with country ways and the country way of talking. I was a city girl, and Timmy had grown up with me. I had always been a person who wanted to speak proper English. As Lisa used to tell me when I corrected her, "Mother, you should have been an English teacher." Ray had that country drawl and in a lot of ways reminded me of Sneedville. I wanted to get rid of those reminders. But, regardless, I loved having Ray with us. I felt like our family had finally come together.

Timmy was now nine years old and had never had to share anything in his life, including me. He loved going to my mother's house and playing with Mike, but Mike lived with Mother. Timmy also liked going to Sneedville and playing with Ray, but Ray stayed there. Now that Ray was going to be living with us, it was going to be different for Timmy—and for all of us. It didn't take long before Timmy and Ray had a jealousy thing going. Both vied for my attention.

Ray had a habit of not always telling the truth, so whenever he told me something, I took that into consideration. They argued and fought. One tried to outdo the other. Not pleasant! But they loved each other and would fight a circle saw blade for each other. That feeling between them has continued throughout their lives.

We enrolled Ray at Hermitage Hills Elementary. He got along well in school with his classmates, but he had to work hard to catch up with his class. Ray is probably the most loyal friend anyone could ever have. He is always the first person to help a person in need. He loves his family, is always dependable, and loves to tell you a joke. Ray is a person you can count on.

Whenever Jimmy went out of town, I would drive the boys to Aunt Jessie's café. Timmy had always been Aunt Jessie's favorite. She would make everyone a hamburger and give us Cokes. Aunt Jessie and I always talked while the boys played.

Once when Jimmy returned from out of town, Ray said, "Daddy, we went to Aunt Jessie's when you were gone and Mother drank Wiedemann's Fine Beer." Shit hit the fan! I told Jimmy, "I did not drink beer. Ray is lying." Well, Jimmy believed him. He immediately told me, "You are never to go there again and take these kids." I thought but didn't say, "You just sit there and watch me. I am going."

I decided right then and there that I was tired of Jimmy Martin telling me what I could or couldn't do. I was tired of being treated like a child. I also didn't like Ray's lie. I was never able to get the smell of beer past my nose. (I still don't like the smell or the taste.) I did stick my tongue in it one time and it gagged me. And I also don't like the smell on anyone else after they have had a beer.

Ray was in his glory. He had told Dad I did something wrong, and Dad was praising him for telling him. Ray had this adoration for Jimmy and still does. He was desperately searching for his daddy's approval. Jimmy never believed that I didn't drink that beer. But if he had thought about it, he would have known it was a lie, because I didn't like any kind of alcoholic drinks.

After Timmy and Ray had settled down and weren't fighting as much, Jimmy became more loving to me. We went fishing at Old Hickory Lake and did some swimming and picnicking. We were having fun as a family. Often, Jimmy knew someone who had a boat, and I got to go skiing. We were back loving Nashville.

In 1964 Roy, Norma, and their kids, Kay and Keith, came down to see us from Anderson, Indiana. Timmy and Kay were the same age, as were Ray and Keith. Norma and I were very close. We were almost the same age. Every time one of us became pregnant, it wasn't long before the other one was pregnant.

We always had such a good time whenever they came to see us or if we went to Indiana to see them. They loved the lake as much as we did, so we took all the kids on picnics and swimming. We also went to the Hermitage, the home of President Andrew Jackson. That was one my favorite things to do. I liked reading the love letters Jackson wrote to his wife, Rachel. Even today I go back to the Hermitage whenever I am in Nashville, and I always read the love letters. I guess I am just a romantic at heart.

Jimmy and I decided we were going to have another child. I still wanted that girl. It didn't take long until I was pregnant with Lisa. It was not an easy pregnancy. I was sick all the time and not just in the early mornings. Whenever I drank iced tea or Coke, I threw it up in strings. I had no idea why this happened and the doctors could never tell me. Years later I learned that one of my kidneys was enlarged and the other kidney was very small. When I was about ten, I had become very sick with typhus fever. I no sooner recovered when I came down with scarlet fever. The doctors believed those fevers had settled into my kidneys and stunted the growth in the left one. As a result, the right one took over and became enlarged.

Even pregnant, I was going on the road with Jimmy quite often. Jimmy suggested that we get Janet (not her real name, and you will see why later on) from Martins Ferry, Ohio, to take care of the boys in our house while we were gone. I thought that would be okay. I wasn't threatened by her. She was definitely not attractive or personable. Not being threatened by her was a huge mistake on my part. Jimmy didn't care what a woman looked like; he would take any woman to bed.

Janet was with us several months and everything seemed to be going okay. She was loyal to the kids. I didn't think she was loyal to me—I found that out the hard way—but I was pregnant with Lisa, and I needed the help.

Early in 1964 Jimmy and I became friends with country singer Billy Grammer and his wife, Ruth, a really great couple. Their hospitality was wonderful. They lived on Old Hickory Boulevard between Franklin and Nolensville Road. When we arrived, I thought it was the biggest house I had ever seen. It sat on top of a hill with a long driveway on a huge, treed lot. The house was a long, ranch-style brick house—definitely a house I wanted to have one day.

They invited us for a dinner of fish that Billy had caught. While Ruth fried the fish, Billy helped get the rest of the dinner ready. Finally, as we were eating, Jimmy said, "Billy, where did you get these fish? They don't have any bones in them." I was mortified. Billy said, "I filleted them." Jimmy said, "I never heard of that kind of fish." I then said, "Jimmy, that means he took the bones out of the fish with a knife." Jimmy said, "Oh," and kept eating.

That night we discussed going together and forming a talent agency. In addition to Billy and Jimmy, we would try to get other acts to go with us. We called it the Gra-Mar Talent Agency. Billy was going to be the procurer of talent and I would do the booking. After the Gra-Mar Talent Agency was formed and all the licenses obtained, we moved across the street from Decca Records and the Wil-Helm Talent Agency to 26 Sixteenth Avenue South. Cedarwood Publishing, Jim Denny Enterprises and Lucky Moeller, Hubert Long, and Capitol Records were a few doors down the street. Zeke Clements and Happy Wilson had an office across the hall from us, and Don Light and *Billboard* magazine had an office upstairs. We were all very friendly.

With this move, I would become the first and only female booking agent on Sixteenth Avenue South, or as it is known today, Music Row. I had also recently been appointed a Kentucky Colonel, an award for public service. This made me not only the first female booking agent on Music Row but also the first female Kentucky Colonel. Red O'Donnell wrote about it in his column for the *Tennessean*.

I know a lot of people would say that Louise Scruggs was a booking agent as well. That's true, and she was excellent at her job. But Louise was more of a manager and only booked Flatt & Scruggs. I had booked people other than Jimmy since I first started. Louise never had an office on Music Row. I don't know for sure, but I would bet that she was a Kentucky Colonel as well. Louise was one of the finest ladies I have ever met. The last time I saw her, she and I and her husband, Earl, were sitting together at Jimmy's wake. We exchanged phone numbers. Next thing I knew, my son Ray called me and said Louise had passed away. Ray attended her funeral.

Quite a few artists stopped by the office daily and chatted. One of those was Mel Tillis and his daughter Pam. I liked Mel. He was a super nice guy— and funny! Billy and I loved having Mel stop by. Pam was as cute as she could be and well mannered. I enjoyed her visits with her dad but never saw her again after those days at Gra-Mar—that is, until she became a well-known singer in the mid to late 1980s. I did see Mel periodically for many years to come.

In August 1964 I booked Jimmy for two days at the Key West Naval Air Station. We drove there, did the shows, and then went on to Tampa for a package show with Carl Smith and Minnie Pearl. There were other people in the show, but I forget who all was there.

The drive to Key West from Nashville was long. We were in our 1959 robin's egg blue and cream Cadillac towing a trailer. There was no interstate at that time. I rode shotgun in the middle seat to keep the driver awake. I had never been to Florida before and I was very excited. We were somewhere in Florida, and I had stayed awake as long as I could when I started dozing off. Bill Emerson was driving and my head fell over onto his shoulder. From the backseat, Jimmy slapped me hard on the back of my head and told me to sit up. I was stunned. When we got out of the car, he said, "What were you trying to do? Make out with Bill?" That's the way he was. I never told Bill what Jimmy had said until recently, when we were talking on the phone.

We rented two rooms at a little motel in Key West, one room for the boys in the band and one for Jimmy and me. The motel looked like something from out of the forties or from the movie *Key Largo*. In those days there was no such thing as booking ahead, especially if you didn't know where you were going to play. And we didn't know Key West.

The boys got their stuff out of the car and went to their room. When Jimmy and I entered ours, we stood in water that was ankle deep. After telling the office about the water, Jimmy came back and said, "They had a hurricane, but the bed is dry. Let's just spend the night, because it's too late to go looking for another place." I was scared to death a snake might be swimming around the room or hiding, so I barely slept that night. As soon as daylight came, we all checked out and went looking for another motel. We finally found one room at the Quality Inn. It was the only room available. Were we ever tired! The guys took the two beds, and I took a pillow with a blanket and slept in the bathtub until showtime. What a trip!

That night we played the officer's club at the naval air station. The place was packed, and Jimmy and the band were well received. The next night we played the enlisted men's club and it was standing room only. If we thought the band was well received the first night, it received double the applause the second night. Everyone loved Bill Emerson's banjo playing. They also loved Jimmy's antics and singing. This was our kind of crowd. We went back to our motel, and the next morning we drove to Tampa.

By the time we got to Tampa, we were all exhausted. I couldn't have cared less if I never saw Florida again. The only bright spot was seeing Minnie Pearl. The first thing she said was "I can't believe you are pregnant again." I explained to her that this one was planned. I loved Minnie. It always made my day to see her. Carl Smith also made the same remark to me when I saw him. I teased him: "Are you keeping up with my pregnancies?" He laughed and said, "No, it just seems like you are always pregnant." The show in Tampa was fantastic. Jimmy and the band encored and he was happy again. After the show we drove back to Nashville.

It had been a very tough trip for me, being pregnant with Lisa and getting bigger every day. Several of us in the music industry were pregnant at the same time, including Loretta Lynn and Brenda Lee. Brenda was often at Decca across the street from my office. Whenever I saw her, she always waved at me. Brenda was tiny and I was tall. We sort of looked like Mutt and Jeff, but we both waddled the same way.

I was busy working at Gra-Mar when Ruth Grammer called me to say that Jim Reeves's plane was missing. Jim had been at the controls of his single-engine plane flying with his business partner, Dean Manuel. Ruth was getting ready to go to Jim's house and wanted me to go with her. I told her I would meet her there. Immediately I called our sitter, Janet, to let her know I would be at Mary Reeves's house. I gave her the telephone number and told her she could call me if there was an emergency. Jimmy and Billy Grammer were out of town.

When we arrived, Joyce Gray met us at the door. Joyce was Jim Reeves's longtime secretary. There were a lot of people around, and I believe they had finally gotten Mary to lie down. Jim's plane had not yet been found. We all sat around and waited.

Even though I was five months pregnant with Lisa, I wanted to be there for Mary and Joyce. Jim and Mary's collie, Cheyenne, seemed to be having a difficult time too. First of all, there were a lot of people there that the dog didn't know, and, secondly, everyone seemed to be making themselves at home.

When Jim's plane was finally found and his and Dean's bodies taken to the funeral home, someone had to go identify them. Mary asked Joyce to go. I told Joyce I would go with her and Ray Baker, one of Jim's band members. The three of us got into the police car and were driven to the funeral home. But after we arrived, Ray didn't want to go in to identify the bodies. I knew Joyce couldn't go in alone, so I went in with her. I will never forget the scene. Even though they were in body bags, the stench in the room was horrible. They had been out in the Tennessee sun for two days, and this was at the end of July, the hottest part of the summer. There wasn't much left to their bodies, but Joyce was able to identify Jim and Dean by their clothing. I was very glad Mary didn't have to see them.

Back at the Reeves's house, I saw Charlie Dick, Patsy Cline's husband. Charlie had his car door open and was sitting on the running board, crying. I walked over and put my arm around him to let him cry on my shoulder. I was crying too. We were both remembering Patsy. I felt so sorry for Charlie. He was so distraught, I was afraid he was going to have a heart attack.

Things were hectic. Now they were trying to plan a funeral. Ruth and I went over to Mary Reeves's house every day. Sometimes we brought things to eat or we made sandwiches for everyone when we got there. Even though I was pregnant, I did what I could to help. His funeral was held at Phillips Robinson Funeral Home, the same place as funerals for Patsy Cline, Cowboy Copas, Hawkshaw Hawkins, Randy Hughes, and Jack Anglin.

Roy and Jimmy standing in the yard in front of their house in Sneedville. Sister Evelyn is in the background. Even then he was singing as loud as he could. The picture was in *Time* magazine.

Jimmy in 1951.

Jimmy and Oscar circa 1955—as usual, horsing around.

High kick—Jimmy and banjoist Rudy Lyles seeing who could outkick the other.

Jimmy with his friends Tivis, Grant, et al. standing by the barn at Jimmy's homeplace. That barn is where I tried to milk a cow.

Me in 1953. Taken in the Arcade in Nashville on my way to the skating rink.

Jimmy and the Osborne Brothers in 1954. This photo was used as their official photo.

Mother, Mike, and Mama when Mike was six months old. The picture was taken in our front yard.

Billie in 1958 when she arrived in Detroit with Timmy.

My Farmer grandparents standing out back of their mattress factory on Fourth Avenue South in Nashville.

Jimmy at Casey Clark's, where he was "King of the Armory."

Timmy, Jimmy, and Hank Williams Jr. after a show in Cleveland, Ohio, in 1962. Jimmy let Timmy ride back to Nashville on Hank Jr.'s bus.

Jimmy showing a crowd how to play. He loved doing this.

Ray, Lisa, me, Jimmy, Buddy, and Timmy. The photo was made at our home in Hermitage in 1966 for an article published in the Sunday magazine section of the Nashville *Tennessean*.

Our family on the front steps of our house in Shreveport in 1959. You can look at my face and tell how happy I was.

Backstage at the Louisiana Hayride in 1959, dressed to the nines.

Front yard in Jacksonian Drive. It was a guy thing.

Me in Nashville in 1968. This was taken outside the courthouse in Nashville, where I worked.

Dan Morgan, Betty Sue Lynn, me, and Wayne. This is the night Betty Sue and Dan were married.

Jimmy and Marty Stuart. Marty was visiting at Jimmy's home as he often did. Whenever Jimmy was getting a picture made, he dressed the part.

Our family—Mother, Michelle, Lisa, Buddy, and me—in 1980. Taken shortly after Lisa and Buddy came to Florida to live with me. Mother came down to help remodel Lisa's and Buddy's rooms.

Ray, me, and Mike at our house on NW Forty-Sixth Avenue in Plantation. This was the first house we owned in Florida.

My five kids in 2000. Taken at the Café de Paris in Fort Lauderdale, where we were celebrating Chuck's retirement from American Express.

Michael James Martin and Bob Smith. The photo was taken in Englewood, Florida. Michael was always happy when he was with Aunt Birdie and Uncle Bob.

Me at work, preparing exhibits for a trial in 2011.

Ray modeling on a cruise ship. He was extraordinarily good looking. Girls chased him, but he could run fast. He also played a great game of tennis.

Friends and family visiting Jimmy in hospice in his final days.

Timmy kisses his father good-bye.

Little Jimmy Dickens with
Jimmy at the end of his life.

9

∫HOWER∫ AND ∫URPRI∫E∫

Pregnancy was rampant in Nashville in 1964. Loretta Lynn, Brenda Lee, and I were all pregnant at the same time. Loretta was pregnant with twins, whom she named Patsy and Peggy. It seemed like all I did was go to showers.

Dottie West gave Loretta a shower first. Her shower was held at Dottie's house off McGavock Pike in Donelson. It was a pretty, well-decorated house in a nice subdivision with neighbors all around. About twenty women were there, all from the entertainment field—Leona Atkins, Jean Shepard, Ruth Grammer, and for the life of me I can't remember the others. But most of the same women attended the shower given for me just a month later.

Mine was given by Leona Atkins. I have the register signed by all the guests. Recently when I was talking to my daughter, Lisa, I asked her about the baby book. She said, "I have it," and she sent it to me. It's now in my cedar chest, safe and sound.

Reading that baby book brought back many memories. I had forgotten who all was at the shower, but here they are: Mrs. Chet (Leona) Atkins; Mrs. Tompall Glaser; Mrs. Jim (Mary) Reeves; Dottie West; Mrs. Chuck Glaser; Mrs. Billy (Ruth) Grammer; Ruth and Paul Charon; Dixie Deen (later Mrs. Tom T. Hall); my sister Betty Gibson; Mrs. Mike Miller; Mrs. Bobby Smith; Mrs. Velma Montgomery; Pat from Decca Records; Mrs. Ernest Ashworth; Sara Hardesty; Mrs. Onie Wheeler; Faye Joiner; Jeanne Pruitt; Reba Dunn;

Loretta Lynn; Shirley Webb; Mary Ann Garrison; and Ann Paulson. Leona gave me the baby book. Mary Reeves gave me a beautiful bunting that unzipped and made a full-size comforter. It's strange, but those are the only two gifts I wrote down in the book. Why didn't I write them all down? I don't really know.

Sometime during the latter part of August 1964, Jimmy was surprised to learn that the Osborne Brothers had been inducted into the Grand Ole Opry. They were not only on Decca Records, having been signed about a year before, but they were now members of the Opry too. The news was devastating to Jimmy. As the years went by, it would be not only the Osborne Brothers that joined the Opry but other bluegrass bands as well, including Del McCoury, the McReynolds Brothers (Jim and Jesse), Buck White (the Whites), and Ricky Skaggs, followed by Alison Krauss and Ralph Stanley. And as each group joined, his being overlooked for the Opry became more and more difficult for Jimmy to digest.

Of course, he blamed me for not promoting him. I tried to talk to him many times about the reasons why, but he wouldn't listen to me. I tried to tell him that his drinking was a problem. His response was "I don't ever have liquor in my house." I would tell him that was true but that he drank every night—everyone knew it. He also didn't try to hide the fact that he ran around with other women. After the Osborne Brothers' induction in the Opry, Jimmy's drinking and staying out became worse. He was blaming everyone but himself. It was like not being able to see the forest for the trees. My trying to talk to him only made things worse, so I shut up.

Jimmy was the type of person who couldn't bear having anyone telling him anything. I think he believed people thought he was dumb because of his lack of education. There was nothing further from the truth. Jimmy was a smart man in many ways. He had good common sense. He could figure things out, but sometimes his view of things became distorted. He was excellent with money matters, even though he didn't understand what he was doing. He trusted people in power or finance to advise him. He believed in them.

On Saturday, November 21, 1964, I went to the Gra-Mar office. Jimmy was out of town. He had gone to Kentucky to go hunting. I wanted to get his new record, "Widow Maker," packed and shipped out to the disc jockeys. I could drop them off at the post office on my way home. I worked all day, nonstop, getting everything done. When I was finished, I stood and looked at the big, heavy bags and knew I couldn't put them in the car by myself. Don Light saw me trying to pull on the bags. He got Happy Wilson, who had an office across the hall, to come help. Don and Happy put the bags in the car, and I was forever grateful.

After I got to the post office, I knew I was a pitiful sight—big as a barrel and trying to get mailbags loaded with records out of a Renault. Not a pretty picture, but hysterically funny. The kind gentlemen who worked at the post office came to my rescue and unloaded my vehicle. I was so thankful, I wanted to hug every one of them.

When I arrived back at home, Timmy and Ray were starving. I had called Janet and asked her to take some chicken out of the freezer. Even though she took care of the boys and the house, she didn't do the cooking or washing clothes. I have always been anal about how both of those jobs should be done. Anyhow, I got the chicken washed and breaded and had started frying it when my water broke. I told Janet to pack a bag for me and said, "Let's get to the hospital." I took the chicken off the stove and left it sitting in the grease.

We lived in Hermitage, about fifteen miles from the hospital. The boys and Janet and I got in the car. I was not in pain, so I drove to Baptist Hospital in Nashville and checked myself in. I had asked Janet to call Jimmy and let him know I was going into labor. I also asked her to call Shirley Webb, Jack Webb's wife and Loretta Lynn's sister-in-law. That was the last thing I remember.

Lisa was born at 11:02 a.m. on Sunday, November 22, 1964, one year to the day after John F. Kennedy was killed. She weighed six pounds, fifteen ounces. She was twenty inches long and had black curly hair.

I had been in labor about eighteen hours, and Lisa had been born breach. I had had a difficult birth, but I never knew it. The doctor had given me "happy gas." It knocked me out and was the best thing ever. I had it with all my children. If I had to go through what women go through today in delivering a child, I could never make another one. It would have happened only once.

When I awoke, Jimmy was standing by my bed with the biggest bunch of zinnias I had ever seen in my life. It would be the first and only time he brought me flowers. He said, "We have a beautiful baby girl." We were both so proud. He gave me a big kiss. That was the sweetest kiss I had had from him in many years. I would never have another one.

I also learned that Shirley Webb had been at the hospital with me the entire time. I loved Shirley and we were great friends. I wish I knew where she lives now. Maybe she will read this book and get in touch with me. I hope so.

You would have thought that Lisa Sarah Martin was the queen who had arrived. Her birth was announced on WSM-TV in Nashville by Ralph Emery and Bobby Lord. The country disc jockeys all across the United States included the announcement of her birth on their daily shows. Red O'Donnell included her birth in his column in *The Tennessean*, and it was also written up in newspapers all across the country. Jimmy and I received a telegram from Sydney Goldberg, vice president of Decca Records, congratulating us on the birth of our little girl. That was thrilling. We also received fruit baskets from Owen Bradley, Harry Silverstein, Pat and Ruby from Decca Records, and Paul Cohen from Kapp Records. Flowers came from Marty Salkin, Leonard Salidor, and Sydney Goldberg, all vice presidents of Decca Records; Jimmy Key and Jimmy C. Newman and New Keys Publishing Company; Neil Bogart of *Cashbox* magazine in New York City; Sara Hardesty and Don Light of Billboard Publishing Company in Nashville; Faron Young and Preston Temple in Nashville; the Hermitage Hills Baptist Church; and the pharmacy in Hermitage Hills. Yes, the queen had truly arrived. She was just the most beautiful baby in the world. Her parents and her brothers adored her, and they still do.

Ray and Timmy were wild about their little sister and were determined to see her walk. They would stand her up and walk her back and forth between them for an hour at a time. As a result, she walked at eight months old and was climbing by the time she was a year old. My sister Betty used to call her "Baby B-Bomb" after the little girl in the Dick Tracy comic strip. Lisa jumped up and down constantly. You just couldn't keep her penned up. She was a mess and we didn't care.

On October 29, 1965, at eleven months, Lisa became a real queen when she walked onto the stage at the War Memorial Auditorium in Nashville and accepted her crown and trophy as the "Queen of Nashville" at a children's beauty pageant hosted by the local VFW. She wore a pink evening dress with a sweetheart rosebud corsage. I made the evening dress because I couldn't find one that was a size nine months. It had a bodice of pink satin brocade, with a pink satin underskirt and net fabric over it. She was absolutely beautiful. The audience just oohed and ahhed at her.

Yes, she was now officially a queen, not only in our household but in the city of Nashville as well. Again, she made all the radio stations, television stations, and newspapers. You know the old saying "Once a queen, always a queen"? That, my friends, is my daughter, Lisa. She is so loved by her family.

After taking off a couple of weeks to recuperate from having the baby, I returned to work. It wasn't strenuous and I was my own boss. So if I got tired, I could go home. I tried to put in a full, eight-hour day. It was wintertime and we needed to get shows booked for the spring. I was lucky enough to book several shows in California—one in Salinas, one in Santa Cruz, and one in San Francisco. We decided to do our own packages, with Billy Grammer, Jimmy and his band, and another star from the Grand Ole Opry. I would set the shows up in the middle of the country as stopovers on the trip back from California. At this time the phone rooms were going strong. They were called phone rooms because you would set up a room with several phones in it. Then your sponsor for the show, such as a VFW, American Legion, or a fire department, would send volunteers from that organization to come in where the phones were set up, call businesses in and around the area, and sell advertisements in the show's program book. Along with publishing their ad, you gave them tickets to the show. The number of tickets given to the sponsor depended on the size of the ad. Usually you could also sell the business more tickets and have them put up signs in their business about the show. In return, the sponsor would receive a portion of the net earnings.

We wanted to promote two shows of our own, starting in Keokuk, Iowa, and the second show in Quincy, Illinois. After making several phone calls, we obtained sponsors for each of the shows. Billy and I hired Cedric Rainwater, who was experienced in that type of promotion, to go to Keokuk. Cedric was well known in the music business as a comedian. He didn't have any work, so we decided to give him the opportunity. I sent my sister Betty to help out, because I knew that she would watch out for our interests.

About six weeks into the promotions and lots of tickets being sold, Betty called and told me that Cedric was using money out of the show funds. She and Cedric had rooms that shared a bathroom—what we would call today a Jack and Jill bath—and she had to keep her door locked because he had tried several times to come into her room. She knew he was skimming, and she told me I needed to fly up for an accounting. I told her not to tell him I was coming. I caught a plane that evening and Betty met me at the airport. It was late, but I was able to get into her room without him finding out.

The next morning, when Cedric knocked on Betty's door, I answered. To say he was shocked would be an understatement. I immediately told him that I wanted to get all the records and the money for both the Keokuk and Quincy shows. After we had breakfast, I started going through the records. There was a lot of money missing. I asked him where the money was, and Cedric couldn't—or wouldn't—tell me. I fired him and bought him a one-way bus ticket to Nashville. I let Jimmy and Billy know what was happening. We hired a girl to come help Betty, and I flew home. She finished promoting the shows and did an excellent job of it.

Upon returning from one trip to Keokuk and Quincy, I arrived home and discovered that some money I had been hoarding for months was missing. Since I had about thirty shoe boxes full of shoes, I had stashed the quarters, nickels, dimes, and dollar bills in the box that had held a pair of brown and aqua shoes in my closet. I did this so that I would know which box held the money I had hidden.

I asked Janet about my money from the shoebox, and she said, "I found it and gave it to Jimmy." I was furious. That was money I had been saving for necessities, and to get away if I needed to. I knew she had to have looked through everything to find the money, or she had seen me adding to my stash. I knew then that Janet was no friend of mine. From that time on, I used the Kotex box in my bathroom to stash my money.

It was now spring and I was putting in a lot of time at the office. A couple of times Jimmy called me to say he and our boys were going fishing when they were out of school. But this particular day, the boys were in school when he called and told me that he and Janet were going fishing. I thought it was strange that he was taking Lisa and Janet fishing. Being my own boss, I decided to close up shop and go home. I wanted to see what was going on. Besides, Vernon Derrick would be in town a little later and the band would be leaving to go on the road.

When I got home Jimmy's car was in the driveway, but there was no sign of anyone around. I eased into the house and heard noises coming from our bedroom. I walked down the hall, opened the door, and was shocked to see Jimmy and Janet having sex in our bed. I was mad as hell. He jumped up, grabbed his clothes, and started threatening me. I thought, "You son of a bitch! You are fucking this creature in my bed while my daughter is in her playpen in the den, and you're threatening me?" I was ready to kill both of them.

I took Janet by the arm and herded her out of the house buck naked. Jimmy was going to take her to the bus station. He got his keys and started for the car. He had already given her some clothes in the yard to cover up. I went and got his 16 gauge shotgun from the closet, loaded it, and walked calmly to the door. I told him, "You put that whore in the car. I have six bullets in this gun. I'm going to put one in each tire and one in each of you. So go ahead and do it." He put the car back in the driveway and told her to get out. By now Vernon had arrived. He offered to take Janet to the bus station. I told him, "No, let the bitch walk."

Janet walked next door and called my friend Jeanne Pruett. She asked Jeanne to take her to the Greyhound bus station. Jeanne called me and wanted to know if it was okay with me to take her to the bus station. I told her what had happened and that I would appreciate it if she did. Jeanne came over and got her, and I never saw or heard from Janet again. I was and am so thankful for a friend like Jeanne. She is a wonderful person as well as a terrific singer and songwriter.

After Janet left there was a succession of Jimmy's girls coming to take care of the kids and the house. No one lasted very long. There were so many, I can't remember their names. I do remember one tall girl from Arkansas, but not her name. Even Timmy and Ray don't remember their names.

Vernon Derrick was probably the best showman Jimmy ever had. He was a joy to watch and to just be around. He was not only a good musician but a really good person as well. We hit it off right away; he was easy to talk to and a lot of fun. I always thought of Vernon being sort of childlike. Jimmy later accused me of flirting and being in love with Vernon. That could not have been further from the truth. Vernon and I were friends, and we remained friends long after we left Jimmy.

Vernon was always early when he came to the house to leave on a show. This one particular day he wanted to know what I was cooking for supper. I told him, "I don't know." He said, "I will go get a beef roast if you will cook it." I told him, "Okay," but I thought, "I have never cooked a beef roast!" While Vernon went to the store, I called Mother and asked her how to cook it and she told me how. Jimmy, Vernon, and the kids loved it. I also made gravy and mashed potatoes. Everything was delicious. Their bellies were full and they were all thrilled. After that, Jimmy started buying beef every once in a while.

Vernon and I remained friends even after I finally left Jimmy for good and remarried. Whenever he was going to be in Florida with Hank Williams Jr., Vernon would call and tell me where they were going to be playing in Tampa, St. Petersburg, Orlando, or anywhere close. He would get backstage passes for my husband, Chuck, and me, and sometimes we invited my friend Jo Walters to go with us. Vernon and Jo had a little crush on each other. If Vernon was in the immediate Fort Lauderdale area, we always called Jo to come over to our house too. It was hard not to like Vernon; he was a good old boy. We saw Vernon on the shows, and every once in a while he would call me or I would call him. Chuck liked Vernon very much and considered him a friend.

The California tour was a disaster. The shows were good, but Jimmy's behavior was getting worse. He was drinking a lot more and now he had started being nasty to people for no reason. He wound up insulting Billy Grammer.

We were all staying at a motel in Oakland, and the promoter was a friend of Billy's. The night before the show in San Francisco, the promoter took all of us out to a Hawaiian-themed restaurant. I had never been to or seen anything like it before. I had my very first piña colada there. We were having a good time listening to the music and talking, but as we were leaving, Jimmy made an insulting remark to Billy. The promoter was standing behind him, and when he heard the remark, he sucker-punched Jimmy in his kidney. I screamed. Jimmy went to the floor. It was several minutes before I could get him up and out of there. I took him to the hospital, where they examined and x-rayed him. The doctor told Jimmy that he had a bruised kidney and couldn't play the show the next night. He had to get lots of rest, or he could possibly lose his kidney. What were we going to do now? The contract called for five people or we wouldn't get paid.

I kept thinking that by the next day Jimmy would be okay. He wasn't. When it came time for the show, I told him, "The contract says five people." He asked, "What are we going to do?" I said, "I will be the fifth person." I walked on stage, did a little moderating, and then stood on stage during the rest of Jimmy's show. After that, Vernon Derrick took over. I have always said, "Thank God for Vernon Derrick."

Billy left the motel right after the show. I didn't see him again until Keokuk, Iowa. I never saw or spoke to Billy again after the Quincy show. The worst part of that night was that because of Jimmy's remark, I lost Billy and Ruth as friends. I had loved them dearly.

I took my typewriter and again went home to do bookings. Regardless of how badly Jimmy and I were getting along personally, I still continued to book him along with several other people. I knew that if I didn't, we wouldn't be able to live. I booked other acts from the Opry, because I liked to book shows. The typewriter was on the desk and I was back in business.

When we returned home from the California trip, Jimmy seemed to be in better spirits. We both knew that Gra-Mar Talent Agency no longer existed, and Jimmy seemed fine with that. Janet was now gone and I was staying at home. I liked that. Whenever Jimmy left to go on the road, Timmy and Ray and I had a great time. We would wax the floors, then put our socks on and run and slide across them, making them shiny. It was a terrific way to get the floors waxed and polished while having fun.

The boys and I played Monopoly. Timmy especially wanted to win. We also played ball in the backyard with other kids from the neighborhood. And often we went to visit Mother and Mike and Aunt Jessie. We just had so much fun.

Jimmy, Timmy, Ray, and I had always liked to go fishing. We started going more and more often to Old Hickory Lake with a picnic lunch. Timmy and Ray swam. I took Lisa in the water and let her play around while Jimmy fished. We had good times.

One day we were at the lake and it had been a great day. We had to walk across high weeds coming and going to where we planned on fishing. After a full day of fishing and picnicking, I was practically running across knee-high weeds to the car. I was carrying a glass water jug when Jimmy yelled at me and said, "Wait up, I have something for you." I turned around and saw he was holding a six-foot-long snake. I was scared to death that he was going to put the thing on me. I was running as fast as I could across the creek when my foot slipped on the moss-covered rocks. As I went down, the glass jug broke and my wrist and hand went into its edge. I didn't know I had been cut. Jimmy saw what had happened and yelled at me to wait. I was *not* waiting. I was running. He then called out to a man who was nearby to stop me. He put the snake down, which turned out to be dead. Dead or alive, I am deathly afraid of snakes. When Jimmy caught up with me, he took a thick Sunday *Tennessean* newspaper and put it under my arm. At the hospital the doctor put forty stitches inside and outside the wrist of my left hand. It was a prank to Jimmy, but it was the terror and ruination of a beautiful Sunday afternoon for me. And I still have the scars to prove it. Ray and Timmy remember it vividly.

Jimmy had his hunting dogs, Bessie and Becky, and in the hunting season he was off with them to hunt. Timmy never liked hunting; he didn't want to kill anything. Ray loved hunting and still does. Jimmy was so happy whenever he was hunting. He brought home rabbits and squirrels, cleaned and dressed, and I would put them in the freezer.

Almost everyone in Hermitage Hills had anywhere from a half acre to an acre of yard. A lot of the parents were in the music business, and their kids went to the elementary school. They played in each other's yards all the time. If you needed your child home, you just went to the front door and yelled their name. We didn't call each other's houses and ask about our kids; we just yelled.

The kids rode their bicycles to the store and back. They didn't have to get out onto busy Lebanon Road. Timmy would ride his bicycle to Jeanne Pruett's house to play. Whenever he and Ray were out, I wasn't concerned. Every kid in the neighborhood was out doing the same things. Looking back, it was a wonderful time for the kids to grow up. Everyone knew each other. My sons and Lisa still keep in touch with their friends from school and the neighborhood.

On any given day, several of the neighborhood kids would come over and play ball in our backyard. I was a pretty good ballplayer. One time we were playing and I hit a fly ball. Timmy was running after it yelling, "I've got it, Mother!" and ran smack-dab into the tree. Even though seeing him run to catch the ball was funny, it was not amusing to see that big lump right in the center of his forehead. I was scared to death that he was seriously injured. We took him to the hospital, where he was x-rayed and treated. Fortunately, he had not sustained a permanent injury. Good-naturedly we called him "Knot Head."

One night the boys and I had been waxing the floors in the living room and hall. We were laughing and having a great time. Jimmy was on the road. And because we didn't have air conditioning in the house, the doors and windows were all wide open. Lisa was in her crib. It was a perfect time to stop to have a cigarette break (back when I smoked).

I sat down on the couch in the den. Just after I lit up, I sensed what felt like a breath on the back of my neck. I knew someone was outside the window. I got up, went into the living room, where the boys were still playing, and told them to close and lock all the windows and doors and not to make a fuss about it. I got up and went to the bedroom, closed and locked the windows, loaded the shotgun, and walked out into the hall. By this time Timmy and Ray had locked all of the other windows and doors except for the front door. I told them to leave that door unlocked in case we had to run out. I told them to go and get Lisa and then reached around and turned the light off in the den. Now the whole house was dark. I figured I could see out but whoever was outside couldn't see in. I pointed the shotgun at the window and said, "I know you are out there. If you want to come in this house, come in the front door. When you do, I am going to blow you to pieces." I then racked up a bullet into the chamber. The sound was very clear what it was. We heard whoever it was take off down through the backyard. The dogs were barking and we heard my clothesline go down. We called the police, who came with their sirens screaming. (I have always wondered why the police do that. I guess they are just letting the burglars or whoever know they are coming.)

The police checked out the house and the backyard. Whoever was outside had been standing on an old wooden crate in order to see into the house and then had run through the clothesline now lying on the ground. The police told me that I should take the kids and go somewhere else to spend the night. I took them to my sister's house in Lakewood. Before we left, I unloaded the shotgun and took it with me.

The next morning, we went back home. I called Jimmy and told him what had happened. He was worried to death about us. So when he got back home, we bought an air conditioner—no more open windows and doors.

A few months later we had another incident occur. My next-door neighbors, Helen Gannon and her husband, Howard, were gone for the weekend. When they returned, they realized that someone had been in their house and rummaged through their drawers. They didn't find anything missing, but then Howard went out to the mailbox to get their Saturday mail. Inside the box he found a pair of Helen's panties. Now we were all really terrified.

Our anxieties were short-lived, because it wasn't too long before the culprit was found. His escapades had escalated and he had been caught. Turned out, he lived across the street. We were all shocked. His name was also Jimmy. He was a nice guy, or so we all thought. In fact, before he started all of this, whenever our own Jimmy would leave, the boys and I and Lisa had enjoyed going outside. I liked sitting on the steps and watching the kids play. Jimmy the neighbor would come over and talk. There was nothing to ever indicate he was a Peeping Tom. He was just a nice guy from the neighborhood. We were all glad when he was caught.

We had lots of good times in Hermitage Hills but also a lot of bad times. Now I was pregnant with Buddy. I didn't want another child, but Jimmy kept on and on about Lisa needing someone to play with. I had been taking every precaution to keep from getting pregnant. We were using protection. I couldn't understand how suddenly I wound up pregnant. To this day I believe Jimmy sabotaged the condoms because he wanted another baby.

After I knew I was pregnant, our home life started going downhill rapidly. Jimmy went from this person who wanted sex every night to taking his elbow and punching me in the ribs or breast if I tried to put my arms around him. He never talked to me. He watched me like a hawk. I didn't understand where all this hostility was coming from. He wanted this baby, but he didn't want me. I was miserable.

One day when we were at Rita and Buddy Lee's house, Rita asked me what was wrong. I wasn't acting like myself. I told her I was miserable and why. I told her how Jimmy was treating me. Rita asked me why I put up with it. She said, "You have a car; just leave." I asked her if Buddy would give me a job if I left Jimmy.

Toward the end of summer I called Rita. Jimmy was out of town and would be gone for three weeks. I told Rita I wanted to leave, and then she had Buddy call me. After talking to him, he said, "Come on over and start work." I immediately went to work for Buddy Lee Attractions as his assistant. We were working out of his basement, but I didn't care. I was earning money, and that money was going to take care of me and my kids.

By the time Jimmy returned, I had rented an apartment and a U-Haul truck and had moved the furniture out of the house. I left him a knife, fork, spoon, and the sofa in the den. I had enrolled the boys in a new school. I was pregnant and Lisa was just a baby; I could take her to work with me. Buddy didn't mind her being there and Rita loved it. Life was good again. I had my kids, I wasn't getting punched in the ribs every night, and I didn't have to be afraid.

I was also earning a salary. I had money and an apartment and my car. But the problem was I wasn't far enough away from Jimmy. Sometimes Timmy and Ray skipped school and walked about five miles home to Hermitage Hills. Jimmy brought them back to my apartment each time they did this. Soon Jimmy was begging me to come back.

I quit my job with Buddy Lee and moved back into our house, but life was never the same. It seemed the abuse just got worse. Jimmy questioned my every move. I could do nothing right. If I was miserable before I left him, there were no words to describe how I felt then. I was pregnant, very unhappy, and stuck.

On Christmas Eve 1965, I made supper for myself and the kids. Jimmy was nowhere to be found. I kept thinking he would come home. After the kids went to bed, I sat down at my desk to look at the schedule to see what I could book after the holidays. I turned on the radio to our country music station (which I believe was WENO), and I heard the DJ talking to Jimmy. He asked, "What do you want for Christmas, Jimmy?" Jimmy replied (and this is burned in my brain), "I have my Christmas present in the car." I didn't know whether he was talking about another woman or a bottle of whiskey. He came home that night just before midnight.

Jimmy had always gone out every day around 5:00 p.m. He would return about 9:00 p.m., either heavily drinking or drunk. When he came in the door, we never knew what to expect. I always cooked supper for the kids and me. I left his food either on the table or on the stove. Sometimes he ate, and other times he left it sitting there.

His elbow in my ribs and breasts seemed to be coming more frequently. I decided that I would not try to initiate any lovemaking with him. Well, that didn't work either. He started accusing me of screwing everyone in the band and in the neighborhood. I was damned if I said anything. And when I didn't say anything or tried to defend myself, he would slap me. I hated what this man had become.

It seemed like sitting on the commode was the only privacy I had. Even then if I was gone too long, he would come looking for me. If *he* went on the commode, he even wanted me to sit there with him. I hated that, too.

One night I was just sitting on the commode fully dressed and crying. I couldn't stand it anymore, but what was I going to do? I was due to have the baby in March. I kept trying to figure out what was causing all this anger in Jimmy. I had really done nothing to him. Then I started thinking about the Osborne Brothers getting on the Grand Ole Opry. I thought back to the time they had been inducted in 1964. It hadn't been long after that when Jimmy had started becoming more aggressive. He was drinking more and staying out later. I believe now that he was taking his anger out on me because they had been asked to join the Opry and not him. I never told him my theory, but as time went on I was sure that was what started all his anger. This wasn't the fault of the Osbornes. They did nothing wrong and everything right. Jimmy just didn't understand why he was being passed over. It had nothing to do with his music and everything to do with his personal habits. Had I been the person I am now, I probably could have handled it better, but who knows. I don't think his not being invited to join the Opry was the only reason for his hostility.

Our son Buddy was born at Baptist Hospital on March 26, 1966. We left Lisa with a sitter, and Jimmy drove me to the hospital with Timmy and Ray. But unlike with Lisa's birth, there was little fanfare. Buddy was an absolutely beautiful baby. Jimmy wanted to name him after his grandfather. He had first wanted Buddy Lee Ease Martin, but I was against that. We settled on Lee Ease, and we called him Buddy.

I had talked to my doctor during the time I was pregnant about tying my tubes. The doctor said I had to have my husband's permission. I talked and talked to Jimmy, but he said no. I went back and told my doctor that Jimmy wouldn't agree to my tubes being tied. I wanted to know what else I could do. I knew I couldn't take pills, because they had to be refilled. I had no money and no insurance. Dr. Huddleston told me he could insert an IUD and no one would ever know the difference. I told him, "If it keeps me from getting pregnant, do it." Little did I know that the IUD would cause me to suffer extreme pain for the next couple of years. Jimmy never knew about the IUD. If he had, he would have beaten the hell out of me and accused me of trying to be with every Tom, Dick, and Harry in Nashville and beyond. Even though I had the IUD, I don't remember ever having sex with Jimmy after Buddy was born.

Jimmy picked Buddy and me up from the hospital and took us home. On the way, things were good. Jimmy was happy we were coming home. Then as we pulled into the driveway, I saw that my car was gone. I asked, "Where is my car?" He said, "I sold it." I said, "You wouldn't dare." He said, "I did." I went into the house and asked the girl who was taking care of Lisa (I forget her name), "Where is my car?" She said, "Jimmy sold it." At that point I calmly turned around, looked at Jimmy, and said, "You just opened the door of someone else's car and told me, 'Get in the car, Barbara'?" I turned around and went to the bedroom. I spoke very little to him over the next six months.

Whenever Jimmy was on the road, I still had to get to the post office. At the time I was also booking people from the Opry. So whenever anyone came by the house to pick up their contract or to pay my percentage for booking a show, I asked them to take me to the post office. If we needed something from the store, Timmy and Ray rode their bicycles to get it. Jimmy would leave home for a week and leave me five dollars to get milk, bread, and cigarettes. Before he returned, we sold Coca-Cola bottles in order to have enough money to live on. This went on for years before and after Buddy was born, and the situation rapidly grew worse.

By this time I despised Jimmy Martin. I felt like I had been a slave to him all those years. I knew he didn't know how to show love. But on the other hand, he could be so great one day, and the very next day he could be hell on two legs.

Over the next six months, I tolerated Jimmy. I went about the business of booking him, but I spoke to him as little as possible. I made no advances toward him, and when he tried to make love to me, I turned away. I was through with Jimmy. I just had to figure out a way to take my kids and get as far away as possible. I had no money, no car, and no one to help me. But I wasn't depressed, because I had a goal in mind: getting away and leaving the prison I had been in for almost fourteen years.

10
GOODBYE

The night before I left Jimmy Martin for good, I cooked supper. After the two older boys and I ate, I fed Buddy and Lisa and left the rest on the table for Jimmy. The boys and I were in the den watching TV when Jimmy came in the back door. The first thing he did was shove the table across the kitchen floor. He wanted to fight.

He came into the den and told the boys to go to bed. He went over, cut the TV off, unplugged it, and turned it upside down. I kept asking him, "Why are you doing this, Jimmy?" He kept calling me a whore. I went to the bedroom to get away from him, hoping he would cool off. He followed me and shoved me down on the bed. Then he jumped on top me, started choking me, and yelled over and over, "Tell me you love me!" Well, when someone is choking you, you will tell them anything they want to hear. Choking me had become a regular thing for him to do since Buddy had been born. All the time he was choking me, he made me tell him that I loved him. And I did it to keep him from killing me. What I really wanted to say was, "I hate, hate, hate you!"

As soon as his hands came off me, I grabbed Lisa out of the baby bed and hit the door. I was barefooted, but I didn't care. I ran as fast as I could across the creek to Gail and Bill Yates's house, holding on to Lisa as tightly as I could. I think it was the only time in my life that I ran through grass and water without being fearful of a snake. I was running fast and scared to death. Now I had a two-legged kind of snake trying to catch me.

Fortunately, Bill and Gail had their door open. I ran inside without knocking. As fast as I got in the house, Jimmy was behind me. Bill told him to calm down. Jimmy was yelling, "Get your ass out here! I am going to hold your head in the creek until you gurgle!" There was no way I was leaving Bill's house.

Gail took me to the bedroom and asked me what happened. I told her. I asked her if I could spend the night with them. Gail could see the bruising on my neck where Jimmy had choked me. I was shaking so badly, I could barely breathe. Gail and Bill said I could stay there and that nothing was going to happen to me.

The next morning Gail let me borrow a pair of her shoes. I knew that Jimmy went to the bank every day about the same time. Timmy and Ray were in school. After Jimmy left I waited a few minutes and went home. I grabbed a diaper bag and stuffed it as full as I could. I grabbed Lisa and Buddy and ran back out into the street. Lisa was walking, but Buddy was still a baby in my arms. He was only six months old. I had no clothes and nothing for them except a diaper bag. I had on a pair of borrowed shoes and my clothes from the night before. I didn't have one cent to my name. I didn't know what I was going to do, but I wasn't staying in the house with Jimmy.

We had just made it to the street when Jimmy came home. He pulled up in the driveway, got out of the car, and walked out into the street. By now Lisa, Buddy, and I were in front of the Gannons' house next door. Jimmy started throwing rocks at me and yelling, "If you leave, you can't come back!" I turned and yelled, "I *am* leaving and I don't want to come back!" He then said, "You can't make it without me." I stopped, turned around and looked right at him, and said, "Honey, you just stand there and watch me." About that time, another rock zinged right past me. I just kept on walking and trying to protect my kids from the rocks flying by.

The kids and I walked to the shopping center on Lebanon Road and into the Laundromat. I didn't have a dime for a telephone call. I had nothing except two babies, a pair of borrowed shoes, and a diaper bag. It wasn't long until Brownie Johnson walked in. He was a musician who lived near us in Hermitage Hills. Timmy had played some music with Brownie at the hootenannies. I don't think I have ever been so happy to see anyone in my life. I asked him if he minded giving me a ride to my sister's house on Broadway near Seventeenth Avenue South. He said he didn't mind at all. I told Brownie what had happened and that I was never going back to Jimmy.

When we got to Betty's, she was shocked to see me. I told her what happened and asked if I could stay with her a couple of days. She said, "Absolutely." Betty's husband, Leo, came home from work shortly after I had told Betty what happened. He said I could stay there as long as I wanted.

The next morning I saw an ad in the paper for a waitress at the Pancake Pantry on Twenty-First Avenue South. I asked Betty if she minded keeping Lisa and Buddy while I went to find a job. Since we were about the same size, she let me borrow some clothes. Betty didn't have a car either. She kept Lisa and Buddy while I walked to the Pancake Pantry, which was only about a half mile from where my sister lived. I applied for a job and was hired. They gave me a uniform and told me I could start to work that afternoon. I went back to my sister's house, changed into my uniform, and headed back to work. I had never been happier about anything in my life. Tonight I would have some money.

I worked at the Pancake Pantry for about three months. During that time I was able to get an apartment for me, Lisa, and Buddy on Sixteenth Avenue. Lois Johnson and Kirk Hansard lived right across the street. Her mother lived with them. I was now closer to work, so my walk to and from was not as far. I worked the afternoon shift, so it was midnight when I walked home. The area was safe, and I was not afraid.

Before moving into an apartment, I asked Betty if she could use Leo's car to take me to Jimmy's house. I still had the key and was hoping he was gone so that I could get a few things for myself, Lisa, and Buddy. I had no clothes for any of us. She said, "No problem."

We got to Jimmy's house about 8:30 p.m. His car was in the driveway. I rang the doorbell and he came to the door. Then suddenly there were two naked young girls standing behind him in the living room. When they ran into the room, Jimmy slammed and locked the storm door. I was livid. I put my foot through the storm door, unlocked it, and went in. Betty was still in the car. Timmy and Ray were in their bedroom and these naked girls were running all over the house. Words cannot describe what I felt. After cussing all of them out, Jimmy threw me out of the house. I landed right beside where a baseball had been left on the ground. I picked up the baseball, leaned back, and, as hard as I could, threw it through the picture window in the living room. Then I went to the car, told Betty to back it out of the driveway into the street, and we waited for the police to arrive.

After the police came, I told them what was going on and that my kids were in the house with two naked girls and Jimmy. The police didn't like that at all. I told them I had left Jimmy several weeks before and just wanted to get some things for the kids and myself out of the house. I told them all hell had broken loose when I discovered the naked girls. They didn't arrest me but told me to leave and to come back at some other time. I never went back for clothes, shoes, or anything. The Salvation Army would become my best place to shop.

Once I moved into my apartment, I was able to get a lady to come sit with the kids while I worked. She was to make their supper and give them a bath before bed. Shortly after she began to work for me, I noticed that Lisa and Buddy were starving when I got home. The cooks at work always gave me food to help me out each night after I had finished my shift. They gave me whatever was left over: bacon, ham, turkey, oranges, and applesauce. I was bringing food home, plus buying other things at the grocery store with my sister every couple of days. I couldn't figure out why my kids were starving, so I decided to find out.

A couple of days later I had the day off. I pretended I was going to work, but I walked around the block and came back. I crossed the street and sat on Lois and Kirk's porch and waited. Sure enough, about an hour later, here comes the babysitter's daughter. She parked and went into the apartment. When she came out, she had two big grocery bags full of food. She and her mother were stealing my food and not feeding my kids. I ran across the street yelling, "Get your fucking ass back in my apartment and leave my groceries. Get out, or I will call the police!" The two of them left in a hurry, leaving my groceries behind.

I didn't know what I was going to do now. I had to go to work, and I had no one to take care of Lisa and Buddy. I took the kids over to Lois's house and her mother agreed to babysit the kids while I worked. Now I could feed my kids before I left, give them their bath, and take snacks and pajamas to Lois's house. This was only temporary until I could find another babysitter, and it was only a thirty-minute walk to the Pancake Pantry.

I had been working there for about three months when Hubert Long came in. We had been friends since I first met Jimmy. Hubert was a booking agent with offices on Sixteenth Avenue. He asked me what I was doing at the Pantry. I told him I had left Jimmy and I needed to feed my kids. He then wanted to know how I got home. I said, "I walked." He said, "Not anymore." From that time on, Hubert picked me up and took me home. He did that until I was able to buy a car about a month later at the Buy Here—Pay Here lot. My life was becoming more stable. I was happy because now I had an apartment, a job, a little money, and a car. I never thought to ask Hubert for a job. I know he would have hired me, but I guess I thought my life working in the music business was over.

The car I bought was a baby blue, four-door Falcon. I didn't really care what color or kind it was as long as it had wheels. My payments were twenty dollars a week. I knew that amount was okay. I was making twenty to twenty-five dollars a day in tips. I could double up on my payments a couple of times a month. The Falcon ran like a champ. I could go to Alabama and visit Mother and Mike. The car was a jewel, and I kept it long after I paid it off.

It was in September 1966 that I finally left Jimmy for good. Buddy was six months old, and Lisa was not quite two. Here I was with five children—two living with Jimmy, two with me, and Mike was with my mother. I would be thirty-one years old in October. I had never had a checking account, had never paid rent, had never had to pay for groceries, a light bill, nothing. But I did know how to balance a checkbook. I had learned how to do that in my high school bookkeeping class, but I had never used that knowledge. I had worked since I was twelve years old, but then the money was all mine. I didn't have to share. Growing up, I used the money to buy new clothes or shoes or material, and Mother made me new outfits. I didn't have to pay bills.

When I was with Jimmy I still worked, but he took my money. He paid all the bills and took care of everything. I went to work, came home, and gave the money to him. When we needed to go to the store, he went with me. Each time we went shopping, he said, "Don't spend over fifteen dollars." I added up prices in my head so that I wouldn't overspend. I knew if I did, he would go off his rocker right in the store. If I needed anything else and he was in the mood, he either took me to get it or he got it himself. I had nothing and owned nothing. But you know what? I never thought about that. It didn't occur to me. Was I dense? I don't think so. Just complacent.

Leaving Jimmy brought me a lot of surprise lessons to learn about life. These were all things I should have known before I left my grandparents and my mother. It took some hard knocks to wake me up—like my car getting repossessed, having to move out in the middle of the night because I owed back rent, and having to pinch pennies to have enough money to buy milk and food for my babies. One day a lightbulb went off in my head. I looked at myself in the mirror and said, "Girl, you have responsibilities. You need to get it in gear and face them." That was when my life really started changing for the better.

I was finding it more and more difficult working as a waitress and trying to make ends meet. I was making chocolate gravy two or three times a week to feed Buddy and Lisa. I just made the regular milk gravy and put some cocoa powder in it, and they liked it. I had learned this from my sister. It was cheap to make and satisfied the kids. I could also make a pan of biscuits for almost nothing. That was much cheaper than store-bought bread.

About this time I met John Denny of Cedarwood Publishing. To clarify, we were friends, never lovers. He suggested that I start the Barbara Martin Agency back up. I told him I had no money and was barely skimping by on what I made as a waitress. John told me he had a building where I could have an office and set up shop. He also moved me to an apartment close to where he lived and set me up with a roommate. Now I had a roommate with a cat named Pyewacit, two kids, and myself. I hated the cat and the roommate, even though she was helping with the rent. She stayed a few months until I could no longer tolerate either, and then she moved. But she left the cat. Eventually I got someone to take the cat.

The new Barbara Martin Agency was located on Seventeenth Avenue South, directly behind Cedarwood Publishing. One of the acts I was booking was Willie Samples, a terrific singer. I had him booked on a package show with Hank Williams Jr. in Guelph, Ontario, and into nightclubs in Ishpeming, Michigan, and Rapid City, South Dakota. Tee Meroney was playing with Willie's band. I went along to try to make friends with the owners of the clubs. I drove to Ishpeming by myself and stopped in Green Bay, Wisconsin, at another club. I was able to book another act in the club in Green Bay for the following month.

Regardless of how hard I was working every day and booking quite a few acts, it was difficult to survive on $20 here and $20 there. The normal rate of pay for newer artists in those days was $100 to $150 a night. There were very few making more than $500 a night, which meant my little 15 percent commission wasn't much money. So the worry of trying to make ends meet was taking a toll on me.

About the second day I was in Rapid City, I woke up in my hotel room and found almost all of my hair on the pillow. I cried and cried. I immediately bought a wig and I wore it constantly. It took almost a year for my hair to grow back in, and that was after I had taken cortisone shots in the scalp. When I returned to Nashville, I showed my scalp to Shot Jackson and he was appalled. I only told a few people about losing my hair. It was devastating, and I was embarrassed. I knew I could trust Shot. By then Shot and Donna Darlene were together. They were my longtime friends. The stress of trying to have my agency and taking care of the kids was too much. I closed the office and got another job.

People kept telling me I should take Jimmy to court and make him pay child support. What they didn't know was that I had never been legally married to Jimmy Martin. Regardless, I contacted a lawyer in Nashville by the name of Robert "Bobby" Jackson, who said I could definitely take Jimmy to court for child support. He also told me that I could move into the Hermitage Hotel and Jimmy would have to pay for it—none of which turned out to be true. Bobby Jackson filed a suit against Jimmy in family court in Nashville. Every time we had a hearing, Jimmy would give me a little money to quiet me down.

One day I was sitting on a bench in the courthouse waiting to go in to see the judge when an old black guy who had worked at the courthouse for many years asked me which courtroom I was going to. I told him. He said, "Ma'am, I hate to tell you, but you are going to lose. You need to be at the other end of the courthouse." I couldn't figure this out, but I soon found out he was right.

Ironically, many years later Jimmy's wife, Teresa, would retain Bobby Jackson to represent her in her divorce from Jimmy. With no children, she got a house. I got nothing for the fourteen years and four children I had given him even though I was the one who had promoted his music and was responsible for his success. I felt like it was my money that had bought her house.

One good thing did come out of my meeting Bobby Jackson, and that was I became friends with Joanne, his secretary. She helped me move to a better place. She also introduced me to Hap Motlow, a major stockholder and founder of the Jack Daniels whiskey company, and to Charlie Galbreath. Charlie was a criminal court judge in the criminal court of appeals for the Middle District of Tennessee from 1968 to 1978. I liked Joanne. She was a fun person.

I remember one afternoon Joanne called me at work and said, "You want to go with me to see Hap Motlow tonight?" I didn't know who Hap was, and I really didn't care to know, but I said, "Sure." After work, I met Joanne and we drove out to Hap's apartment. He was waiting for us. He must have been in his late sixties or early seventies at that time. When you are not yet thirty-three, it is difficult to tell how old someone is, and I really didn't care. I was there with Joanne, and I certainly wasn't going to date him. I liked Hap, and he was a very nice man. He and Joanne had been friends for a long time. We all sat around talking for several hours, and when we got ready to leave, he loaded us up with bottles of Jack Daniels Black. I didn't drink the stuff, so I thought I would just give it away. It was not the last time Hap supplied me with Jack Daniels Black, but my relationship with him was purely platonic. I was never in his company without Joanne.

Buddy and Lisa and I had been living at the new apartment a short time when Lisa started getting sick. I thought she just had a bad cold, but when none of the over-the-counter medications seemed to be helping her, I took her to the emergency room at Nashville General Hospital. It turned out she had pneumonia. I left Buddy with my mother and sat with Lisa day and night. I notified Jimmy that Lisa had pneumonia and was in the hospital, but he never bothered to come to see her.

After she got better, I decided to move again. I found a job in a furniture store office in Lakewood. There was a trailer park nearby. Having never lived in a trailer, I didn't know what to expect, but it looked nice, so I rented it. It was twenty dollars a week, including utilities. I now had bills of forty dollars a week—twenty for the trailer and twenty for the car. I was only making fifty dollars a week at the furniture company. I had to find something else.

While I was living in the trailer, Timmy ran away from Jimmy's house and came to see me. I wanted him to stay with me so badly, but I had no money. What I was making was barely getting us by. I explained this all to Timmy, and he and I both cried. I put him, Lisa, and Buddy in the car and drove him part of the way back home. When Jimmy found out what he had done, he beat the hell out of Timmy. And for a long time after that,

Jimmy would make him sit at the kitchen table and yell at him, "You are just like your mother." He would slap Timmy in the face time after time to punish him for coming to see me. This went on for months. Jimmy's abusive treatment caused Timmy so much pain during his life. I believe it was the catalyst for all of Timmy's later problems with drugs. I know it was the reason he joined the navy as soon as he graduated from high school.

I hated Jimmy Martin, not only for what he did to me but also for what he was now doing to my kids, and there was not a damn thing I could do about it. I had no money, and without money in Davidson County courts, you are up the creek without a paddle.

I knew I was not going to be able to make ends meet working in the furniture company. Mother had moved to Birmingham, Alabama, to be near my grandfather. I talked to Mother, and she said if I went down there, I could get a job and she would take care of Lisa and Buddy while I worked. She had room for us at her apartment. So I loaded up my old Falcon and headed out.

In Birmingham I was able to get a job immediately as a keypunch operator at Associated Grocers. I worked from 3:00 p.m. till 11:00. And because of the shift differential, my pay was one hundred dollars a week. What a change, going from fifty to one hundred dollars a week! I was thrilled. I was able to pay Mother to watch Lisa and Buddy. And I was able to buy groceries. I was also keeping up with my Falcon payment and had extra money to spend.

Mike loved having his little brother and sister there, and Lisa and Buddy loved Mike. They also loved their grandmother. Things were going well for all of us. But as usual, Mother couldn't keep away from the bottle. She was going out to drink on the weekend. She would come home on Sunday afternoon in time to sober up. I hated that, but I couldn't live her life. She was there on Mondays when Mike had to go to school and I had to go to work. At the time, Mother was only in her early fifties.

While we were living in Birmingham, I began having problems with my periods. I was in and out of the hospital for months. The bleeding was profuse. I would get a shot to stop it, and a few days later I was back in the hospital, pouring blood. The doctors couldn't decide what was causing it. I certainly was not having sexual relations with anyone. I was skinny as a rail, and my eyes were sunk back in my head. I looked horrible and I felt just as bad. It would be over a year before this problem was resolved.

After a while I decided Alabama was not for me. I called my friend Jerry Johnson Colmus in Nashville to see if I could stay with her until I could get started. With me gone, Mother wouldn't go out drinking, because she would have no one to watch the kids. I drove to Nashville to Jerry's house. I had taken a week off from work, so I didn't have much time to search for a job without losing the Birmingham one. I also wanted to get back to Lisa, Buddy, and Mike.

It was in the summer of 1968 when I applied at the courthouse for a job as a keypunch operator with the Metropolitan Government of Nashville. I was immediately hired and assigned to the finance department. I would be working the afternoon shift for a salary of $350 a month. It was a small cut in pay from my Birmingham job, but I had very good benefits, including hospitalization for Lisa, Buddy, and myself. I was elated. I rented a nice one-bedroom furnished apartment at the Madison Square Apartments for $90 a month. Even though the apartment number was #M-13, I didn't care, because I wasn't superstitious. I was so very happy. I was around the corner from my best friends, Jerry Johnson Colmus and her sisters, Wilma Lee Cooper and Peggy Gayle Leary.

Jerry was the first woman to travel overseas with the USO. She played bass and sang for Roy Acuff as one of the Smoky Mountain Boys. Wilma Lee and her husband, Stoney, were and had been on the Grand Ole Opry for many years. Peggy Gayle was a singer and the cutest little thing you have ever seen. But even though she was little, she could get her feathers up too quick to talk about it.

Mother didn't want me to move back to Nashville, but I hated Birmingham. I told DaddyHollis I was going back to Nashville and that I had found a job and rented an apartment. Before I left Birmingham, I traded the Falcon for a 1968 Mustang. What a mistake! My old Falcon was paid for, and now I had payments of ninety dollars a month. I wasn't thinking when I did this. I just loved the turquoise-and-cream-colored Mustang, and I had to have it. I was still thinking like a spoiled-rotten child.

I missed Mother and Mike, but I liked my job at the courthouse. I had a great babysitter who lived in the apartment complex and didn't charge me very much. I had my friends Wilma Lee, Jerry, and Peggy. And I had made new friends from the apartments, Wanda, Roy, and Roberta Bounds; Wayne Johnson; and Harold Young. I had reconnected with my friend from grammar school, Birdie Lee Smith, and her husband, Bob. And I had my lifetime friend Opal Taylor. I loved all of these people.

Once I started working at the courthouse and receiving a paycheck, I tried to decide how I was going to make my pay last all month. Metro paid only once a month. I had a babysitter to pay $20 a week; rent of $90 a month; my phone bill, which was about $5 a month; gas to get back and forth to work of $20 a month; and a car payment of $90 a month. A total of $225 had to be paid before I put milk and food on the table. I couldn't make it. I had to get a part-time job.

I had worked as a waitress at the Holiday Inn on James Robertson Parkway for Miss Sally, the manager. I loved Miss Sally and she liked me. We were both Memphians (as people from Memphis are known). I knew I could make enough working part-time to supplement my pay. I called Miss Sally, who told me to give her a couple of days and she would see what she could come up with. I told her okay.

By now the Mustang had been repossessed, and I had bought another car from the same Buy Here—Pay Here lot where I had purchased the Falcon. This time it was an old Mercury station wagon. It ran well and there was more room for the kids. My payments would be less than half of what they had been on the Mustang.

A couple of days later Miss Sally called and asked me to come by the Holiday Inn when I got off from work. I was working days and had been for about three months. When 4:30 came, I flew out the door. I practically ran across the Woodland Street Bridge to get to the parking lot, where my car was in the Metro employee parking lot.

When I arrived at the Holiday Inn, Miss Sally wanted to know if I was hungry and I told her no. We then sat down to talk. She asked me if I wanted to work on Wednesday nights and Saturdays as the bartender. I told her I didn't know anything about being a bartender. She told me she would give me a book. At that point she told me to be there Saturday at noon. She gave me my uniform and told me to wear knee-high black boots. Now I had to get some boots. I hugged her and left. I went shopping and found a very cute pair for thirty dollars. They were expensive, so I hesitated buying them, but knew I had to have them. I kept those boots for forty years. I finally did give them away—it was one of those things I wish I hadn't done. They were so comfortable, and I loved wearing them.

Saturday morning I couldn't wait to get to the Holiday Inn. I got Lisa and Buddy up early and took them over to Jerry Johnson's house. They were going to stay with Jerry on Saturdays while I worked. After I got off from work, I slept there.

Jerry had two Pekingese dogs named Peeper and Punkin. I hated those dogs. They were the two dumbest dogs in the world. They ran off all the time and couldn't find their way home. Poor Jerry would be out in the pouring rain chasing those dogs down Grapevine Street and along the Cumberland River in Madison. I told her all the time to just let them go. Anyhow, when I came in at 2:30 in the morning, I tried to be very quiet. The kids, Jerry, and Peggy would all be sleeping. The minute I sat foot in the door, the yappy-yappers would start barking and nipping. They would follow me up the stairs to the one that creaked, and then they would really cut loose. Finally, after everyone was up and after Lisa played with them, they would shut up. I swore I was going to gag them, but I never did.

I loved my part-time job in the Gold Record Room at the Holiday Inn. True to her word, on my first day there Miss Sally gave me a bartender's book and told me to make and taste every drink in there. I started doing just that, and by the time the bar opened I could make quite a few drinks. The tasting didn't last long, because I couldn't stand the taste of all that liquor, and I thought, "If a drink isn't correct, someone will let me know." I must have done all right, because not a soul complained, and after about a month, she added Fridays to my work schedule.

My bartender's outfit was a short gold dress with black mesh sleeves, and I wore black knee-high boots with a one-inch heel. My hair was long and naturally dark, dark brown, and I kept it immaculate and fixed at all times. Miss Sally told me I looked very good in the outfit. I knew I looked good too.

That first night I was doing really well making drinks, opening beers, talking to the customers, and listening to the music. Ed Bruce was the singer and guitarist. I was busy and enjoying my work when one customer asked me for a Rusty Nail. I thought he was joking, so I said, "We don't have any rusty nails, but if you go down the railroad tracks behind the motel, you might find some." I thought he was going to fall off the bar stool, he was laughing so hard. He then told me how to make a Rusty Nail, with Drambuie and Scotch whiskey with a lemon twist. After that, he came into the bar a couple of times a week and was a great tipper. That's one drink I never forgot how to make.

Ironically, a lot of Nashville policemen and detectives came into the lounge. One of those was a detective by the name of Paul Godsey. The reason I am mentioning him is because a couple of years later, without knowing their relationship, I would marry his nephew.

The filming for the TV show *Hee Haw* was in the beginning stages. It was being filmed at the old WLAC studios just down the street on James Robertson Parkway. After the crew finished for the day, the musicians would stop in at the Gold Record Room. At various times we had Buck Owens, Roy Clark, the Hager Twins, and Jackie Phelps, and at least one of the girls was usually there. Almost everyone on the show, whether they were on the televised portion or just working behind the scenes, stopped by at one time or another.

Ed Bruce was a good singer and songwriter, and everyone in Nashville seemed to like him. Ed worked there the entire time that I worked as bartender. He went on to star in movies and to be a big recording artist. One thing I can say about Ed is that he was a gentleman. I never saw him do or say anything wrong or use a dirty word.

I continued at the courthouse, and at 4:30 on Wednesdays and Fridays I went into the bathroom, changed into my Gold Record outfit, put on my coat over it, and went to work at the bar. I was making anywhere from $100 to $150 each week in tips. I also got to eat supper there. I was able to pay Jerry and Peggy for babysitting on those nights, and that money helped them. Money was scarce for them, too, in those days. Neither of them was able to work, and Jerry was getting paid very little for working the Opry with dobro player Cousin Jody. We were all making out with the money I made at the Holiday Inn.

The bar was also like being out socially. Even though I wasn't dating anyone who came into the bar or worked there, I got to know a lot of people. That meant I now had people to talk to, and I made the most of it.

While bartending one night, I had a telephone call from Audrey Williams, Hank Williams's ex-wife, telling me that Tennessee governor Frank Clement had just been killed. I liked Frank and had met him several times through people in the music business, including Audrey. I told Audrey that I was working until two in the morning and wouldn't be able to come to her house. I said I would call her the next day, which I did. After I hung up

the phone, I told Ed that our governor had just been killed. But because
of my schedule, I was unable to attend Frank's funeral with Audrey. I also
didn't think I belonged there. I was so sorry to hear of his passing. I always
thought of him as one of the good guys.

I had reconnected with Birdie and Bob Smith at the Dusty Road Tavern
on Woodland Street. Birdie was my lifelong friend, despite the fact that
we had not seen each other in years. We immediately reconnected. It was
a good feeling.

Sometimes if I got off early from the Holiday Inn, I stopped by the Dusty
Road. It was owned by Bobby Green, an ex-prizefighter. He was a small
man who smoked his cigarettes in a holder. It was always hanging out of
his mouth. Before I started at the Gold Record Room, I often borrowed five
dollars from him to hold me over until payday. Whenever I went in after
work, he always had a hot dog for me. Sometimes he charged me, but most
times he didn't.

Because I was a single woman, people at the Dusty Road were always
buying beers for me. They naturally assumed when you are in a beer joint,
you drink beer. I didn't drink beer, so I asked Bobby to just hold them back.
He would then give me a Coke instead. One time I had about ten beers
waiting for me. I told him to just forget it or give them to someone else. I
guess all the beers I gave him back paid for all of those free hot dogs.

Bob and Birdie stopped by the Dusty Road every afternoon after work.
Birdie was just learning to play the bass, and it was good practice for her
when they jammed. Sometimes if Harold Young, Roy Bounds, Wayne Johnson, Charlie Hardeman, or other musicians were there, they would all jam.
I loved it. I also loved to hear Wayne sing. He was a good singer and a really
good guy. I dated Wayne for quite a while and my mother loved him, but
the relationship was not meant to be. Wayne had an ex-wife he just couldn't
stay away from. They had been divorced for years, but he kept staying on
the scene. I liked Wayne as a friend but didn't want him as a boyfriend.
He and I stayed in touch for many years and was another person who died
much too young of kidney failure.

I was working two jobs and taking care of Lisa and Buddy, and I was trying
to have a life of my own. It became difficult to find a minute to stop by the
Dusty Road after work. Sometimes I would take Lisa and Buddy with me.
They loved the hot dogs, and Birdie was crazy about both of them. The Dusty

Road was not like most beer joints. Bobby ran a clean place—no cussing, no fighting, no drunks—so taking the kids there was okay. Besides, they liked the music.

One day while sitting at the bar at the Dusty Road and the kids weren't with me, I met a man by the name of Bill from Cookeville, Tennessee. I had seen Bill there many times but had never talked to him. He was nice-looking, and I knew he worked for a local manufacturer as a supervisor. I also knew he was interested in me, because Bobby Green had told me. Bobby liked him and said he was very nice, and Bobby's recommendation was all I needed.

By spring I was having more problems with my periods. In the summer of 1969 I had one continuous period and was in and out of the emergency room. The doctor said I had to have a D & C. I called Jimmy and asked him to take Lisa and Buddy because I had to go in the hospital. I made him promise that he would give them back and that I could have them on weekends until I recovered. He promised. Mary Ann Garrison was living with him and she would care for the kids. I had nothing against Mary Ann, but I felt sorry for her. I wanted to tell her to run, not walk away from him.

During my recovery, the first weekend I went to get the kids, everything was fine and I picked them up with no problems. The next weekend, Mary Ann brought them out to my car with their suitcase. When I got to my apartment and opened the suitcase, it was empty. I had to go out and buy everything for them again, including toothbrushes. When I went to pick up the kids a week later, no one was at Jimmy's place. I called and no one answered. That week, Jimmy served me with papers for full custody. I knew then I would never get Lisa and Buddy back. He had taken my kids again. I was broken.

I started stopping at Dusty Road every afternoon when I didn't have to go to the Gold Record Room. Dusty Road was across the street from the Metro parking lot, so I would pick up my car, drive it across the street, and park in front. For me, it wasn't about drinking, because I didn't drink beer; it was about being around people.

Bill and I started talking. The more I saw him, the more I liked him. But I thought there was something strange going on. Every Friday after work, he would go back to his home in Cookeville. I asked, "Bill, are you married?" He said no. So then I asked him, "Why do you go home every week? Why not spend some weekends here?" He would give me one excuse after another. I didn't believe him. And as my good friend Doris would say, "Lo and behold!" The truth was revealed.

My friend Jerry Johnson Colmus was going to be playing in Cookeville. We decided when she accepted the gig that this was our opportunity to find out about Mr. Bill. I bought a blonde wig and went with her. We stopped at a place to have some coffee, and I looked up his name and address in the Cookeville phone book. The first thing we did when we hit the city limits was go by his house. It was actually a double-wide mobile home on about an acre lot—very homey, clean, and nice. Sort of like Bill. But sure enough, there were swings in the yard. Jerry and I started yelling at the same time—"Gotcha!"

Jerry was playing in the parking lot of this big supermarket. They had a trailer set up where she could change clothes to get ready. I went into the trailer, put on my wig, and some glasses and baggy clothes. I looked just like a blonde hick. I stood to the side of the stage where I could see the crowd. It wasn't long before I spotted Bill with his family. Bill knew Jerry, so I was surprised he was standing close to the stage. I guess he didn't think she would recognize him. Right then and there, I knew how I was going to handle this situation.

Monday afternoon, Bill called and wanted to stop by. I said, "Sure, I will be home about five-thirty. He said, "I will see you then." I said, "I can't wait." When Bill came into my apartment, I said, "Did you bring your wife and kids?" He said, "What are you talking about?" So then I gave him the rundown. I told him I had seen his double-wide and knew about his trip with the wife and kids that afternoon to see the show. I told him, "I could have spit on you. You were that close." Then I told him to get out. I never saw Bill again, nor did he ever come to the Dusty Road again. All I could think about was the old saying "Liar, liar, pants on fire."

After my D & C, I returned to working both of my jobs. But the D & C had not helped. I was still having long, heavy periods. I would bleed through everything. The dark circles under my eyes were back. I was tired and anemic all the time. I weighed about 110 pounds, quite skinny for someone five foot, seven inches tall. This had been continuing on and off for almost two years. I had to do something.

11

LIFE AFTER JIMMY MARTIN

I was having such a good time working at the courthouse and at the Gold Record Room, and I knew a lot of people. So when the annual Disc Jockey Convention in Nashville rolled around, I decided to stop by the Andrew Jackson Hotel, where the convention was being held.

I walked into the lobby and ran into Charlie Louvin and Audrey Williams. I stopped to talk and hugged Audrey. They were happy to see me. About that time, Jimmy came into the lobby and straight over to me. He asked, "What are *you* doing here? You don't have any business here." I asked him to go away. He kept telling me to get out. I had all I was going to take and I slapped him as hard as I could. He cussed me. I went out onto the street, I was so embarrassed. I wanted to find a rock and crawl under it. I kept apologizing to Audrey and Charlie, who followed me out. Charlie said, "Hold your head up high. He deserved it." Audrey put her arms around me and said, "You should have killed him a long time ago." She then suggested that she and I go to the Black Poodle Lounge in Printer's Alley. I was happy to get away, so we took off for the Black Poodle.

The Black Poodle was the meeting place for musicians. Willie Nelson, Kris Kristofferson, Roy Orbison, Carl Belew, Faron Young, Webb Pierce, and just about everyone stopped by at one time or another. Sometimes the booths were packed with entertainers. At that time, they weren't the megastars they would later become. They were able to move around freely, have a drink, and no one would bother them.

When Audrey and I walked in that night, Bob Osborne was standing at the bar. I walked over to say hello. The place was packed, so he said, "Let's go over here and sit down on this step." It was by the exit door. I will remember that night as long as I live.

Bob and I sat on the step, and I told him what had happened and that I had slapped Jimmy. He said, "Good for you." I said, "I could just kiss you for that." He said, "Why don't you? I have been waiting twenty years." We kissed and kissed and kissed. I think I had been waiting on that kiss since the night on Glover Street when Jimmy went out the back door of our house and returned three days later. We left immediately, got into Bob's car, and drove to the parking lot of a laundry on Woodland Street. We sat in the car talking and hugging and kissing and hugging and kissing and talking. That night was incredible. I didn't want it to end. But it was a happy ending to a night that had started out so badly.

The next day I realized that I had forgotten to tell Audrey I was leaving. I called her and told her what had happened. She was thrilled for me and for Bob. Bob and I started seeing each other as often as we could. He went to the Dusty Road with me. We loved being together. We always had lots to talk about, and we couldn't keep our hands off each other.

A month or so later, Bob and his brother, Sonny, had a gig playing at the Black Poodle. At that time Benny Birchfield was playing with them, and Benny was dating Jean Shepard. Jean and I had been friends for a long time. We went to the Black Poodle every night and would sit together and talk and listen to the music. I still consider Jean my friend and would do anything for her. She is one of the best women I have ever known. With Jean, just as with me, what you see is what you get. She is a good, kind person, totally unaffected by stardom.

Bob was happy I was at the shows. But I knew that Sonny was not happy with my dating Bob. I didn't care. I liked being with Bob.

Then one night Bob's wife, Pat, showed up. Even though we had all lived together when Timmy and their son Robbie were babies, I really didn't like her that much. I was sitting with Jean when Pat joined us. We all made small talk, mostly about the kids. Pat didn't stay long, and I was glad. I don't think she ever knew that I was dating Bob. I certainly was not going to tell her, and I didn't think anyone else was going to either.

When Bob and Pat, Jimmy, and I had been living together in Detroit, I had never thought about any kind of relationship between Bob and me. I knew Bob was loyal to Pat. I never saw him try to go out with anyone. But Pat and Bob didn't have a touchy, feely type of relationship. I had never seen him put his arm around her or kiss her, nor did she show any love for him. I knew their relationship was tenuous at best. From the time Bob and I first kissed, we had that feeling. It felt right for the time being. I knew it was not going to be a long-term relationship. I never wanted nor thought of Bob divorcing Pat. I liked her, but we were never best friends. Pat and Bob did divorce a couple of years after he and I broke up and I had married Charles "Chuck" Stephens.

Several years after Bob and Pat were divorced, Pat became friends with Randy and Linda Reed, who lived across the street from her on Harbor Drive. And the Reeds just happened to be best friends with my husband, Chuck. When Pat found out I was married to Chuck and that he and I were coming up to see the Reeds, Linda told me that Pat couldn't wait for us to get there.

After we arrived, Pat came over to join us and we had a wonderful conversation. She wanted me to come to her house and look at her divorce papers. I looked at Chuck. He knew the story about Bob. I tried to find excuses not to go, but Linda had told her I was a paralegal. So I went to Pat's house to see the papers. She wanted to know if she had been treated fairly in the divorce settlement. I told her she had come out very well. After that, whenever I was in Nashville, Pat would always come over to Randy and Linda's house.

Getting back to when I was first seeing Bob, things were going so great for us. We loved being together, and we were having fun. Pat had been out of town and Bob took me to see his house on Harbor Drive. Then Bob broke the news to me that Pat was pregnant. I couldn't believe my ears. He had been sleeping with Pat while he was sleeping with me. I felt betrayed, and it was over. Thinking about it now, I was the one doing the betraying, not Bob.

In November 1970 I started dating Chuck Stephens. He had come to work as a programmer at Metro. I always kidded around the office about any of the new guys who came to work. When I saw him, I asked my girlfriend Carolyn Morelli, who was my boss Ken Smith's secretary, if he was married. She said no. I said, "Let me see his resume." She gave it to me, and after I read it I said, "No kids, divorced, college education, and good looking. I think I will just marry him." She laughed and said, "Oh, yeah? You're not going to marry anyone." Then she said, "He has been asking about you, too."

Chuck and I hit it off right away. I was always in the computer room, wiring a board or collating something. At that time the clothing style for women was short skirts, sweaters, and boots, and that's what I usually wore to work. They looked good on me and I knew it. One day I was having a dinner party and I asked him if he would like to come. He said yes. I gave him my address and told him to be there at 7:30 p.m.

I had several people coming over that night, including Tee Meroney and his girlfriend, Harold and Alline Young, Wayne Johnson, Roy and Roberta Bounds, and now Chuck. I was making steak, biscuits, salad, and baked potatoes. Chuck arrived right on time and I introduced him to everyone. When it came time to leave, Chuck and Wayne were trying to outlast each other. Wayne had already emptied the garbage, taken it out, and helped put the dishes away. Finally he left. Chuck asked if he could pick me up for work the next day. I lived in Madison, and he lived across town off Franklin Road, about twenty miles away. I mentioned that to him, but he said he didn't care. He wanted to pick me up. I said, "Okay."

The next morning he was right on time. That night after work he got his first dose of the Dusty Road Tavern and he loved it. He met Bob and Birdie, and Wayne was there again, as were Harold and Alline and Roy and Roberta. Chuck was a beer drinker and fit right in with the crowd. We had a great time. He would continue to pick me up each morning and take me home every night. I was no longer working at the Holiday Inn and was only working at the courthouse.

A night or two before Christmas, we went out to dinner with Chuck's roommate and lifelong friend, Gus Gourieux, and Gus's girlfriend, Denise. Chuck took me home and I asked him in to have a drink. When I walked through the door, I wished I had not asked him in. I could tell Bob had been there. There were notes all over, including in the bathroom. They all were signed, "B for B." He had left a present for me: six coffee cups with a rack. I still have two of the cups and the notes. They are very personal. I have never, ever shared them with anyone (nor will I). Chuck asked me who had the key to my apartment. I told him it was just a friend who sometimes stopped by to change clothes if he didn't have enough time to go home.

Bob and I would continue to be in a relationship until January 8, 1971. And on that very day, Chuck Stephens arrived early at my apartment for us to get married. Roy and Roberta Bounds were going to Springfield with us to be witnesses. My girlfriend Wanda came over that morning to help me get ready. As I was sitting at the dresser putting on my makeup, I was crying my eyes out. I told her, "I don't want to do this." She said, "You have to. You have all these people waiting." I had purchased a two-piece navy blue silk suit at the Salvation Army on First Avenue for two dollars. It fit perfectly. I put on my suit, looked at Wanda, and said, "Okay, let's go do it." It would turn out to be the best thing I ever did. But at the time, I didn't think so.

I was not in love with Chuck when I married him. I liked him as a friend. I had no desire to sleep with him. But I wanted a stable home with my children back and to be with someone I could count on. I knew Chuck was a good man, and I could have all of those things. But I wasn't ready to completely give up Bob, regardless of what he had done. I loved Bob with all my heart.

Chuck and I drove to Springfield, Tennessee. It was snowing, and I don't like riding in a car in the snow. Neither of us had any money, because payday was not until Friday. Chuck had a Bank of America credit card, and we used that to pay for our blood tests and to get our licenses. We had already used it at Service Merchandise to purchase our rings. With Roy and Roberta Bounds standing up for us, we were married in the judge's chambers. Later that evening the four of us along with Bob and Birdie Smith went to the New Orleans Restaurant on Eighth Avenue North to celebrate. I still have the champagne bottle with the coasters from our wedding night dinner. After dinner we all went to the Dusty Road, where everyone joined in to help us celebrate. Everything went on the credit card.

On our wedding night, Chuck and I were in bed (this was the first time I had ever slept with him) when the phone rang. I reached over and it was Bob. He said, "Hold on, I want to sing you a song." I said, "Wait, Bob, I have something to tell you." He said, "Let me sing this song." He sang "Long, Lanky Woman," and my heart broke. He sang a couple more songs before I could tell him I had gotten married. He couldn't believe it. I couldn't believe it. It still makes me cry, remembering that conversation forty-five years ago. Then I thought, "How am I going to give Bob up?" I was so mad at him for getting Pat pregnant, and that's how I justified getting married. I was good at justifying my mistakes. (I still am.) After that night, Bob would call me periodically at the office just to make sure I was okay.

Monday morning rolled around, and Chuck and I went back to work at Metro. When we told our boss, Ken, that we were married, we got the shock of our lives. He said one of us would have to leave, because there was a policy with Metro that married couples could not work together. I was mortified. Chuck had only been working there since November, but he made more money than I did. So guess who got the ax? Me. I lost the job that I dearly loved.

I will always believe that losing my job was not because of a Metro policy but because of Ken Smith. He had often asked me out, and I always denied him. Ken was married and my boss. But I was not interested in him. When he let me go, he told me that my marriage wouldn't last. I ignored him. Then about ten years later, Chuck and I were in a shopping center, and as we walked past a store, Chuck said, "There is Ken Smith." I went into the store, walked over to him, and said, "Hello, Ken." He said, "Barbara." Chuck walked up and I said to Ken, "You remember my husband, Chuck?" Ken turned red in the face. I was elated. I have to say, I looked fantastic the day I confronted Ken. I had on my Norwegian silver fox coat, and, being tall, I looked elegant. That really gave me satisfaction after what Ken did, or at least what I think he did.

Chuck and I had been married about a month when we decided to move to the Berkley Hills Apartments in Madison. We would have three bedrooms, because I wanted to be able to petition the court to have visiting privileges with my kids. I thought now that I was married and, within a month after being terminated at Metro, I had found a good job working for a consulting company and was living in a large apartment, I should be able to get visiting privileges. I could not have been more wrong. The court denied my petition. I didn't understand it; neither did Chuck.

While living at the Berkley Hills Apartments, Chuck and I both started school at the University of Tennessee at Nashville. I would be working toward a bachelor's degree and Chuck toward a master's. I loved going to school. I felt like I was doing something for myself at last. Chuck could not have hated school more. One of his classes was accounting, but he could not even balance a checkbook. He was ready to give up on accounting when I took over and started doing his homework. I have always had a flair for numbers but never had the opportunity to use it except for memorizing telephone numbers. I told him, "I will do your homework. Then if you get A's, you can flunk the exams and still pass." And that's what we did.

During the time we lived at the Berkley Hills Apartments, Chuck's mother gave us two little poodles. They were a cute brother and sister. We would close them in the bathroom with their food and water when we went to work. Dumb as we were, we didn't remove the toilet paper or the towels. What a mess we had! The dogs loved to chew on the legs of our new furniture. I could not tolerate that and they had to go. We were happy to find someone to take them.

We still wanted a dog, just not the yapping poodles. We decided to get a Doberman. The first one we found, we loved. We took him to the vet to have his ears clipped, and he died from heart worms during surgery. The vet was devastated. We then got a more mature dog and named him Ace of Spades. We took him to the same vet and got his ears clipped. They were beautiful.

Chuck and I bought brand-new furniture shortly after we married. We had a smoked-glass dining room suite with smoky acrylic chairs and white leather seats. To make the dining room suite more glamorous, we bought a fake bearskin rug with long white fur. It was gorgeous and complimented the dining room table and chairs. Just the look I was trying to achieve. It was stunning!

One day when we came home from work, Chuck let Ace out of the bathroom to take him out the back door to the yard to do his business. But before Chuck could open the back door, Ace squatted and went right on our bearskin rug. I yelled, "Get him! Get him!" Chuck looked at me and said, "Too late." This time the dog stayed and the bearskin rug went to the dumpster.

We decided to buy a house. I liked Nashville's Parkwood area, because I liked Chuck's aunt and uncle who lived there with their children. His cousin Jimmy also lived there. We found a very nice three-bedroom, two-bath house with a fenced-in yard on Spears Road. I was already planning how I was going to decorate it before we even bought it. The house was twenty thousand dollars. We could finance it through the Veterans Administration with no money down, and our payments would be two hundred dollars a month. Now Ace was going to be a yard dog with a big doghouse.

Before we moved in (this time my name was legally on the house) we painted all the rooms. I still had hope that I would get Lisa and Buddy back and have visiting privileges with Timmy and Ray. I had bought a beautiful canopy bed for Lisa when we moved to Berkley Hills. Now I had it set up in the corner room. I made a mirrored dressing table for her room. I made a skirt for it similar to the evening dress she had worn when she won Little Miss Nashville. It was white tulle with a taffeta underskirt and pink ribbons. The bedroom also had a beautiful white eyelet bedspread and canopy cover with curtains to match.

I also set up a room for Buddy with twin beds, so if Timmy and Ray came to see us, they would have their own bed. I had it decorated in a style for boys. I also thought Mike could use it when he came up too.

I petitioned the court for visiting privileges. Once again I didn't even get to court. They sent an investigator out. Chuck and I both met with him, and he went back and denied our request. *Why?* we kept asking ourselves. Chuck had a spotless reputation, a college degree, and we were married, owned our own home, both had good jobs, and were both attending school. So why? We just didn't understand the reasons they had for turning us down.

I was so proud of the rooms I had created for the kids. Unfortunately, they would never get to see them. When we sold the house, we sold the furniture. I never wanted to see Lisa's bedroom or Buddy's bedroom again. I knew then that Jimmy was never going to let me see my kids or let them come to live with me. It had now been three years since I had seen them.

Chuck and I still had a lot of good things happen while we were living on Spears Road and also a lot of bad. I still talked to Bob occasionally, and one day he and I decided to meet at the motel across the street from Madison Square Shopping Center. I wanted to see Bob so badly I could taste it. I missed him terribly. I decided that I would tell Chuck I was going shopping.

That afternoon after work, I said to Chuck, "I am going to go shopping, okay?" He said, "You don't have to ask me if it's okay for you to go shopping. You are a grown woman; go wherever you want to go. I trust you." With Jimmy I had been used to asking permission to do anything. But with Chuck a new world had just opened up to me.

I left home and started to Madison Square, knowing I was getting ready to cheat on my husband. The problem was, I just *couldn't* cheat on him. I never went to the motel, nor did I call Bob to let him know I wasn't coming. I knew that if I had, I wouldn't have left him. He called me at work the next day to find out what happened. I told him and I never heard from him again. I did get a couple of birthday cards just signed "B." But I have never stopped thinking about him.

Chuck's parents had moved to Orlando the day he graduated from Litton High School and left for the navy. Nashville was his home and he didn't want his parents to move, but they had an opportunity to open a wholesale florist business in Florida and they went. Chuck and I visited them in the summer of 1971. They lived in a beautiful little house in Winter Park. I got to know the area fairly well during that visit and I liked it. His parents then came to see us in Nashville for Christmas, but they brought bad news. Chuck's mother, Mary, had just been diagnosed with lymphoma.

After their visit Chuck's parents returned to Orlando and sold the house where they had lived since 1956. They then moved to an apartment. Mary started chemotherapy treatments, which seemed to be helping, and for Christmas 1972 Chuck and I took his grandmother, Granny Lou, from Nashville to Orlando to see them.

Granny Lou was a real pistol. She was in her eighties and was four feet, ten inches tall. She was always dressed to the nines. Everything had to be her way. If she didn't get things her way, she would not speak to you. She lived in the projects on Eighth Avenue North and had a nice one-bedroom corner apartment. She was one of the first members of the Monroe Street Methodist Church. She and her husband had lived in North Nashville most of her adult life. When he died, she moved to the projects, or in polite terms, subsidized housing.

As a treat for her birthday, I took Granny Lou to the Teddy Bart show on WSM-TV. She watched Teddy every day. I thought she would enjoy seeing his show, so I called Teddy, whom I had known forever, and told him I was bringing her. I also mentioned that it was her birthday. During the show Teddy walked over to Granny Lou with the microphone and started interviewing her. He said, "You are here with your granddaughter—how nice." Granny Lou said, "She is not my granddaughter; she is my grandson's wife." Teddy looked at me and I rolled my eyes. Then Granny Lou said, "She never takes me any place. She just leaves me at home." About that time, I was looking at Teddy to cut off the questioning. Teddy was so shocked that he finally said, "Thank you, Mrs. Stephens, and have a happy birthday." I had never been so embarrassed in my life. This went out over television for all of Nashville to see.

I was so pissed at Granny Lou that I wanted to just pick her up and fling her across the parking lot. She was very proud of herself and was walking like a banty rooster. When I got Granny Lou to the car, I said, "If you think you didn't go anywhere before, watch what is coming now!"

Driving down to Orlando for Christmas, Granny Lou, Chuck, and I would stop at Cracker Barrel restaurants to eat. Granny Lou liked their restrooms, because they were clean and they had good lotion for your hands. Me, I liked their veggies, and I still do.

We arrived at Mary and Charles's apartment and were very surprised. Mary had lost so much weight, she could barely get around. I told her not to worry about anything; I would take care of all the cooking and cleaning and Granny Lou. That eased her mind a little. The chemotherapy treatments were taking their toll on Mary.

The first morning we were there, I made coffee and sat down to have my first cup. Granny Lou came in and sat down at the table. She looked at me and said, "Carolyn, I will have my tea now." Carolyn had been Chuck's first wife. I looked at her and said, "My name is not Carolyn, and if you want a cup of tea, get up and make it." And that was the way it was for the rest of our stay. She continued to call me Carolyn just to piss me off.

The day after Christmas we started getting ready to leave and return to Nashville. Granny Lou started saying she was not going back to Nashville; she was staying there so that she could help Mary. Mary had already called me off to the side and said, "*Please* take her with you. I cannot stand to have her here." I told Mary, "Don't worry; she is going if I have to carry her." Despite Granny Lou's arguments, the three of us left the next day and headed back to Nashville. During the entire trip she did not speak one word to Chuck or me, nor did she get out of the car until we reached her house. I told Chuck to just let her fume.

For Christmas we had bought new curtains for her apartment. When we got her situated in her apartment, I told her, "Granny Lou, I will come over next week and hang your new curtains." She said, "I don't want them." I said, "I don't care if you want them, I am going to hang them." I did and she liked them.

I know it sounds like I didn't like Granny Lou, and at times I didn't. But I didn't let that stop me from inviting her to our house for dinner and all the holidays. I knew she was lonesome. She was never left out of anything and she would make several more trips to Florida with us.

Chuck was an only child and he was terribly worried about his mother. Her health had continued to go downhill. In the spring of 1973 Chuck and I moved to Orlando. We found a house in Casa Grande off Holden Avenue with orange trees. I was thrilled to have a house where I could just go outside and pick an orange off the tree. I found a job as a secretary with Hewitt Realty, and Chuck went to work for Sun Bank.

By now his parents had bought a place in Seminole, Florida, a suburb of St. Petersburg, which was a short ride away from Orlando. Mary continued to take her treatments in Orlando. Before each treatment, she and Charles would stay with us. We always had a good time the night before her treatment, but immediately following her treatment the next day, she went directly home.

As an only child, Chuck was a restless soul, sort of like my mother. We had such a good life in Orlando. We both had good jobs we liked, and I had lots of friends from my job in the real estate office. We played tennis in a foursome and I played singles on the weekends. I was in great shape and wanted to stay that way.

Mother came down to see us and brought two of my nephews. We took them to Disney and they were ecstatic. Mother stayed for a week. I loved having her there, and Chuck got along with the boys really well. But it wasn't long before he wanted to return to Nashville. His mother was feeling better and her treatments had ended for the time being.

12

ALL MY CHILDREN

Back in Nashville, we moved into an apartment in Madison that bordered I-65. I hated the apartment but knew it would not be long and we would be moving again.

It was wintertime and Chuck decided that he no longer wanted to work as a computer programmer but wanted to go into construction. This is a man who once told me he wanted something mechanical for Christmas. I laughed at him and said, "What, a pencil?" He didn't know one end of a hammer from the other. But as it turns out, he got a supervisor's job for a major construction company. I knew it was because he had a degree and not from his knowledge of the business.

Chuck worked in construction for about three months. One day he came home and was muddy, cold, and worn out. He looked at me and said, "I can't stand this cold. Let's move back to Orlando." He knew he could go back to Sun Bank. So he gave his notice and we packed up and moved back to Orlando.

In Orlando we rented an apartment at Oak Ridge Apartments. I loved, loved, loved this apartment. I was still in touch with my friends from the real estate office and could have gone back to work there but decided I was going to Martin Marietta and apply as a keypunch operator. I was hired and stayed at Martin until they had a layoff. Being a new hire, I was laid off. But before that happened, I was able to take their programming classes.

The programming was so easy for me. I really liked it but knew that if I was hired as a programmer I would wind up as Chuck's boss. I knew that would not be good for my marriage, so I never pursued the field.

We (or at least I) had so much fun in Orlando. After I was laid off, my friend Wilda Gernt and I played singles tennis every day. After tennis in the mornings, we would go for a swim and then have lunch. Wilda went home and she and her husband, Richard, came back after dinner each evening and the four of us would play doubles. This was our schedule five or six days a week.

Chuck and I were back in Orlando for about nine months when I heard from Timmy. By then, Chuck was again tired of Orlando and wanted to return to Nashville. I didn't want to go back, but he was insisting. And now I had a granddaughter in Nashville.

I had not seen Timmy since before he graduated from high school. Prior to graduation, he was working at Moore's Supermarket in Hermitage Hills. I bought him a present, and Chuck and I drove to Moore's. I went in and talked to him. We hugged and talked for quite a while. It was the first time I had gotten to hug my son in six years. I couldn't hug him enough. He walked outside and I introduced him to Chuck. The next time I would hear from him, he would be in the navy.

Later Timmy wrote me a letter from Chicago and told me that he had met a girl by the name of Jodell. She was also in the navy and they were dating. He told me she was originally from Waianae, Hawaii. I then received a letter from Jodell telling me that she and Timmy had gotten married and were expecting. They had been transferred to Annapolis, Maryland. The next letter I received from them was when we lived in Orlando and Timmy wrote to tell me about the birth of my first granddaughter, Michelle Sunshine Martin, born at Annapolis Navy Hospital. I was thirty-eight years old. Shortly thereafter, I received another letter telling me they were both now discharged and had moved back to Nashville. They had rented a trailer in Old Hickory, a suburb of Nashville.

We returned to Nashville and moved into a townhouse on Old Hickory Boulevard in Madison. I don't remember the name of the townhomes, but they are still there.

The first thing Chuck and I did after we settled down into our new home was to go and visit Timmy, Jodell, and Michelle. I couldn't wait to see my first granddaughter. We went over and knocked on the door of their trailer.

Jodell answered and we went in. We hugged and talked for quite a while. Michelle was only about six months old. I picked her up and hugged her and talked to her. When we got ready to leave, I said, "Does Grammie's baby want to go?" You have never in your life seen a child so excited and jumping like she was. I left her there that day, but I wanted them all to go with me. The trailer had really gone downhill since I had lived there shortly after I left Jimmy. There were roaches everywhere, including inside the refrigerator. I almost gagged when I saw all of those roaches. It was not a good place to live.

I liked Jodell. She was a beautiful, personable young woman. I had my reservations about her housekeeping skills but kept those to myself. I have always been a person whose house was spotless. But I knew that Jodell was my passport to knowing what was going on with Lisa and Buddy, and I was hoping she would be able to take pictures of them and give them to me.

It didn't take long for Jodell and me to devise a plan. I would buy new outfits for Lisa and Buddy, and she would take them over to Jimmy's. The plan worked like a charm. She had them try on the outfits so that she could see how they fit. Then she took pictures of the kids in their new outfits. From then on, and as long as we lived in Nashville, Jodell was my eyes and ears in Jimmy's house. She will never know my gratitude for her helping me.

Being back in Nashville also meant being with my other sets of eyes and ears, Wilma Lee, Jerry, and Peggy. Wilma played quite a few shows with Jimmy, so she saw the kids often. Jerry was usually on the road with her.

It wasn't long before Wilma Lee told me she would be playing the bluegrass festival in Adams, Tennessee, with Jimmy. I was hoping Lisa and Buddy would be going with their daddy. I told Wilma I was going in disguise. I brought out my disguise clothes, including my old blonde wig, and went to the show. I walked all around with my hat and my glasses, and no one ever knew who I was. I stood right next to Jimmy's girlfriend at the time (coincidentally named Barbara), right in front of the stage, and next to Lisa and Buddy. I took lots of pictures.

My son Ray had married Darlene Duncan and was still playing shows with Jimmy. I didn't know where he and Darlene were living, but I was hoping it wasn't with Jimmy. Jodell told me about Darlene and Ray. I assumed Jodell had told Darlene about me, because one day I received a call from Darlene. Jimmy was out of town and she wanted to come over. I quickly told her where we lived.

When Darlene got to our apartment, I thought she was the prettiest little lady I had seen in a long time. She was small—about five foot, two inches tall—with waist-length black hair. She was adorable. She played with Michelle as we talked. After she left, I was sorry to see her go, since I liked her so much. But I knew it wouldn't be long before I would see Ray.

In the meantime, my son Mike had married Cathy Chambers. It was a beautiful wedding. Mike had been in the ROTC in high school, and immediately upon graduation he had joined the National Guard. He wore his uniform when he got married, and he looked so handsome and skinny. Three months after Michelle was born, Mike and Cathy would have their first child, Hollie. Now I had two granddaughters, and I wasn't even forty years old.

Chuck and Mike had bonded at Mike's wedding. Mike felt like he had a father at long last. Chuck called Mike his son. They would remain very close for the remainder of Chuck's life. Mike still gets teary-eyed when he talks about his dad. I gave him Chuck's Cadillac and Mike treasures it. He drives it all the time.

Once Michelle was born, I was babysitting for Jodell. I didn't work, so I could take care of Michelle every day. She was already staying with us most of the time anyway. Chuck and I bought her a playpen and a high chair. I put her in the high chair when I was cooking, gave her a spoon and a plastic bowl, and told her to bake me a cake. She would stir and stir. Then when it was about time for Chuck to come home, I put her in her playpen. She stood there and waited for him. When he walked through the back door, she would start jumping up and down, waving her arms, and saying, "Dah, Dah." He was her *Dah,* not her *Daddy.* She knew the difference. To this day, he is still her Dah and she loves to cook. Michelle took her first step in that apartment, and I was lucky enough to catch it on film.

Chuck was an only child and an only grandchild. The only children he had been around were cousins. He didn't like babies. He associated them with snotty noses and cereal running out of their mouths. He had never diapered a baby either. But his opinion changed when he saw Michelle. He did everything for her and loved it. This was his little girl. He started reading her stories every night when she was only six months old, and this continued until she was in the third grade. He became her protector throughout his life, so much so that several times we almost divorced because of her.

Life was peaceful around our house. No fighting, no screaming, lots of talking and listening. I was so happy. I had Timmy back, with Michelle and Jodell, and an inside track on Lisa and Buddy. Mike was in our lives. Now I was just waiting on Ray.

Then one day I heard a knock on the door, and there was Ray. I almost fainted. I couldn't believe he was standing there. I couldn't hug him enough. He was having a very difficult time. Darlene had left him for the band's banjo player. He couldn't believe that nor could I. So he moved in with us. Now I had Mike, Timmy, and Ray in my life, and I would never let them go. I was so happy.

Ray's room faced the back, where we parked. He had made friends with a basset hound next door that he called Droops. Ray would make these crazy sounds out his window to get the dog to start howling. Droops would come over to Ray's window when he heard the sounds and just look up and howl. It was the funniest thing, and being the joker Ray was and is, he thoroughly enjoyed it. And Chuck? He loved it all too.

13

LIFE IN FLORIDA
AND THE KID/ RETURN

In October 1975 Chuck was hired by Bell Helicopter to go to Tehran, Iran. We were going to take our granddaughter Michelle with us. Our friends Dick and Wilda Gernt were already living there. They were originally from Jamestown, Tennessee, but had lived in Orlando before moving to Tehran.

In Iran, Wilda was catering for the American families living in Tehran. I was going to join her in the business. Then the shah fell and they had to leave Tehran quickly. Wilda and Dick hurriedly moved to Rabat, Morocco, and Chuck and I moved to Miami.

Ray and Timmy were going to move to Miami with us. Jodell was back from a visit to family in Hawaii, and she and Michelle were going to Miami, too. We had a plan. Once the U-Haul truck was loaded, Ray would drive the truck; Chuck and I would drive our 98 Oldsmobile, which we called the Big Red Machine—what a wonderful car—and Timmy and his family would take their Gremlin. We were going to caravan to Miami. Here come the hillbillies!

Ray was the lead vehicle on the way down to Miami. We were almost at the end of the Florida Turnpike when we saw him head off on the westbound part of the turnpike heading to Key West. We tried blowing the horn and waving but to no avail. We figured he would find out he was on the wrong road and turn around.

We decided to wait for him at the termination point of the turnpike in Miami. While there, Timmy explored the banks of a nearby canal. I didn't know what he was looking for, but I assumed it was alligators. After about twenty minutes, here came Timmy grinning like a possum. He was thrilled because he had found all kinds of like-new electrical equipment. It looked like someone had dumped their stolen merchandise in the canal. Timmy is a very lucky person. I always told him that if he fell in a bucket of shit, he would come out smelling like a rose. You remember the old saying? Well, it was true for Timmy.

In the meantime we were all laughing like hyenas, because every time we stopped for food or gas on the way down, Ray would say, "Just follow me, boys; I know the way." We teased him about that for a long, long time. In good spirits, we would say, "Ray knows the way . . . Not!"

In Miami we found a Howard Johnson's motel on LeJeune Road and checked in. We had three rooms—one for Ray; one for Timmy, Jodell, and Michelle; and one for Chuck and me. Another thing we found close to the motel was a fantastic Italian restaurant by the name of Red Diamond. We all fell in love with their food and the garlic rolls. It is no longer there, but I keep looking for it every time I go down LeJeune Road.

Chuck had to report for work on Monday, and Jodell and I were designated to look for an apartment. She and I looked all over Broward and Dade counties for an apartment. But mostly we were sightseeing. We even went to the beach in Hallandale. We were amazed to find women sitting at the beach in their fur coats, because we were both in shorts and sleeveless tops. This was before the condos were on the beach. There was only the water tower. Finally, we found and rented an apartment in Fontainebleau Park in Miami. It was a townhouse that started on the second floor, with no elevator.

Both boys began looking for a job as musicians. Timmy quickly found one with Maria and Dick Velasco and their band. They had to leave immediately to play the Hilton Hotel in Baltimore. They also needed a bass player, so Timmy suggested Ray. The only problem was that this was a pop music band and Ray couldn't read music for the bass. He could read music for the trumpet, just not the bass. Timmy and Ray sat up all night in Ray's room, and Ray learned to read the music for the bass. The next day both boys left to go on the road for six weeks. That left Chuck, me, Jodell, Michelle, and the U-Haul truck full of heavy furniture. Chuck recruited some guys from work and they helped us move in. With every piece of furniture they took off the truck, he cussed Timmy and Ray for leaving us.

The apartment had three bedrooms, so both boys and Jodell and Michelle would live with us. Once we got moved in and settled, I started back to school at Miami Dade Community College and was also attending Broward College. I would take Chuck to work in Coconut Grove each morning, and then I would head to school. Usually Michelle and I would go pick him up in the afternoon. Jodell was working as a waitress, so I took care of Michelle while she worked, and Jodell took care of her when I was in school.

When Ray and Timmy returned, Timmy and his family moved out and rented a place in Hollywood, Florida. Hollywood is about halfway between Miami and Fort Lauderdale. Timmy and Ray continued to work with Maria Velasco in clubs and venues around Miami and the surrounding areas.

One night they were playing at the Holiday Inn in Hialeah, and Chuck and I went to the show. Timmy sang "Color My World," the most beautiful version I had ever heard. Chuck, who was a music aficionado, remarked, "That is the kind of music Timmy should be singing. That was incredible." Not too long after that, Timmy and Dick Velasco had a falling out. Timmy moved on, but Ray continued to play for Maria and Dick. Even today Ray continues to be friends with Maria and calls her whenever he is in South Florida.

Timmy was then hired by Vi Velasco to play drums on the *Emerald Seas*, a cruise ship out of Miami. Vi is Maria's sister, and she didn't hold Timmy's altercation with her brother-in-law against him. After Timmy started playing on the *Emerald Seas*, he told us he could get us a family discount to go on the four-day cruise to Nassau for twenty-five dollars. Chuck and I talked about it and decided we better go before Timmy was no longer working on the ship. Good thing we did, because he only stayed on board about six months.

We had so much fun on that cruise. Timmy played his snare drum each night in the dining room to "Yankee Doodle Dandy" behind waiters carrying trays of baked Alaska. Just joking with him, I told him not to limp like they did in *Yankee Doodle Dandy*, the movie, where the drummer always walked with a limp.

Timmy then started playing music with Jerry Elmore and his band around South Florida. Jerry was a terrific person. He was also a good musician, schoolteacher, family man, and friend. Timmy, Jerry, and the band stayed together two years. Timmy and Jerry remained great friends right up until the time Jerry passed away in 2013. Timmy remains in touch with Jerry's wife, Delores, and their family. During the time they were together, Chuck and I loved going to their shows.

Ray was playing music with Maria Velasco and her husband around Miami and South Florida. They were also playing some cruise ships, and then they were booked on the *Stella Solaris* sailing out of Piraeus, Greece. They were on the *Stella* for over a year sailing the Mediterranean, Egypt, the Holy Lands, and Turkey. Ray made quite a few friends in those countries and continues to stay in touch with them. When he was playing the cruise ships out of Miami, they always came in on Saturday, and Chuck and I would go and pick up Ray. Most of the time they went right back out later that afternoon.

Timmy and Ray decided they were going to form their own band. They would call themselves the Martin Brothers. They played clubs around the area for quite a while. Then they got a contract with Carnival Cruises. At that time there were only two Carnival ships, the *Carnival* and the *Mardi Gras*. They would be on the *Carnival*.

Chuck and I were able to go on the *Carnival* for a week. We were treated like royalty because of Timmy and Ray. We were on the main deck with an outside cabin, and Chuck always had Blue Ribbon beer iced down in the trash can. The guys kept it filled to the brim. That was a great cruise and we only paid $150 for the two of us for a week.

Both Timmy and Ray had girls in every port. Ray was always introducing me to his "fiancée." One of those fiancées was Shari Arison, whose father owned Carnival Cruises. I will never forget when she told me her father worked for the cruise line, and I asked, "What does your father do?" Shari said, "He's the president." I was flabbergasted and said, "That's a good job." It was all I could think to say. I liked Shari; she was down-to-earth. But that relationship didn't last long. Ray left her for a blackjack dealer. Oh, well, we now tell Ray, "Honey, you missed that ship."

Timmy left the cruise in Puerto Rico after meeting Cindy. It would be years before he returned to Miami/Fort Lauderdale. He and Jodell divorced and he later married Cindy. Jodell continued to live near us in Plantation. Timmy and Cindy lived in Colorado for a while, where he played music. They then moved to Tennessee. They were married only a couple of years before getting divorced. Timmy stayed in the Gatlinburg area playing music at the Gatlinburg Social Club.

I loved Miami, but Chuck wanted to move to the Fort Lauderdale area—in particular, Plantation. One of his friends from work lived in Plantation. We wound up buying a house right around the corner from his friend John. Our house was located on Northwest Forty-Sixth Avenue. It was a one-story, with colonial-style pillars on the front porch, three bedrooms, two baths, a two-car garage, and a beautiful patio and pool area. We were in heaven.

Before we could move into the house, there was a lot of work to do. The people who previously had owned the house had two standard-size poodles living indoors. Fleas would attack when you walked into the house. The lady had raised orchids in the garage, and the garage door had never been opened. The backyard was covered by a trellis for hanging potted plants. The place was a jungle and had never been painted, but we got it for a bargain.

Ray tackled the backyard with a vengeance and also tore up all the carpet. Chuck worked on the garage, and I was doing the inside. The three of us worked on the house for about three weeks before we could move in, but when we did it was beautiful, with fresh carpet, tile, and paint. I had also wallpapered the kitchen and made a valance to match. And I had personally laid new tile on the front porch and stoop. I was so proud of myself, since I had never laid tile before. I go by there today and look at my tile on the front porch. It's still there.

The day we were moving into our new house (to us it was new), I was holding the front door open for Ray and Chuck as they were bringing furniture into the house. While standing there holding the door, a big lizard ran up the leg of my jeans. I started screaming and jumping around and ran for the bedroom. My screaming scared Ray and Chuck to death. Ray ran after me and into the bedroom. I was standing there jumping up and down. The lizard was running from one pant leg to the next inside my jeans. Ray said, "Mother, take your jeans off." I said, "I can't do that, Ray. You are standing there." Ray turned his back to me and said, "Now take your jeans off." I did, and the lizard ran free. We laugh about it now, but it wasn't funny at the time.

Once we were living in the house, we started riding to work in Miami with a friend of Chuck's who worked at Ryder System, John Geraci. By now

I was working as a paralegal for a large firm in Miami. One of the attorneys was Thomas Scott, who would later become attorney general for the Southern District of Florida. I loved Tom. He called me Della, after Della Street on *Perry Mason*, and I called him Turkey Scott. John was a good artist and had drawn a picture for me of a turkey judge and turkey lawyers in the courtroom. I had it framed and gave it to Tom. He loved it.

I had only been at the firm a couple of months when Tom told me he was moving to Fort Lauderdale to go to work for Clay Shaw. This was before Clay became a congressman. Tom wanted to know if I would move with him if he could get me into the firm. I told him I would. Unfortunately, Clay's firm didn't have an opening, but Tom started asking other people about a job for me. He was determined to get me to Fort Lauderdale.

A week or so after Tom had started working with Clay, I had a call from an attorney by the name of Harry Hinckley. Harry told me who he was and said, "Can you start work on Monday?" This was on a Friday. I told him, "I don't know you. Plus, I have to give notice." He then said, "I will wait for you to get here." I called Chuck and told him what was happening. That afternoon after work, Chuck and I went to see Harry.

I liked Harry and he liked me. Also, it turned out that he and Chuck were fraternity brothers at Pi Kappa Alpha, and they shared the same birthday. Karma or what? Those coincidences really sealed the deal.

On Monday I went back to work and told Joe Womack, the attorney I worked for, that I would be leaving in two weeks. I told him I was going to work for Harry Hinckley. Joe knew Harry and said if I wanted to leave earlier, I could. I did, and reported to work in Fort Lauderdale.

Working for Harry Hinckley and his colleagues, Chuck Shores and Sam Tyler Hill, would turn out to be the best job I had ever had. I loved Harry, his wife, Cathy, and the entire firm. Everyone got along, and Harry knew how to treat people. We had a receptionist, Maggie, who was about eighty-five at the time. She couldn't hear it thunder. If she was in the back making copies or whatever and the phone rang, someone, including the attorneys, would yell, "Maggie, the phone is ringing." We all loved it and her.

Harry was a generous man. On Easter, Secretaries Day, or just a whatever day, Harry would come around and give each of us a hundred-dollar bill and say, "Go buy yourself a new outfit." We received Christmas bonuses, too. And every Friday, all of us, including the attorneys, gathered in the kitchen for a late afternoon glass of champagne, or a piece of birthday cake, or some other snack, and yakked and laughed.

Harry was appointed circuit court judge, and we had one bang-up robing party at the Lauderdale Yacht Club. Chuck was mad at me that night, because Sam and I were going from one bar to another, Sam pulling me along. Then we were clogging, and that really took the cake with Chuck. He was a very reserved person and didn't like people making a spectacle of themselves. He thought Sam and I were doing just that. There were probably ten of us clogging together, and we all stayed on the dance floor at least an hour or more. I didn't care what Chuck thought. He could have joined in. We were all having such a good time. The next day, I had a whopper of a headache. I know some of the others did, too.

Harry is long gone. I went to his funeral and cried. He was a wonderful person, friend, and employer. I don't know what happened to Chuck Shores, but when I was working I would see Sam Hill from time to time. We always hugged and talked for a few minutes. Sam was equally as good a person, friend, and employer as Harry. I worked with Harry and Sam for seven years. During that time, after Harry became a circuit court judge, Sam became head of the firm.

While I worked for Sam Hill, I began receiving calls from Lisa. This all happened because my sister Billie and her husband, Woody, went to a show Jimmy was playing in Michigan. Ray was playing with Jimmy at the time. He introduced Lisa and Buddy to Aunt Billie and Uncle Woody. Lisa and Buddy then started questioning Ray about me and wanting to know what I was like. Ray told them, "Here is her phone number; call her and find out for yourselves." When I received that phone call, I thought I had died and gone to heaven.

Lisa continued to call me. When Jimmy would leave to go hunting or to look at dogs, she would call me from the neighbor's phone. Soon we were talking about Lisa and Buddy moving to Florida. But in order to do that, we had to involve Jimmy's sixteen-year-old babysitter/mistress, Teresa Sutherland. Teresa and Lisa were almost the same age. Teresa was born in September 1963, and Lisa, our daughter, was born in November 1964. (Jimmy had been born in August 1927.) It didn't take many conversations to get Teresa totally on board, not knowing at that time she had a hidden agenda. She would have Jimmy all to herself—no more kids around.

Once Teresa was involved, a plan was devised. Ray and I flew to Nashville. Teresa was going to let us know when Jimmy left the house. Ray then went and picked up Lisa and Buddy. Our plans were to fly out that night.

Ray and I flew to Nashville and got a room at what is now the Super 8 Motel on Central Pike in Hermitage. After we checked in, Ray called his longtime friend Mr. Benz to come by. He also called Charlie Cushman and J. T. Gray. Charlie and J. T. are both bluegrass musicians, and J. T. now owns the famous "Station Inn" in Nashville. At various times over the next day, all three of them visited us at the motel.

The following day, Teresa called and said Jimmy was going to be out that night. She would call us when he left, and she said Lisa and Buddy were ready. Around 8:00 p.m. Teresa called. Ray drove to Jimmy's house, picked up Lisa and Buddy, and was back at the hotel in about forty-five minutes. Ray and I were already packed and ready to go to the airport.

When they walked into the hotel room, I was never so happy in my life. We all hugged and hugged. I couldn't get over the fact that I now had *all of my children*. It had taken me ten years, but it was worth the perseverance. Ray reminded me recently that the first thing I said was "Ha, ha ha. I've got them now."

That night we flew back to Fort Lauderdale, where Chuck and Michelle picked us up and took us home. When Buddy and Lisa walked into the house, they couldn't stop talking about how beautiful it was. Our swimming pool thrilled them. The house was decorated nicely, we usually had dinner on the patio, and we went out to eat often. They were not used to living like we lived. They also weren't used to someone just coming up and hugging them. I have always been a hugger. My mother was a hugger. I will never forget Buddy sitting on the sofa in the den and saying, "I will never let anybody talk about my mother again." How I wish that had been true.

I enrolled Lisa and Buddy in Plantation High School. Buddy would now get to play junior varsity football, and Lisa joined the chorus. I took them shopping at Burdine's and Jordan Marsh and bought new clothes for them. They were happy and so was I.

At the time of Buddy and Lisa's arrival, Michelle was six years old and in the second grade. She had always been superintelligent and excelled in school. She had been the center of our attention all of her life. Now, for the first time, she had to share. That was not a good thing for her.

Our house had only three bedrooms. We now had Lisa, Ray, Buddy, and Michelle with us. We needed another bedroom desperately. We decided to turn the garage into a room for Buddy. Ray was working the cruise ships and was only home on Saturday. We sent Mother and her newest husband, Clayton (whom we despised), airplane tickets to come down and help renovate the garage.

When they arrived, Mother was thrilled to see Lisa and Buddy. She had not seen them since they had gone to live with Jimmy. I told her we wanted to turn the garage into a bedroom. No problem. It didn't take long for the job to be completed and move Buddy. By now we already knew Buddy was a slob. A friend of mine at work was making signs for children's rooms out of fabric and stuffing them. I ordered one that said "Pig Pen" and hung it on his door so that every time anyone went in or out, there it was. The garage room suited Buddy perfectly. We put an air conditioning unit in the window. Now he had his own private space.

Before we finished the garage, Ray came home and said, "Mother, I have something to tell you." I was in the kitchen making dinner. I said, "Okay, Ray, what is it?" He said, "Mother, I am going to get married." Ray was twenty-five years old, so I said, "It's about time." Well, Chuck had been cleaning the pool and listening to the conversation. He yelled and said, "What did you say, Ray?" Ray went out to the pool and told Chuck. Chuck was livid. He threw the skimmer down and said, "What the hell do you want to do that for?" Chuck didn't want him to move out of the house. Chuck loved Ray and didn't want him leaving home. Chuck was mad for a week.

I asked Mother, who was excellent at upholstering, to cover a headboard for Lisa's bed. She and I went to Cloth World and picked out a white fabric with tiny roses on it. Mother not only made a beautiful headboard and vanity stool, but she also covered them in clear plastic so that they wouldn't get dirty. Then she painted the drawers of the vanity to match the headboard and stool. Mother was a gifted artist and could do anything she wanted to do.

While Mother was in Plantation, we had a family picture made. It turned out to be a very good one. I look at it today and think of those very good times.

On November 22 Lisa turned sixteen. We bought her a new outfit and took her out to her favorite restaurant, Yesterday's. We let her order whatever she wanted, which always included escargot (she had eaten it for the first time in Fort Lauderdale at Café de Paris and loved it). It was a beautiful night, and she and Chuck danced together. That made a beautiful memory.

In the meantime, Jimmy had filed suit for the return of Lisa and Buddy. My first thought when I got served with papers was "You are now in my territory." I didn't think about it at the time, but he was living with a sixteen-year-old girl, Teresa, who, now that the kids had moved out, was no longer a babysitter. Had I thought better, his life might have turned out differently, because I would have reported it. Regardless, he didn't win. Lisa and Buddy would stay with me. And he could keep his sixteen-year-old.

Before we answered the petition, Sam, my boss, asked me about Jimmy. I told Sam that Jimmy was an alcoholic—functioning during the day but had to have those drinks at night. I pulled up his driving record from the State of Tennessee. I had no more than brought it up on the screen when it disappeared. I tried getting it back up and couldn't. I then called the State of Tennessee to explain that we needed his driving record for a lawsuit in Fort Lauderdale. I was told that they had no record of him having a driver's license. The records were gone. I told Sam about it and he was amazed. I said it was a typical example of Jimmy Martin's political power at the time. I knew that Jimmy was paying off some political people in Nashville, because Ray and Timmy had told me. They had seen him doing it numerous times. He also had friends who were judges and attorneys.

Once the petition was served, I knew I had to tell Chuck that I had never been married to Jimmy. I had never told him, and I knew he would find out when we went to court. I had already told Sam Hill, and it wasn't a big deal with him. I was hoping it would be the same with Chuck. *Not so!* I had never seen Chuck so mad in my life. He was pacing like an animal around the patio. I thought he was going to divorce me. I just sat there. Finally he came over, sat down with me, and said, "Do you have anything else to tell me?" I said, "No. That's it." He put his arms around me and gave me a kiss and a hug. He was okay.

I came home from work one day and Lisa was sitting and watching TV. She looked like she was pissed. I asked her, "What's wrong?" She said, "You're not supposed to be married to Chuck; you're supposed to be married to my daddy." I said, "Lisa, if I were not married to Chuck, I still wouldn't be with your daddy." That ended that conversation and it never occurred again.

Christmas 1980 was absolutely wonderful. We had our usual huge tree standing in the living room. Chuck, Lisa, Buddy, and Michelle all decorated the tree. I made homemade boiled custard and started baking. We had lots of Christmas presents around the tree. I always had a Christmas present, usually a large box, beautifully wrapped with no name on it. It would drive the kids crazy. They couldn't wait until Christmas morning to see who got the no-name present. It was someone different each year. After we opened the presents on Christmas morning and picked up all the paper, Lisa, Michelle, and I started dinner and set the table in the dining room. It was the best Christmas of my life. I had my children back.

Everything was going well until one of Jimmy's fans showed up in Fort Lauderdale and called Lisa. Lisa wanted to know if she could go and spend the night at their house. They had a place on the east side. I told her she could go, but I would take her over there so that I could meet them. That was a huge mistake on my part.

After Lisa returned the next afternoon, she went in and was going to pack her clothes to go to Ohio with these people. She knew their son, who was in the service. She said, "I'm going to marry him and we're going to have five kids." I said, "No, you are not. The only place you are going is back to your father." I then called Jimmy, and the first thing he said was "I don't want to talk to you, Barbara." I said, "This is about our daughter, and you *are* going to talk to me." I told him what was happening and said I was putting Lisa on a plane to Nashville that night.

Lisa ran into my bedroom, then closed and locked the door. I asked her numerous times to open it, but she wouldn't, so I kicked it in. She was yelling and screaming at me that she was going to Ohio. I got her on the floor, sat on her, and held her arms to make her listen to me. I said, "You are *not* going to Ohio, but you *are* going to Nashville. We don't live like this, and you are not going to cause all this chaos and tension. You will not go to Ohio and get married at sixteen years old." She was on the plane to Nashville that night. The next time I saw her was at her high school graduation. After her graduation, she returned to Fort Lauderdale. She was going to go to the University of Tennessee at Martin in the fall. In the meantime, she worked for a law firm over the summer. I knew the manager of Conrad, Scherer & James and was able to get her an interview. Lisa excelled at her job and loved the legal field. She would have made an excellent lawyer.

We had such fun over the summer. Lisa, Michelle, and I went shopping and bought clothes for Lisa to go to college and for Michelle to start fourth grade. Plus we had so many good times just swimming and being together on the patio. I thought, "Why did we have to waste two years before we were able to enjoy each other's company?" And, "Why did I let her spend the night with those people from Ohio?" That second question, I could answer: because I didn't want to be like Jimmy Martin and never let her do anything.

Despite all the problems we had in adjusting to each other over the years, I wouldn't trade getting my kids back for the world. Would I have done some things differently? Absolutely! I felt so guilty about the years we had lost that I gave everything I could to them and to Michelle. I let them manipulate me, almost ruin my marriage, and practically break me before I woke up one day, and said, "Why am I doing this? You are stupid. This has to stop." And I stopped it. I stopped feeling guilty. It wasn't my fault that I had not been able to see my kids or participate in their lives. Those hundred-dollar bills Jimmy was doling out to pay off people in the justice system (if you want to call it that) and Jimmy's revenge for my leaving him had been the cause of it. Timmy and Ray had seen the payoffs and knew who had been paid. I had nothing to feel guilty about as far as Michelle was concerned. Chuck and I had given her everything, including private school, dance lessons for eleven years, a home, love, and advantages none of the others had. No more guilt!

14

LETTING GO OF JIMMY MARTIN

Chuck and I were on our way home from London, England, in March 2005. We had spent a week with our friends Peter and Jan Mitchell, who lived in Weymouth. Peter was having a party to celebrate his seventieth birthday, and I didn't want to miss it. Peter and Jan are like my brother and sister. We met in China at a train station around 1990 and are best friends to this day.

On our way back home, Chuck and I had to change planes in Detroit, and we had quite a wait before boarding for Fort Lauderdale. We were sitting there when my phone rang. It was my son Buddy. Buddy said that Jimmy's bladder cancer, which had been diagnosed approximately a year earlier, had spread and he had been put in hospice. There was no hope for him. Buddy was in Nashville and said he had called Jimmy's ex-wife, Teresa, to let her know. I told him that calling her was a very big mistake and that it would come back to haunt him.

At the same time, I told Buddy about a friend of mine, whom Buddy knew, whose mother had had bladder cancer. A noted urologist from the University of Miami had performed surgery on her and made something called a neobladder. I didn't know the specifics, but I do know it involves making a bladder by taking out a part of your intestine. My friend's mother is still alive and well, and it's been about twelve years since her surgery. I told Buddy to tell Jimmy about the procedure. I could get in touch with the doctor for them. I don't know if he ever discussed it with Jimmy or if it was too late for surgery once Jimmy found out the cancer had spread.

Jimmy went home from the hospital under hospice care. The only thing anyone could do now was to make him comfortable. Lisa took a week off from work to care for her father. Buddy was there from Florida. Ray lived close by and was there on a daily basis. Ray had been going to Jimmy's house almost daily for years. Jimmy's and my granddaughter Michelle came from Hawaii to be with him too.

During the time the family was with Jimmy, numerous visitors came by to see him, including Bob and Sonny Osborne, Little Jimmy Dickens, Marty Stuart, Eddie Stubbs, and many more. He received a solitary rose in a vase from the Grand Ole Opry. Jimmy was very happy with the flowers people sent and that people came out to see him. The single rose meant more to him than anything—it was acknowledgment.

By the end of February, Teresa arrived at Jimmy's home. Jimmy and Teresa had been divorced seven years and she had gone on to have another relationship. She had two sons through this other relationship.

Jimmy had signed a will years before. Buddy read the will to Jimmy and explained what it said. When Buddy was finished, he asked his father, "Dad, is this what you wanted?" Jimmy said, "Hell, no." Until Buddy read and explained the will to Jimmy, he had not understood where his money was going after he was gone. Buddy then got in touch with a friend of Jimmy's who is a judge, and the judge referred him to Jeff Herring.

Jeff Herring is a well-known and well-respected probate attorney in Nashville. He was called to the house to prepare a last will for Jimmy. At this time in early March, Jimmy was very coherent. He met with Jeff privately and they discussed the will. On March 25, 2005, Jimmy signed the will prepared by Jeff Herring naming his son Lee (Buddy) Martin as sole trustee. Jeff Herring retained the original will.

Two weeks after arriving in February, Teresa began weaving her web to get everyone to leave the house, leaving her alone with Jimmy. The first person to go was Lisa. Lisa, being the feisty person she is, had called Teresa in Pennsylvania and told her not to return to her daddy's house. Teresa then called Buddy, who in turn called Lisa. Buddy was mad at Lisa for telling Teresa to leave. Lisa went home and Teresa returned on March 12, 2005, to Jimmy's house with her kids. On April 8, 2005, Buddy had to return to Florida to go back to work. He gave Teresa Jimmy's checkbook.

Jimmy had been put in home hospice because the cancer had spread from his bladder to other organs. During the time that all of Jimmy's children were there, accusations had been made like "Lisa is trying to kill her dad with the medication"; "You are not going to die, Jimmy. You don't need the pain medication"; and "The medication will kill you."

On April 13, 2005, Jimmy was seen in the emergency room at the Summit Medical Center in Hermitage. He was released and sent home. That same day Dwight Dillman, the current owner of Bill Monroe's festival grounds in Bean Blossom, Indiana, where Jimmy had been named "ambassador," went to Jeff Herring's office and picked up Jimmy's original will. Dwight is not a member of the family, but he supposedly did this at Jimmy's direction. Jimmy had already met with Jeff the previous month and told him what he wanted in the will. Jimmy had put Teresa in his will after asking Buddy what to do. Buddy told him to treat her like one of the kids. And he did. In a way, Teresa *was* like one of Jimmy's kids. She had been with him on and off since she was sixteen and he was fifty-three. Now his money would be split five ways.

After Buddy left for Florida, Teresa brought her two sons by another man to Tennessee along with her father. They were all living at Jimmy's house. Then Dwight Dillman, his girlfriend, and Rick Fowler started coming to the house every day. Rick came by the house occasionally while the kids were there, but Dwight and his girlfriend did not come over when the family was around.

One day Jimmy called his longtime friend Jay Hunter to ask him to pick up and install a new kitchen stove. Jay told him, "No problem. I will be over shortly." When Jay arrived at the house, Dwight got Jimmy into his car and they left. While they were gone, Jay was busy trying to get the stove installed when Teresa started trying to tell him how to do it. Jay told Teresa, "If you think you can do it better than me, here. I will go home." Shortly after, Dwight returned with Jimmy. Jimmy looked at Dwight and told him to pay Jay. That was not like Jimmy. Jimmy never asked anyone to pay his bills for him. Jay told Jimmy there was no charge. The strange part is that no one in the family knew where Dwight had taken him. Then, for Jimmy to ask Dwight to pay Jay makes one wonder if Jimmy gave Dwight money. At Jimmy's funeral, Dwight came up to Jay and again asked him how much was owed for putting in Jimmy's new stove. Jay told him, "Jimmy doesn't owe me a damn thing."

Ray was our eyes and ears to find out what was happening at Jimmy's. He would drive past there every day two or three times. He started noticing that Jimmy was going off with Dwight, but he never found out where they went.

When Dwight returned to the house with Jimmy's will, one of them (if not all) began telling Jimmy, "Buddy can sell your house and there would be nothing you could do about it." He was also told, "Buddy has stolen some of your money." Jimmy became so agitated that he called Buddy at home and asked him, "Buddy, can you sell my house?" Buddy said, "Yes, Dad, I could, but I would not." Jimmy asked him about taking his money, and Buddy said, "Dad, I have not stolen anything from you. All of your money is there."

During this time, Teresa had read Jimmy's will and found that when she died, her children would not get her share of the money. The following week, Charlie Sizemore, a local attorney and a bluegrass musician, was called to the house to meet with Jimmy and draw up a codicil to the will. Charlie went and told Jimmy he could not do that. (Later, when the will was being contested, Charlie would testify, "I saw what was happening and did not want to be a part of it." Charlie is and was an ethical attorney.)

After Charlie's visit, Rick Fowler called his friend Grant Smith, another local attorney in Springfield, and asked him to come and meet with Jimmy, which he did. After the meeting, Grant prepared a codicil that added Teresa's two sons and also added Rick Fowler and Dwight Dillman as co-trustees with Buddy. Jimmy gave Grant Smith all of his financial papers. Those papers have never been returned to the family.

On May 1, 2005, Teresa wrote a check from Jimmy's checkbook for five thousand dollars payable to Grant Smith with a note on the check saying, "For the benefit of Jimmy Martin Estate." That same day, she wrote two additional checks to Grant Smith—one for twenty-five hundred dollars with the note "Attorney Fees" and another for two thousand dollars with the note "For the benefit of Teresa Martin." On May 10 another check was written for three thousand dollars, but payment was stopped. From the first time Grant Smith visited Jimmy, he either went to the house or to the hospital every day for the remainder of Jimmy's life.

Jimmy was admitted for the final time to Summit Medical Center around the third week of April 2005. During this hospitalization, Grant Smith prepared and had Jimmy sign a form that revoked Buddy's durable power of attorney. On that same day, Jimmy also signed a codicil granting power of attorney for health care to Teresa Martin and to Grant Smith. And an alternate power of attorney was signed and given to Rick Fowler. All of these documents were signed in the hospital. They were prepared by Grant Smith and notarized by either Grant or his wife.

During Jimmy's hospitalization, our son Ray and his wife, Susan, were denied visitation. This was a devastating blow to Ray, because he had always been very close to his dad. Ray called Buddy and me. I sat up all night thinking about what we could do. The following morning, I called Buddy and said, "We need to file a conservatorship over Jimmy to get those people out of the hospital." Buddy and I flew to Nashville that day.

Jimmy's good friend Jay Hunter was also denied visitation. Jay pushed them aside and told them, "Jimmy is my friend and I am going in to see him. To hell with you," and went in to Jimmy's room. As Jay tells it, he didn't stay long, because he knew they were going to call hospital security to make him leave. Jay was at the hearing to appoint a conservator and was ready to testify.

Another one of Jimmy's good friends, Red Roberts, was also denied visitation. Red had been with Jimmy when he first learned he had bladder cancer. Red had also gone with Jimmy and driven him to and from his chemotherapy treatments. Not being able to see him now was a devastating blow to Red. Jimmy and Red had fished together and had been buddies for over fifty years. The good news is that Red did get to see Jimmy before he died. Red testified at the hearing to get a conservatorship over Jimmy.

Nancy Cardwell, formerly with the International Bluegrass Association, had written articles about Jimmy and they were friends. She lived nearby in Donelson and had visited with Jimmy on several occasions at his home in Hermitage. Nancy was there at Jimmy's hospital room the night Ricky Skaggs came to see him. Jimmy had been angry with Ricky at one time because Ricky didn't want to record a particular song with him. Now Ricky wanted to make things right between the two of them and told Jimmy that the reason he hadn't wanted to record the song with him was that the key was too high, and he simply couldn't sing as high as he used to when he was a younger man. Jimmy accepted Ricky's explanation, and the two of them talked and prayed together before Ricky left the hospital room.

In April 2016, I attended a show at the Parker Playhouse in Fort Lauderdale starring Ry Cooder, Sharon White, Cheryl White, and Ricky Skaggs. The show was fantastic, and the harmony between Ricky, Sharon, and Cheryl White was incredible. When I heard Ricky sing the high tenor part, I thought back to what he had said to Jimmy in the hospital. I think he was appeasing Jimmy to keep him from being upset. I thought what he told Jimmy was very nice and pacified Jimmy in his dying days.

On May 9, 2005, Jimmy's sister Hazel and her son, Terry, came to Nashville from Morristown, Tennessee, to see Jimmy before he passed. Hazel and Terry were denied admittance to Jimmy's room. Buddy, Ray, and I met Hazel and Terry at Famous Dave's in Hermitage. Hazel was devastated that she could not see her brother. The next time she would see him, Jimmy was in his casket.

Buddy called Jeff Herring before we left Fort Lauderdale to ask about getting a conservatorship over Jimmy. Jeff didn't do that kind of work, so he referred Buddy to Kathy Everette, another attorney in his office. That same day, Buddy called Kathy and arranged for her to meet us at our hotel. We then called Lisa and Ray and asked them to come to our room to meet with Kathy.

That evening Kathy Everette came to our room and met with Buddy, Lisa, Ray, and me. At the time, Timmy was living in Florida and wasn't available in person, so we put him on a conference call. We explained to Kathy what was going on and why we needed a conservator appointed as soon as possible. We needed an emergency hearing. Kathy was retained. On May 10, 2005, Judge Randy Kennedy issued letters of conservatorship over Jimmy and appointed Cliff Sobel as conservator.

Later that day at Summit Medical Center, Grant Smith and Cliff Sobel arrived at the hospital at the same time. I thought this was suspicious—the newly appointed conservator and the person who had persuaded Jimmy to sign papers arriving at the same time. My legal training told me something wasn't right. It looked too much like the "good ole boys" getting together.

When they got to Jimmy's room, Buddy told Grant Smith that Grant would no longer be Jimmy's attorney. Grant immediately requested a competency hearing on Jimmy so that Jimmy could sign a second codicil. The second codicil to Jimmy's will was never produced. We still don't know what Grant was trying to put in the second codicil, since the first one only added Teresa's children along with Dwight Dillman and Rick Fowler as co-trustees with Buddy.

Teresa Martin was served with a legal order to stay away from Jimmy Martin, and she was removed from his house by the process server. Her father, who was still staying in Jimmy's house, was also removed. Once she was served, Teresa was in such a hurry to get the papers, as well as one of Jimmy's guitars and other items she had stored in Jimmy's limo, which always stayed in the driveway, that she jumped into the limo and sped away, forgetting her kids and her father.

All of this was going on—the greed to get Jimmy to sign his money and properties over to people outside the family—while he lay there dying. But in order to do that, they, including Teresa, Dwight and his girlfriend, and Rick, had to alienate and isolate Jimmy from his children. They were able to do that by denying them access to Jimmy in the hospital. No one was allowed to visit him unless they said it was okay. They had someone sitting with him day and night, making sure no one in the family could talk to him.

The greed and isolation didn't stop there. They were telling Jimmy that he wasn't going to die and that he didn't need the pain medication. Despite his pain, they also fired hospice. When Buddy asked Dr. Beckman, Jimmy's doctor, "Why was Dad taken off hospice?" the doctor just shrugged his shoulders. He was no longer dealing with the family but with outside influences.

I never went to Jimmy's room to see him or try to make amends. I could have gone, but I didn't want to upset him on his deathbed. So I sat in the lobby and waited on Ray and Buddy. I was only there in support of my children and to write checks for whatever they needed.

After Teresa was barred from the hospital, Buddy and Ray sat beside their father in the hospital every day and night. Jimmy never asked about Teresa, Dwight, or Rick. He was very happy that Buddy, Ray, and Lisa were there, and his friends also came over to see him. Jay Hunter sat with him the night before he was moved to hospice. Jimmy was always afraid of dying alone. He even had stated to the doctors and nurses that he did not want to be alone. Now he had nothing to fear, for his children were all there, except Timmy, who was working in Florida. They were the ones who had loved him and only wanted love from him.

During those two short months of March and April 2005, Jimmy was physically and mentally abused. He was manipulated—pain medication was withheld and hospice was fired. He was brainwashed by people who put suspicions in his head—that his family had stolen his money and that his daughter was trying to kill him. This brainwashing would have been difficult enough for a healthy person to undergo, much less a man who was seventy-seven years old. He was already afraid of dying alone. To continually tell him lies in order to alienate him from his family and friends was inhumane. All just to get his money! How does one live with oneself after doing something like that?

Before he was taken to hospice the final time, Jimmy told Buddy he had signed some papers. Buddy said, "Don't worry about it, Dad." Buddy didn't want to upset Jimmy. That was his love for his dad.

Jimmy Martin died on May 14, 2005, at the age of seventy-seven. The world lost a fantastic entertainer, and my children and grandchildren lost their father and grandfather.

After Jimmy died, Buddy called me and wanted me to come to Nashville to be with Timmy, Lisa, Ray, and himself. I talked to Chuck, and he agreed that I should go and be with them. I was still working part-time and had payroll obligations to make. I talked to my boss and told him I had to go to Nashville. I prepared the payroll for two weeks, grabbed my laptop, and headed to Tennessee.

Jimmy had been taken to the Phillips-Robinson Funeral Home on Gallatin Road. He had been friends with Gale Robinson and his father, Gale Robinson Sr., for years. Gale Jr. is a judge in the Metropolitan Nashville Courts. His father was also a judge until his death. Buddy and I met with Gale Jr. to make the arrangements.

Jimmy had always told everyone that his funeral and everything was paid for. All they had to do was bury him at Spring Hill Cemetery. As it turned out, he had paid for only the marker and the plot but nothing else, including the embalming, casket, opening and closing of the grave, and the container. Again I was there with the checkbook.

Jimmy's body was moved to Hermitage Hills Baptist Church for viewing. It was the church where Timmy and I had been baptized at the same time, so it was like coming home to walk into the church. All of Jimmy's family from Sneedville attended the viewing. Earl and Louise Scruggs sat with me. I think every bluegrass musician in Nashville came except Bob and Sonny Osborne. I know that Marty Stuart and Connie Smith, Doyle Lawson, J. D. Crowe, and Eddie Stubbs were there as well as many other people.

While I sat in the front row with Louise and Earl, I looked over at Jimmy in his casket. At that moment I felt so sorry for him, because he could have had a wonderful life instead of one filled with the pain and heartbreak caused by alcohol, women, and his insecurities. He had spent his life chasing a dream to be on the Opry, and when he found out that wasn't going to happen, he began digging a hole and putting up a defensive "I don't care" wall that he could never overcome. Looking at Jimmy now, I didn't feel any love, only sympathy and heartache for him and for our children, who had lost their father.

The funeral service was held at Cornerstone Church on Old Hickory Boulevard in Madison. The huge church was filled to capacity with country music artists, bluegrass music artists, radio and television personalities, the Nashville legal community, family, and fans. My sister Billie came, even though she was very ill at the time, pale as a ghost, and walking with a cane. I was so proud of her. The entire service was filmed. I have never seen the film, produced by George Goehl, but would like to have a copy.

Buddy, who is a terrific speaker and writer, led the service. Several groups sang hymns, and Timmy sang, a cappella, "Lord, I'm Coming Home." There wasn't a dry eye in the house. It was beautiful. Timmy told me he had spent the night before sitting in the field behind Jimmy's house alone, rehearsing the song. He said, "I wanted it to be perfect, because Dad would be mad if I messed it up." I cried. Jimmy's casket was taken out of the church as his Decca recording of "The Last Song" was played.

Jimmy was laid to rest at Spring Hill Cemetery in Madison. His neighbor across the street in the cemetery is Roy Acuff. Hank Snow is nearby. Louise and Earl Scruggs, Kitty Wells, and Johnnie Wright have since departed and are buried nearby. Our grandson Michael James Martin, Timmy's son, who was killed by a hit-and-run driver while riding his bicycle, is resting behind his grandfather, together with my mother, grandmother, and my daughter-in-law Susan's mother, Jimmie Dean Browning. I will be nearby when my time comes. The cemetery will be jumping then.

You would think that once Jimmy died, it would be a simple matter of probating his will. Not! *Nothing* was ever simple with Jimmy Martin.

Almost immediately after Jimmy's death, Grant Smith filed the codicil to the will he had written in probate court. The case was assigned to Judge Randy Kennedy, who is the only probate judge in metropolitan Nashville and Davidson County. This is a county of almost two million people with *only one* probate judge for its entire population. There is something wrong with this picture.

Buddy asked Gale Robinson for the name of a good attorney we could retain to represent Jimmy's and my children. Gale recommended John Reynolds. He's a nice guy, but nice guys finish last. This is one of those times we should have been careful about what we asked for.

During one of the hearings, it was brought to the court's attention that Grant Smith—the attorney who had drawn up the powers of attorney and the codicil to the will and who had a second codicil in the wings waiting—was listed as a witness, meaning he had a conflict of interest. The court agreed but continued to allow Grant Smith to participate in the trial anyway. And the court continued to pay him. During the forty years I worked as a paralegal, witnesses did not go into the courtroom until after their testimony. And furthermore, witnesses were never paid.

Grant claimed he was Jimmy Martin's attorney, but Buddy had already fired him and a conservator had taken over. He represented no one. Teresa had her own attorney, George Duzane, who worked on a contingency fee. George also had a conflict of interest, because he had represented Ray in a divorce. Now he would be representing Teresa against Ray. Judge Kennedy did not see a conflict there.

The last I heard, Grant was paid $88,388.92 by the court and $9,000 by Teresa Martin written out of Jimmy's checking account. There have been other payments since that time, not including payments Jimmy made to him. I never saw the bills, so I couldn't swear this was true, but family members have related this information to me. And remember, Grant was a witness who should not have been participating in the lawsuit and should not have been paid.

The matter went to trial the end of July 2009 before Judge Kennedy. Remember, he is the only probate judge in Davidson County, Tennessee. The testimony was clearly in favor of the Martin children. Attorney Jeff Herring testified about going to Jimmy's house and meeting with Jimmy privately, following his instructions in preparing the will, and Jimmy signing the will.

Charlie Sizemore, a well-respected and ethical attorney in Davidson County, testified about the scene at Jimmy's house when he went to meet with Jimmy about preparing the first codicil. He testified as to Jimmy's mental and physical condition at the time and about the people at the house. He advised the court that he could see what was happening in Jimmy's house and that he wanted no part of it.

Despite all the witnesses' testimony and the law in Tennessee favoring the Martin children, Judge Kennedy ruled against both the Martin children and Teresa. He allowed Cliff Sobel to continue acting as trustee, and further he allowed Grant Smith to continue as an attorney and awarded him additional attorney's fees. This ruling and waste of Jimmy Martin's hard-earned money is a disgrace to the court system.

There was so much going on in this case from day one. The attorney representing the family, John Reynolds, was late on everything he had to file. He never put up an argument at any of the hearings either myself or the family attended. All of this is in the transcripts of the hearings and depositions on file. If you go to the Davidson County courthouse and review the transcripts on file, which are public records, you will agree.

In the beginning of the case, I was in constant contact with John Reynolds. Buddy, Lisa, Timmy, and Ray authorized me to assist John in their case. I sent letters to John, outlined the medical records, did a timeline, and offered to do a PowerPoint presentation for the trial but was told it wasn't necessary. None of the information I had sent nor the pleadings or suggestions were ever used. Eventually I was cut off from receiving transcripts and pleadings. This happened shortly after John sent me a transcript of one of the hearings. I went through the transcript, pointed out the errors, and made comments. That had been my job for almost forty years as a paralegal. I knew what should or should not have been done. One would think an attorney would use that knowledge, especially since they could get it for free. I think I was cut off because I knew too much.

It is now 2017, twelve years after Jimmy died, and the probate of Jimmy's will and the codicil he signed is still being held up by the courts. Even after a lengthy trial with all the testimony favoring the Martin children, Judge Kennedy refused to name Buddy as administrator. Clifton Sobel remained as the court-appointed trustee until the new trustee for Jimmy's estate brought a lawsuit against him for malpractice.

Many thousands of dollars were paid—more than two hundred thousand dollars, not including the amounts paid by Lisa, Buddy, Timmy, Ray, and

Teresa to their individual attorneys. Lisa and Buddy paid John Reynolds eighty-five thousand dollars. Timmy paid around ten thousand dollars. Ray refused to pay and took the matter before the Tennessee Bar Association. We do not know the amount of money that has been paid to the court-appointed trustees, who have done nothing, including forcing the return of Jimmy's mandolin from Tim Dillman, Dwight Dillman's brother. Jimmy had loaned the mandolin to Tim prior to his death but had left it to Lisa in his will. Tim claims that Jimmy gave him the mandolin. But if that were so, why did he give it to Lisa in his will signed on March 25, 2005, just two months before his death? Ray was there when the mandolin was *loaned* and is a witness to the transaction.

The money that has been squandered on attorneys' fees, court costs, and fees for court-appointed trustees was a direct result of greed. If Teresa had not been greedy and wanted her two children in the will, as well as having Dwight and Rick involved, that money could have been split five ways. Her children would have benefited more with that split than by trying to put them in the will. Buddy was the one who called and told her Jimmy was dying. And he is the one who allowed Teresa to stay there while he sent his sister home. Why couldn't she trust him to do the right thing? No, instead she threw her alliance to Dwight Dillman and Rick Fowler, two people who had no business involving themselves in family matters. As a result, she cost herself, Lisa, Buddy, Timmy, and Ray a lot of money and heartaches. Her actions benefited no one but the court and the attorneys.

Jimmy scrimped and saved and worked hard to accumulate his estate during his lifetime while living like a pauper. Promotion of Jimmy Martin, his records, and films lies dormant; nothing in that regard has been done since he has been gone. This in itself is a tragedy. What happened to the estate of Jimmy Martin and his children was not fair. They did not receive justice.

15

THROUGH IT ALL, NO REGRETS

Today I sometimes sit and think about the men I have loved and the "what ifs" of my life. Whenever I loved someone, I loved them with all my heart. The love for that person never completely went away. With Laney Cobbolino, I did hear about him from my sister Billie, who lived in Detroit and saw him occasionally. With Jimmy Martin and Bob Osborne, I saw them on TV or heard about them from my children. My love for Bob was a different kind of love from what I had for Jimmy. With Bob there was also friendship. My heart still does a little pitter-patter when I think about him. If I could say anything to him after all these years, I would say, "I hope you are healthy. I hope you are happy. I wish you a long life." And as the old 1920s song asks, "Do you ever think of me?"

It is always so easy to look back and see what you should have, would have, or could have done with your life by the choices you made. But at the time, and particularly if you are still young, absolutely no one can tell you that you are making a mistake. I am not blaming my mistakes on being young, even though I think my youth was a contributor. I take full credit for each and every decision I have made, whether it was good or bad. I know I hurt a lot of people with some of my decisions, including my children.

Leaving Jimmy when I finally did was something I felt I had to do. I knew that he could make a mistake and choke me to death without meaning to do so. Don't get me wrong. Jimmy was not always vicious. He could be the most caring, tenderhearted man in the universe. He was a kind man who would help anyone. His problems were almost always associated with his drinking. His mental problems were self-induced by things he didn't understand—things like being passed over for the Grand Ole Opry. He would have never said he thought his drinking and moral problems were reasons for that. Because of his inability to look at himself and his actions clearly, he started saying, "I'm not good enough to be on the Grand Ole Opry." The old saying "The best offense is a good defense" is what he was doing. He was getting at the Opry people before they got to him.

The groups the Opry was hiring were family-oriented. They were not drunks. They didn't beat their wives and kids. And they didn't brag about how good they were or how bad they were. If Jimmy had been able to stop and think about all of those things, I think his life would have turned out differently; the problem was that he didn't have the education or the ability to do so. While Jimmy was very intelligent with a lot of common sense, he didn't have that capability.

When Jimmy and I were together, it was a roller-coaster ride. There was never a day during the entire time I lived with him when I felt like he loved me. Do I think he loved me in his own way? Absolutely! Many people, including members of my family, tell me that he loved me. We had a great sex life, and he loved my being able to book and promote him. But he wanted to possess me like a stick of furniture. I always thought I didn't exist as a person to him, but I knew he was proud of the way I looked and my ability to book him. Thinking back, I can only remember one Christmas present he gave me: a five-dollar manicure kit. I almost cried—not from happiness, but from disappointment. I just thought he could have gotten me something a little nicer and more personal. I am sure there were other things he bought me, but just not at Christmas. Jimmy's Christmases when he was growing up were nothing like mine. He thought buying a lot of presents was a waste of money. In his mind, he bought everything we needed all year round.

After I started having kids with him, I wanted a home for them. Jimmy wanted that, too. He just didn't know what it took to keep a mother and father together. He had grown up in a family that did not put their arms around him and hug him and tell him they loved him just for the hell of it. It was a farm family in the '30s: work hard, eat, sleep, and go to church. That was their lifestyle.

Here was this extremely talented singer, musician, and showman with no education and no idea of how to deal with ordinary life, keep a family together, or get on the Grand Ole Opry. Jimmy was a tormented man who thought that everyone wanted something from him or was out to steal from him. He trusted people who did just that while he didn't trust his own family. He was a control freak. He had to be in charge of the money, the house, people, everything—the whole nine yards. Say one word in opposition to what he wanted, or try to explain that what he was doing was wrong, and he would knock the shit out of you. It could be me, or his kids, or someone else. He was like a fighting rooster, ready to strike at any time.

As for our home life, I don't think Jimmy ever realized how he treated me during the time I was with him—or, from what I understand, how he treated the other women in his life. And even if he did, he would never admit it. I never thought about why he beat the hell out of me or choked me until I was blue in the face. At the time, I thought it was because he was drunk or just plain mean. I now think it was both, as well as his lack of self-esteem. He had confidence in his music, just no confidence in himself.

It took me years to realize that if I had stayed with Jimmy, I probably would have died. During the last several years before my leaving, he became more and more aggressive. Around five in the afternoon, come hell or high water, Jimmy was going to drink beer. It didn't matter who was there. Then the wait began to see what kind of mood he would be in when he came home. Sometimes he was okay, but other times he was in a rage. It was sort of like being in a rain shower and suddenly the rain turns into a violent storm. That is the way he was when he drank, and oftentimes he was that way sober.

As the old saying goes, "You get more flies with honey than with vinegar," but Jimmy didn't know that. If he had treated me with the tiniest bit of respect, I would never have left him. I wanted to be there, not because I loved him, but because I had four children by him. I believe, though, he thought I loved him so much that I would take anything he dished out. What he didn't know was that by the time I left him, I had not been in love with or in lust for him in a very long time. I had lost all feeling for him in Wheeling.

There was a short period of time before I got pregnant with Lisa when everything was wonderful between Jimmy and me. We were talking and having fun. There was no fighting. I almost fell in love with him all over during this time. But when I got pregnant with Buddy, all of those good feelings were lost once again. Again he became a person I didn't like. At that point I would no longer take his abuse. Regardless of what it cost me, I had to get away.

Jimmy's escapades with Bill Monroe's daughter, Melissa, were the beginning of his not being brought into the Grand Ole Opry family. Subsequently, his abuse of alcohol, his constant crying about not being on the Opry, his abuse of his family, and, most importantly, the vulgar, foul-mouthed person he became were all factors that led to his not being made a member. I know he said, "They think I'm not good enough to be on the Opry." That defensive, looking-for-sympathy statement did nothing for me. He knew and I knew why he was not on the Opry. His behavior had caused that.

I once read an article where Opry manager Bud Wendell was asked how he went about deciding on hiring new acts to become members of the Opry. He stated—and this is not a direct quote—that he looked for people who could be counted on to be there and to give a good performance. Stable, dependable people. Jimmy Martin was not stable. You could depend on him to be at his job, drunk or sober, but that was the problem: drunk or sober he went onstage. The last time he made a guest appearance on the Opry, they literally had to drag him off the stage. Ray told me how embarrassing it was. I was also told the same story by someone, not a musician, who works at the Grand Ole Opry.

Jimmy was an extraordinary entertainer. He knew how to teach music even though he could not read music. I saw him more times than I can count showing a banjo player or a mandolin player how to get the correct rhythm for a song or where to make an emphasis. With our kids, he would sit for hours singing and teaching them. He liked to show people how to play and how to sing. Then he could brag about it. And he would brag to everyone who would listen.

In 2000 or 2001 I took my grandson Michael Martin to see his grandfather play at a festival in Dunellon, Florida. Ray had left tickets for us to get into the show. Of course when we got seated, Michael wanted to immediately go and see his grandfather on the tour bus. Michael was about twelve or thirteen at the time, and I felt it would be perfectly safe for him to go to the bus alone. Plus, I could see all around. I continued to watch the show. Michael returned to his seat when Jimmy was getting ready to go on stage. Rhonda Vincent was the act ahead of Jimmy. I noticed that after she ended her show, half of the audience left, and they did not return when Jimmy took the stage. Even though I had not been with Jimmy for many years, the audience's walking out on him bothered me. I felt sorry for him. He was sober that day and gave a good performance, but his reputation had preceded him.

While Michael and I were in Dunellon, Jimmy hung back and looked at me from a distance. He had done this in Alabama as well when my son Mike and I had attended a show there. At that show Ray again left tickets for us. Also at that show, while introducing the band, Jimmy said, "This is my son Ray Martin. You can see how good-looking he is. His mother was beautiful." Ray then popped up and said, "And she still is. She is sitting right over there." I thought Jimmy was going to lose his teeth, because his mouth fell open so far. He had not known I was there. After the show, Jimmy was very friendly with Mike, but he never spoke to me.

I often think about what a wonderful life Jimmy and I and our kids could have had together. We could have been the best family band and singers around. There is Timmy, who plays drums and has a beautiful country music voice. Ray plays mandolin, bass guitar, and sings. And Lisa is also a terrific singer. Together they had beautiful harmony. Even Buddy, who is an excellent writer and master of ceremonies, could have joined in. And I was a fantastic booking agent and manager. We could have had it all. Had we been able to accomplish this, I believe Jimmy most likely could have been on the Opry.

Some time ago I spoke to Alan Munde, who had played banjo with Jimmy. I wasn't there when they played together. I asked, "What was the most difficult part of your association with Jimmy?" He said, "The culture." He said it was a complete culture shock after he went to work for Jimmy. Alan is college-educated, as are his mother and father. He said that Jimmy's background was foreign to him. I can definitely understand that now. But in all honesty, while living with Jimmy, I couldn't see that we were any different. After I left him and became better educated, I saw my past life for what it was.

Now I can look back and see that Jimmy's emotions were always on the surface; whether he was having a good day or a bad day, you would know it. Jimmy told everyone about his problem with his brother Roy and how his brother had borrowed money and never repaid it. Jimmy and Roy didn't speak for many years. Before Roy died, though, they did get together with their brother, John.

At the time Roy died, Chuck and I were in France. When we returned, Lisa and Ray told me about Roy's death. I immediately called Roy's wife, Norma, and said I had just found out. She invited me to come see her. I went and spent the weekend. We had a really great time just catching up. During our conversations, I learned that Roy had treated her like Jimmy had treated me but not nearly as badly. I was shocked, because, unlike Jimmy, Roy had graduated from high school and college. I guess education doesn't always matter; it's the scars from childhood or young adulthood that pave your way as an adult or family person.

I believe that Roy's and Jimmy's mistreatment of women, whether verbally or physically abusive, or in my case both, was the result of their mother marrying again while they were so young. She then had three babies with her second husband quickly. The babies received all of the attention while Jimmy and Roy received none. I believe that subconsciously they were punishing their mother through Norma and me.

It was well known among band members that Jimmy hit and embarrassed our sons Ray and Timmy in front of them. He often criticized them on stage. Even though Jimmy probably thought this was okay, it wasn't—not with the band members nor with his audience. It became the fodder of gossip among musicians and, I am sure, the fans as well—another reason for his not being on the Opry.

Ray and Timmy tried for years to please their dad. The relationships would be okay for a while, and then something would happen to make Jimmy angry. It never took much. Even with his kids, those thunderstorms were never far away. You could be laughing and talking one minute, and then one word could set him off. The next minute you were running for cover. Ray and Timmy both carry physical and mental scars as a result of their mistreatment.

Lisa and Jimmy were like oil and water after she grew up. As a child, she was Jimmy's little angel. Then, as an adult, she could do nothing to please him, even though she continued to try desperately. The problem was that she was a woman and they were too much alike.

Buddy always wanted to play football, but Jimmy didn't want him playing. He was afraid Buddy would get hurt. I think Buddy, as the baby of the family, had it better than the other kids. He didn't seem to carry the scars and resentment the others had. When Buddy came to Florida to live with me, he finally had his opportunity to play football, and he was quite good at it. Even after high school, Buddy continued to play on the sheriff's team. Buddy's son is now a quarterback at Eastern Illinois University on a football scholarship.

Jimmy helped anyone in need. He was basically a kind person. There were times I was with him when we learned about musicians in financial trouble, who were about to lose their houses. I would talk to Jimmy, and he would tell me to call and tell them he could lend them money to save their house. One was Josh Graves. No one, including Josh and many others, ever failed to repay Jimmy for his kindness.

As the years wore on, and particularly after I left, Jimmy's drinking habits escalated. He went from drinking beer to hard liquor. He was thrown out of all the beer joints and bars in Hermitage. The liquor store where he was a regular customer sent a beautiful bouquet of flowers for his funeral. In fact, it was the largest one there. We all had a good time with that, especially Ray. Jokingly, Ray said, "Don't buy stock in that liquor store; it just went down." How many people get flowers for their funeral from their favorite liquor store?

I still think about the good days our family had together. We always enjoyed going to the lake whether we were in Michigan, Louisiana, or Tennessee. I can still see Timmy sitting in his little rocking chair trying to sing at only six months old while Jimmy leaned over, singing to him. The time we went roller skating in Shreveport and played pop the whip on skates. And when I learned to water ski. Fishing was such an important part of our lives. The horse races in Wheeling were so special, even though we threw away a lot of money. There are so many good memories: The first time Timmy sang on WWVA and how proud Jimmy and I were of him. The births of our children. Watching Jimmy perform and the crowds cheering him on. Sitting with him at the fair conventions and him helping me at the table and organizing the brochures. Being in bed together before all the animosity started. Going to see Timmy and Ray play baseball. The look on his face after Lisa won the Little Miss Nashville contest when she and I walked on stage. Those are just a few of the volumes of good times that I remember, and I often wondered where that man went. That was the man I loved and admired.

I can understand Jimmy being denied a spot on the Grand Ole Opry. He wasn't someone that you could count on arriving sober every Friday and Saturday night. Or count on going out on stage to give a good performance without rattling on and on about nothing. Or, in later years, to do his show and leave the stage. He was also known to make sarcastic remarks to other entertainers. He was the kind of man who would slap his wife or kids in front of anyone or cuss them out in public. Regardless, Jimmy was a persecuted soul, with himself as his own persecutor. He didn't know that what he was doing was wrong. I am sure he thought that other people on the Opry, including Bill Monroe, publicly ran around on their wives. But they were never punished. Then again, maybe he never thought of that aspect of his life. With Jimmy—and I am not a psychiatrist or psychologist—I believe it was all about sex. The women he met and slept with meant nothing to him. He probably didn't remember their names half the time. It was the power to get any woman he wanted that made him behave like he did. He was the star.

I believe Jimmy Martin's actions were a perfect example of what *not* to do to become a member of the Opry. I know it wasn't his music that kept him off. The embarrassment he felt after people he had worked with and who had worked for him were invited to be on the Opry when he himself was not was more than he could bear. Here was a man who had hit records like "Widow Maker" and whose music was loved around the world by those who loved music not being invited to be part of a show that he idolized. He was humiliated. Would he have admitted it to anyone? The answer is, as Jimmy would put it, "Hell, no." Jimmy was a man who might have listened if someone in power had talked to him about his actions. And he was a man who knew all those people in power.

Jimmy Martin was not the first musician who was a womanizer, who treated his family badly, or who was a drunk. Yet other musicians, like Hank Williams, George Jones, Johnny Cash, Bill Monroe (not a drunk but he did have girlfriends while he was married), were still on the Grand Ole Opry. I name these because they are the ones most people know about. Their reputations did not preclude them from being made part of the Opry family. So the question is, Why not Jimmy Martin? I believe the reason was that Jimmy had gone out with Bill Monroe's daughter—not just once but numerous times. And as Bill himself said, "Jimmy will never be on the Grand Ole Opry as long as I live." That started the war, and Jimmy's later behavior finished it.

But isn't the Grand Ole Opry supposed to be about the music? Jimmy Martin was a man of music! His entire life and his very soul were dedicated to music. He deserved to be on the Opry for his music. Now he is dead. It's too late for him to clean up his act. That dream of being made a member of the Opry can never be accomplished.

In my opinion, he should have and still could be put in the Country Music Hall of Fame. He devoted his entire life to music. He had several hit records. He was an extraordinary entertainer for fifty years with fans all over the world. His place in music history needs to be preserved. He's not here to accept the honor, but his children, his grandchildren, and his great-grandchildren are still living.

Do I feel bitterness toward Jimmy for the way he treated me all those years? Absolutely not! I wouldn't trade my time with him for anything. We had four beautiful children together. He never had that with any other woman. Did I regret leaving him? Not for one minute. My life turned out to be beautiful. I say, "Rest in peace, Jimmy Martin. You were loved!"

In the spring of 2006, Chuck and I were spending time at our house off Indian Lake Road in Hendersonville, Tennessee. Hendersonville is a suburb of Nashville, and quite a few of the people on the Grand Ole Opry live there. We were there for the sole purpose of gutting and remodeling our house. I had decided I wanted to get the kitchen cabinets resurfaced rather than replaced, since they were made of good wood from the 1970s. I called the SLI Construction Company to come out and give me an estimate for the work. A few days later a man by the name of Charles Lilly Jr. came to my house. In talking with him, I found out he had played music with my friend Billy Walker on the Grand Ole Opry. Of course, talking about the kitchen went to the wayside and we were soon totally engrossed in discussing the music business.

A couple of weeks later, my son Ray called and asked if I wanted to go with him to the Opry. I hadn't been in a long time, and I immediately said yes. Chuck didn't want to go, so I met Ray closer to the Opry, left my car, and rode over with Ray. When we walked backstage, the first person we ran into was Amy Grant. Ray introduced me to Amy and we walked with her to her dressing room, where her husband, Vince Gill, was sitting. Ray introduced me to Vince. We all talked a few minutes, and Ray and I left.

We then walked to a room where a lot of people were sitting around, mostly entertainers. I was talking with someone when Billy Walker came up, put his arms around me, and gave me a big hug. Billy and I were happy to see each other. We started talking and I told him about Charles Lilly coming to my house. We laughed about what a coincidence it was.

Billy was a popular entertainer at the Opry and a lot of people wanted to talk to him. After we were together at least an hour, I said, "Billy, all of those people are waiting to talk to you." Billy said, "I want to talk to you." I told him, "They are your fans and I am only your friend." Billy said, "I don't care. I want to talk to *you*." Billy would go, do his segment on the show, and come right back to me. He did that for the remainder of that evening.

During the time I was talking to Billy, I heard a loud voice saying, "I heard Barbara Martin is in the house. Where is she?" I walked over to Jean Shepard and Benny Birchfield and said, "I am right here." We grabbed each other and hugged. We then talked a few minutes before Jean had to go. I love that woman—and Benny, too. But Jean is just Jean. No airs about her. I am so thankful I got to see her that night.

It's amazing how things work out. This was the first time I had been to the Grand Ole Opry in several years. When I went there that night, I didn't know that I would be spending almost the entire evening with Billy Walker. I was so glad I was there, because a couple of weeks later, on May 21, 2006, Billy and his wife, Bettie; Charles Lilly Jr.; and Daniel Patton were killed in a rollover accident on their way back to Nashville from Alabama. Ray and I attended their viewings and funerals. Another sad, sad occasion in my life.

Here I am. My son Mike is married to a beautiful woman, Donna. He has three daughters and recently retired as a full colonel from the air force. Donna has a son and daughter. Two of Mike's daughters, Hollie and Brooke, graduated from the University of Alabama, and one, Rachel, graduated with a pharmacy degree from Samford University in Birmingham, Alabama, where she now teaches pharmacy. He has four grandchildren and Donna has six grandchildren, so together they have ten. This is a blended family that works. Everyone is treated as "our child or our grandchild." No one is treated as a stepchild. Education is very important in their family. Both Mike and Donna have master's degrees.

James Henry (Timmy) Martin Jr. is divorced. He has three children living and five grandchildren. His son Michael James Martin was killed by a hit-and-run driver while riding his bicycle in Fort Lauderdale. Michael is buried directly behind his grandfather at Spring Hill Cemetery in Nashville. Timmy's daughter Michelle is a realtor in Fort Lauderdale. She has two sons and a daughter. Michelle's mother, Jodell, remarried and had two more children; she lives in Wainae, Hawaii. Timmy's daughter Jamie lives in Coker, Alabama. She graduated from college in June 2015 with honors and a degree in paralegal studies. His son Jeremy also lives in Alabama. Timmy drives a tractor trailer and sometimes a bus for other entertainers. He is an excellent singer as well. He cut an album but never released it. I think it is very good and I play it all the time. Everyone who hears it wants a copy.

Ray and his wife, Susan, and their daughter live in Mt. Juliet, Tennessee, approximately five miles from Jimmy's house. Their daughter, Lindsey, is in her third year of college and is seeking a degree in art history. She is a terrific artist and entrepreneur. She already has a business selling her paintings and doing custom artwork. She is an honor roll student and teaches art to handicapped students in her spare time. Ray was employed by country artist Clay Walker for several years and in 2014 left to work with Travis Tritt. Susan is an activities director for a nursing home and has worked there for many years. The residents love her.

Lisa is married and has three children—two girls and a boy—and three grandchildren. Her oldest daughter, Sarah, graduated from Tennessee Tech University with a degree in science and a secondary degree in mathematics. She teaches eighth-grade mathematics in Gallatin, Tennessee. Sarah's husband, Nelson, is a musician. They have an adorable son, Cash. Lisa's daughter Samantha has a beautiful little girl, Braelynn. Samantha is a terrific singer. Clint, Lisa's son, has a little boy named Jaxson. Lisa is a family services coordinator for Habitat for Humanity. She teaches future homeowners how to be homeowners. Her husband, Ken Adkison, is employed by United Parcel Service. Lisa and Ken were born in the same hospital, two days apart. They went to high school together but never dated. I guess it was meant for them to be together. Their daughter Samantha sang at their wedding. They now live in Hendersonville.

Lisa graduated magna cum laude from David Lipscomb University at age forty-eight. Both she and Sarah are planning to pursue their master's degrees. She continues to sing occasionally at bluegrass festivals and is mentioned in the Bluegrass Hall of Fame and Museum for her participation on the album *Daughters of Bluegrass*. Lisa started singing with Jimmy when she was five years old. Clint also sang with his grandfather.

Lee Ease (Buddy) is married to Heather and has two children. As I wrote earlier, his son, Bud, is in college on a football scholarship and is a quarterback at Eastern Illinois University. His daughter, Chandler, is still in high school. She is on the school volleyball team as well as a traveling team. Buddy was employed for over twenty years in law enforcement and retired in 2015. He continues to be involved in football and is an offensive line coach for St. Thomas Aquinas High School. He loves being involved with kids. He and his wife are partners in a contracting business. Heather is also one of the best cooks around. They live in Weston, Florida, a suburb of Fort Lauderdale.

As for me, Chuck and I lived a wonderful life together. I grew to love him very much. He was the gentlest soul in the world and had a dry sense of humor that kept me in stitches. He loved all of my children, especially Mike and Ray. I always told him he shouldn't have favorites, but he did. He would only laugh at me and say, "I don't have favorites."

I lost my beloved husband of forty-one years on February 28, 2012. He suffered from Alzheimer's. He was in his eighth year with that dreaded, debilitating disease. One of the worst things in the world is to watch your loved one's mind slip slowly away. I watched him try to do something as simple as putting his underwear in a drawer but not being able to find the drawer. It was heartbreaking. Fortunately, he didn't die from Alzheimer's. He died in my arms of a massive heart attack. He was scheduled to go to the cardiologist on the Friday before he died. When I came home from work, he told me he had canceled the appointment because he didn't need to go. I was beside myself, because the appointment had been difficult to get.

The day he died, Chuck and I had the most amazing time. I went to my gastroenterologist that morning for a checkup, stopped at Whole Foods and picked up a couple of chicken salad sandwiches, came home, and we had lunch. During lunch, Chuck and I were talking about my retiring. I had already given notice that my last day of work was going to be March 1. I was joking around with him, and I said, "Do you think you will be able to put up with me twenty-four/seven?" He said, "I may have to take a Xanax." I said, "Maybe two or three." We laughed and laughed. Then we talked about who loved whom more and about the road trip we were planning. We had just taken delivery on a brand-new 2012 BMW 535 with all the bells and whistles. We were going to just drive wherever we wanted and stay gone for as long as we wanted to. That night, Chuck was already dressed when he woke me up and said, "Take me to the hospital." I told him, "I will call 911." He didn't want that; he wanted me to drive him. I did. And an hour later he was dead in my arms at the hospital.

I continue to live in Plantation, Florida. Life without Chuck has been difficult. Thank God, I have many, many friends in South Florida and all over the world. I am very active socially. I belong to the Italian American Club in Hollywood, the Over Fifty group at St. Gregory's Catholic Church in Plantation, the Chopin Society of South Florida, Friends of the Library in Plantation, and the American Polish Cultural Society in Miami. I am neither Italian nor Polish, but I have lots of friends who are descendants of both. That's my reason for being involved.

Chuck and I traveled the world and I still continue to do so. I have been on six of the seven continents and am looking forward to going to Antarctica.

My friends know they can call me if they need help. I am always there. I am healthy as a horse, having survived two bouts of cancer—colon in 1994 and bladder in 2013. I take no medications and I am a health-walker. Retirement didn't change me. I am still a type A personality. I have to be doing something all the time. But it keeps me younger and on my feet. That *is* what I am trying to do—stay on my feet.

16

JIMMY MARTIN'S FAMILY

On Wednesday, August 27, 1927, the temperature was bordering 71 degrees, the gully was hot, not a leaf stirring, and mosquitos were buzzing. It was a night when another member of the Martin family would be born. This time the child would become world famous when he grew up. Sneedville would honor him with signs entering the town proclaiming "The Birth Place of Jimmy Martin, King of Bluegrass."

That day, Sarah Burchett Martin gave birth to James Henry (Jimmy) Martin. His father was Ease Martin. At the time he was born, Sneedville's population consisted primarily of poor farming families. His mother and father and his three older siblings lived down a dirt road in what we would call today a shack. They were a dirt-poor family, but somehow Ease Martin had managed to obtain another piece of land up the road from where they lived. Ease had planned to build a new house for his family on the land.

Sarah Burchett and Ease Martin already had three children, Euna, Hazel, and John, when Jimmy was born. Then, in 1929, Roy was born. Roy would make five children for Ease and Sarah.

On March 12, 1931, tragedy struck the family. Ease suddenly became very ill and later that day died as a result of pneumonia and fever. Sarah was left with five small children. Jimmy was not yet four years old, and Roy was only two. They were also left with the land where Ease was planning to build a home. The father's death proved to be a devastating and lasting loss to Jimmy and his baby brother, Roy.

Fortunately, Ease's parents, John and Milly Givins Martin, lived nearby at the time of their son's death. John ran the little country store at the entrance to the road where Ease and Sarah Martin lived and where their land was situated. He would help Sarah and the children with their needs until Sarah remarried.

On November 29, 1932, Sarah married Ellis Johnson, who was four years younger than she. Ellis and Sarah had three more children, all girls—Erma, Evelyn, and Edria. Sarah and Ellis continued to live in the home where Sarah and Jimmy's father had lived until Ellis built a house on the land that had belonged to Ease. They lived in that house until Sarah's death on November 17, 1963. Even though Sarah was only sixty-one at her passing, I always thought of her as much older.

Euna, the oldest of the Ease Martin children, was eighteen when Sarah gave birth to Erma, her first girl by Ellis. Jimmy was only seven. He always told me this was a terrible time for him, knowing his mother had given birth to a baby. Over the next four years, she would give birth to two more girls. Each time she gave birth to another child, it would prove to be more and more disturbing for Jimmy. He and Roy were no longer the babies; they were now middle children. The precious little time they previously had spent with their mother would now have to be shared with the babies. Jimmy would carry this resentment the rest of his life.

After Jimmy's grandmother, Milly Givins Martin, died, his grandfather, John, continued to live in the Martin family home with his sisters, Net and Maud. The Martin family home was a white, two-story, Civil War–era house with a front porch that ran the length of the house. A balcony ran across the entire second floor. The house had two chimneys and two front doors. We always went in the door on the left side. When you walked into the living room, which also had a bed in it, there was a big fireplace on the left. This is where we sat in the hard-backed wooden chairs. I don't believe I ever went past the living room, but I do know that the kitchen was behind that room.

Net and Maud were both what the folks referred to as "old maids." They were sweet little old ladies, looked and dressed like Mother Whistler except for the bonnet, and always had a toothless grin. Net had a huge goiter on her neck. Jimmy was crazy about his two old maid aunts. We never failed to go to Sneedville without stopping to see them. Jimmy would start singing and joking with them as soon as we walked through the door. We usually stayed a couple of hours, sitting, laughing, and talking. Net and Maud lived in the Martin family home until their deaths.

All of the children from the original Martin family—Euna, Hazel, John, Roy, and Jimmy—are deceased. Jimmy's brother John and his sisters, Euna and Hazel, all married and raised their families in and around either Sneedville or Morristown, Tennessee. Roy Martin joined the air force, and when he returned home, he married and moved to Anderson, Indiana. He and his wife had four children. He was the only one of the Martin children who graduated from high school and went to college.

Several years ago my son Buddy called me to say he had someone he wanted me to meet. When I arrived at his house, I was introduced to his "cousin," Brenda. When I asked whose child she was, I was told that her father was Roy. I then called Norma, Roy's wife, who told me Roy always said Brenda was not his. But later on I spoke to Thelma, Roy's aunt, who knew Brenda's mother, Dot, and Dot's mother. Thelma said, "Well, the family secret is finally out." Thelma had known about Brenda since Dot was pregnant.

Brenda is a wonderful person. She is married and, ironically, her husband worked at the courthouse in Fort Lauderdale, across the street from where I worked for thirty years. I would often see him at the courthouse whenever I went over. But I didn't know that he was married to my children's cousin. Brenda is a beautiful lady. She has four children, all successful and living in Plantation. She has lived within a mile of Buddy and me for over thirty years. You just never know who is around the corner. She has not been accepted by her brothers and sisters. Her mother passed away recently.

Thelma Burchett Fields is the baby sister of Jimmy's mother, Sarah. Thelma was married to Oscar, who passed away several years ago. They have two children. For over forty years, Thelma and Oscar worked for General Motors and lived in Flint, Michigan. Thelma is now into her nineties and lives in the Morristown, Tennessee, area near her daughter. She is a sassy lady, smokes long cigarettes, and drives her new Buick sports car to the beauty shop in Sneedville to get her hair done. She lives alone and does her own housework and cooking. In September 2015, I spent a couple of wonderful days with Thelma and we toured Sneedville. It was sad to see the old Martin family home torn down, as well as the house that Ellis Johnson built. I was fortunate enough to go to the beauty shop with her, but I did the driving.

In October 2016, I again visited Thelma for two days. We again went to the beauty shop in Sneedville. The beauty shop is owned by Dorothy Gibson (my maiden name is Gibson). Dorothy and I became acquainted and I really enjoyed getting to meet her. I also met Dorothy's sister-in-law, who knew Jimmy from their school days. That was a lot of fun, and Thelma enjoyed our conversation as much as I did. Thelma has been a longtime customer of Dorothy's. After Thelma's hair was done, she and I rode all over Sneedville reminiscing again. When I left Thelma's home to return to Florida, she gave me four quarts of home-canned tomatoes that she and her daughter, Tammy, had canned over the summer. Yummy!

Jimmy's half-sisters Evelyn and Erma went on to have successful marriages and children. They lived and raised their families in and around Sneedville and Morristown. Erma passed away a couple of years ago. Her children still reside in the area. His half-sister Edria married Paul Williams (given name Paul Humphrey), a mandolin player. At the time of their marriage, Paul played music with Jimmy. Paul and Edria have one son. After Paul retired from music, he went to work for the post office, eventually retiring from there. Paul and Edria live in the Morristown vicinity and play music part-time.

Before Jimmy joined Bill Monroe, he had a daughter by a girl who lived in Sneedville. I never knew about her until my son Ray told me. At the time he met her, she lived in Mississippi.

I *did* know that before he met me Jimmy had a daughter who lived in Michigan. He always told me that the mother claimed she was his. I had seen pictures of this child and her mother, but I never met nor saw her the entire time I was with Jimmy, although Ray has.

Close to the end of writing of this book, I received a Facebook message from a lady in Shreveport, Louisiana. She sent me a picture of a man who looked to be in his late fifties. She told me that Jimmy had had an affair with a lady by the name of Norma Jean and that she'd had a baby boy by him. She told me that Jimmy had gone to the hospital to see Norma Jean when she had the baby. He had subsequently sent her Christmas cards throughout the years. She also said that Norma Jean had told her son the truth—that Jimmy Martin was his father—before her passing. Me, being the technology expert that I am (just joking), accidentally deleted the message, so I couldn't follow up on it. This would all have occurred, if it did occur, about the time he was writing songs like "She's Left Me Again" and "It's Not Home Unless You're Here" because I had left him.

All of these claims about children he fathered amaze me. Jimmy loved children. He always wanted to have more, so why didn't he acknowledge the children that he supposedly had already fathered? He certainly acknowledged and was proud of all the children he had with me. Ray, Timmy, and I have discussed this, but none of us can explain it. I guess only Jimmy could answer that question, and, unfortunately, he is no longer around.

Ray told me that Jimmy had told him about a woman he had seen in Shreveport. Ray said he met her when they appeared on a Louisiana Hayride reunion show, but Jimmy never mentioned having any children by her or any other woman in Shreveport.

Hearing about a child he may have fathered in Shreveport has really bothered me. I think this one bothered me more than the others, because Shreveport is where Jimmy asked me to marry him. Shreveport is where he and Paul Williams wrote songs about my leaving and his professing his love for me. After I had returned from Detroit the last time, Shreveport is where we had so much fun.

Sleeping with other women, regardless of whom he was living with, was a pattern that existed throughout Jimmy's life. I believe it was not about the women or the sex; it was about the attention he was getting. Or he was using the women as a punishment of his mother and the love he failed to get from her. Who knows? I certainly don't. It certainly would have been good fodder for a professional psychiatrist. I believe they would have had a field day evaluating him. Opportunity missed! Jimmy took all his reasons with him. And now we will never know why he did the things he did.

Regardless, Jimmy was a goodhearted guy. He was a complex individual to begin with and was made worse with all of life's anxieties and disappointments throughout the years.

EPILOGUE

I always knew that Jimmy was a rambling man, but I hoped he would change. Just like I hoped he would change his mind about Mike coming to live with us. Neither of those things happened. He continued to be a rambling man throughout our time together. Most probably, he continued rambling while he was involved with other women after I left him. But the rambling after I left is more than I need or want to know, and, as they say, a leopard never changes his spots.

The one thing I know about Jimmy—and I am 100 percent sure about—is that he loved his children, his animals, his friends (some of whom he had for over fifty years), his music, and, very importantly, he loved the people who loved his music. He appreciated his fans more than any entertainer I have ever known.

Regardless of his self-destructive ways, Jimmy was a man who was passionate about his music. He was also a humble man, one who thought he couldn't let anyone know he cared. But he did care desperately, and he would cry tears about things that hurt him or about people who, in his mind, failed him. I was one of those people, and he hated me until his dying day for leaving him. In his mind, he did no wrong. He could also act like and be a bully at times. Yet, I think the caring side outweighed the bullying side of him. I would not have thought that in 1966, because I was hurting. I was giving up everything to save my life. But in writing this book and thinking about things from a different perspective, I believe it is true.

What a journey writing this book has been, both good and bad. The things I learned about myself and Jimmy, reconnecting with people I had not seen nor spoken to in years, were incredible. The bad part was finishing the manuscript and sending it away. It was like my baby had left home. Surprises—I've had a few of those as well.

One of those surprises was the message regarding a child Jimmy supposedly fathered in Shreveport, Louisiana, during the time he was on the Louisiana Hayride. Since receiving the message, losing it, and being contacted again, I believe this is in all likelihood true. The glove fits!

My son Ray spoke to him, Jimmy Goins, and believes he is Jimmy's son. He was born in Shreveport in July 1959. This would have been during the time Jimmy and I were there. I returned to Shreveport the latter part of September 1958 after Jimmy had been to Detroit to talk me into returning.

I have now had an opportunity to get to know Jimmy Goins and his fiancée, Patricia Atley, and we have become friends. Photographs of him remind all of us (Ray, Buddy, Mike, and me) of Jimmy Martin. I am told that he loves to sing and is very good at it. He continues to live in Shreveport. His mother, Norma Jean, married, and together she and her husband raised Jimmy. I understand that Jimmy Goins was not told who his biological father was until he was twenty-five years old. He chose not to contact Jimmy Martin at that time. After his mother's death, he and Patricia found me and contacted me. In reading Norma Jean's journal and looking through her things, Jimmy and Patricia found that Jimmy Martin had sent Christmas cards and autographed pictures to her over the years. I was also told that he visited the hospital when Jimmy Goins was born. Patricia and Jimmy seem like genuine, down-to-earth good people, and I am looking forward to meeting both of them and their families in person.

Toward the end of this journey, my publisher introduced me to Nancy Cardwell, who would become one of my editors and my friend as well. During our very first conversation, Nancy related that she had visited Jimmy Martin at his home and in the hospital during his final days and was his neighbor when he first was diagnosed. Nancy is a former executive director of the International Bluegrass Music Association and was a longtime friend of Jimmy's. She was also the author of an article that Jimmy had dictated to her and published in *Bluegrass Now* magazine in 2005. The article was titled "On My Mind: The King of Bluegrass" and was actually a final letter from Jimmy to his fans thanking them for their support through the years. I thought it was an excellent article and could hear Jimmy saying the words Nancy had written.

My family and I will all remember Jimmy Martin for his kindness to others, his love for his fans, his family, his animals, his music, and the Grand Ole Opry. I could never forget him and will always have a special place in my heart for him and the good times we had together. I look at our children and I see him. I listen to them sing and I hear him. Our grandchildren and great-grandchildren also sing. When I listen to them sing, I think of him and would love for him to hear them sing again. I will also always remember him as a rambling man. That memory will be without bitterness. I have learned throughout the years to let bygones be bygones.

As Jimmy told Nancy, "So let's keep on believing and keep on loving, and we'll all be together as one." He had faith in God to the end, as do I.

INDEX

BARBARA MARTIN STEPHENS worked for many years as a booking agent and promoter, first for Jimmy Martin and then for numerous other bluegrass and country music performers.

The Incredible Band of John Philip Sousa   *Paul E. Bierley*
"Maximum Clarity" and Other Writings on Music   *Ben Johnston,*
    edited by Bob Gilmore
Staging Tradition: John Lair and Sarah Gertrude Knott   *Michael Ann Williams*
Homegrown Music: Discovering Bluegrass   *Stephanie P. Ledgin*
Tales of a Theatrical Guru   *Danny Newman*
The Music of Bill Monroe   *Neil V. Rosenberg and Charles K. Wolfe*
Pressing On: The Roni Stoneman Story   *Roni Stoneman, as told to Ellen Wright*
Together Let Us Sweetly Live   *Jonathan C. David, with photographs*
    by Richard Holloway
Live Fast, Love Hard: The Faron Young Story   *Diane Diekman*
Air Castle of the South: WSM Radio and the Making of Music City
    Craig P. Havighurst
Traveling Home: Sacred Harp Singing and American Pluralism   *Kiri Miller*
Where Did Our Love Go? The Rise and Fall of the Motown Sound   *Nelson George*
Lonesome Cowgirls and Honky-Tonk Angels: The Women of Barn
    Dance Radio   *Kristine M. McCusker*
California Polyphony: Ethnic Voices, Musical Crossroads   *Mina Yang*
The Never-Ending Revival: Rounder Records and the Folk Alliance
    Michael F. Scully
Sing It Pretty: A Memoir   *Bess Lomax Hawes*
Working Girl Blues: The Life and Music of Hazel Dickens   *Hazel Dickens*
    and Bill C. Malone
Charles Ives Reconsidered   *Gayle Sherwood Magee*
The Hayloft Gang: The Story of the National Barn Dance   *Edited by Chad Berry*
Country Music Humorists and Comedians   *Loyal Jones*
Record Makers and Breakers: Voices of the Independent Rock 'n' Roll
    Pioneers   *John Broven*
Music of the First Nations: Tradition and Innovation in Native North
    America   *Edited by Tara Browner*
Cafe Society: The Wrong Place for the Right People   *Barney Josephson,*
    with Terry Trilling-Josephson
George Gershwin: An Intimate Portrait   *Walter Rimler*
Life Flows On in Endless Song: Folk Songs and American History   *Robert V. Wells*
I Feel a Song Coming On: The Life of Jimmy McHugh   *Alyn Shipton*
King of the Queen City: The Story of King Records   *Jon Hartley Fox*
Long Lost Blues: Popular Blues in America, 1850–1920   *Peter C. Muir*
Hard Luck Blues: Roots Music Photographs from the Great Depression
    Rich Remsberg
Restless Giant: The Life and Times of Jean Aberbach and Hill and Range
    Songs   *Bar Biszick-Lockwood*
Champagne Charlie and Pretty Jemima: Variety Theater in the
    Nineteenth Century   *Gillian M. Rodger*
Sacred Steel: Inside an African American Steel Guitar Tradition   *Robert L. Stone*

The University of Illinois Press
is a founding member of the
Association of American University Presses.

———————————————————————

Composed in 10.25/14 Chaparral Pro
by Lisa Connery
at the University of Illinois Press
Cover designed by Jennifer S. Holzner
Cover photo: Barbara and Jimmy, summer 1953.
Manufactured by Sheridan Books, Inc.

University of Illinois Press
1325 South Oak Street
Champaign, IL 61820-6903
www.press.uillinois.edu